ARMEN KHACHIKYAN

HISTORY OF ARMENIA

A Brief Review

ԷԴԻԹ ՊՐԻՆՏ
EDIT PRINT

Yerevan, Armenia

UDK 941(479.25)

Scientific Editor
Dr. Aram KOSYAN

Armen Khachikyan.
History of Armenia: a brief review.-Yerevan.:
Edit Print, 2010.- 264 p., 10 maps.

The book is adressed to Armenian's in Diasphora and to readers living in varrious countries who are interested in history and culture of Armenia.

The translation and publication of this book was partly funded by a grant from the United States Department of State.

Author of maps Robert H. Hewsen.

ISBN 978-9939-52-294-4

FOREWORD

Armenians live in every corner of the world. Many of them wish to know more about the history of their ancestral homeland and contributions of the Armenian people to the world civilization, but few are fluent in Armenian, and many, in fact, hardly even read in it. Many young Armenians born outside of the homeland speak no Armenian at all, and have never been to Armenia, having only heard about it.

I am often asked to recommend a book in English on the Armenian history. There are, indeed, a great number of English-language books and articles on various topics of the Armenian history, published during the last two decades. Many of these sources, while useful and important, focus only on one or a few subjects. They hardly can offer an English reader a full and inclusive understanding of the Armenian history. As for more detailed reading on the History of Armenia I usually recommend a definitive publication - Robert H. Hewsen, "Armenia: a historical atlas", (2001) - a trustworthy and comprehensive, heavily illustrated book with maps, chronology, bibliographical references and index.

Yet doubtless is the need to have an English-language book that would offer a brief, comprehensive overview of the history of Armenia, to help the foreign reader develop an in-depth understanding of the complex issues of our history. This review is designed to serve exactly as such a reference point for the general public interested in the history of Armenia. It offers a brief overview of significant events and developments in the history of the nation, and is easy to read, carry, browse, and refer to.

It can also be a useful reference source for foreigners visiting Armenia, including diplomats and international develop-

River Tigris starts in the foothills of the Armenian Taurus Mountains. It crosses the Armenian Plateau from west to east and, after taking in several tributaries, turns south, towards and into the Persian Gulf.

River Chorokh begins in the mountains of Eastern Pontus and falls into the Black Sea, streaming across the Armenian Plateau before turning north and into the Black Sea.

The keys of River Kur begin in the mountains of Northern Taurus. The river first streams north, then turns sharply towards east, and again south-east, heading towards the Caspian Sea. Large sections of the Kur River form the natural northern and north-eastern frontiers of the Armenian Plateau.

River Arax takes start in the picturesque mountains of Byurakn (Bingöl). It streams down across the central part of the Armenian Plateau from west to east, making numerous curves, and merging finally with River Kur before falling into the Caspian Sea. Arax has several large tributaries, including rivers Akhurian, Hrazdan and Vorotan. Arax has played an important role in Armenia's life throughout history, and carries an enormous symbolic value for the Armenian people, who often refer to it as 'Mayr Arax' (Arax the Mother).

The Armenian Plateau is also home to numerous lakes and other natural water reservoirs, the largest of which are **Urmia, Van and Sevan.**

Armenia is often called a "country of mountains." The entire land-

Karahunj – the Armenian Stonehenge

mass of the Armenian Plateau is an imposing natural architectural system of dazzling mountain ranges and stand-alone peaks. Along its northern and north-eastern frontier, it includes a number of spurs of the Smaller Caucasus Mountain Range, which in turn form separate mountain systems, such as the Gugarats, Bazum, Geghama, Zangezur, and Artsakh Mountain Ranges.

The north-western frontiers of the Armenian Plateau stretch along the Armenian Taurus, a Mountain System with numerous spurs and rocky enclaves such as Zeitun and Sasun. Running parallel, but much north, is Northern Taurus, a Mountain Range dividing the waters of Euphrates, Kur and Arax. In the south of the Armenian Plateau are the Kotur Mountains - a range extending straightly north-south between the lakes Van and Urmia.

Towering right in the middle of the Armenian Plateau is the Biblical Mount Ararat, the summit of which, according to the Holy Book, harbors Noah's Ark. Soaring 5,165 meters above the sea, into the zone of eternal freeze, Ararat is the highest point of Asia Minor and the Middle East. The snow of Ararat feed thousands of fresh-water springs year-around, giving life to an amazing ecosystem famous for the uniqueness and diversity of its flora and fauna. On the slopes of Mount Ararat, many varieties of modern domestic livestock roamed in wild, along with onagers (Ecuus Hemionus), mouflons (Ovis Musimon), panthers, and many other rare, now-endangered species. From Mount Ararat and across the central expanse of the Armenian Plateau runs Armenian Par – a mountain range splitting the Plateau somewhat into Northern and Southern halves.

Further decorating Armenia's skylines are stand-alone peaks of Sipan (4,443 m), Aragats (4,095 m) and Nemrut (2,150 m) -- the only functioning volcano in the region.

The Armenian Plateau is rich in natural resources. Historically famous are the gold mines of Sper and Sotk, silver mines of Armenia Minor, and salt deposits of Koghb, Kaghzvan, and Nakhijevan. In addition, the territory of the Armenian Plateau is also rich in iron and color metals, coal deposits, as well as a variety of construction stones.

Mt. Sipan at Lake Van,
with Akhtamar Island on the foreground

The climate on the Armenian Plateau is continental and dry, with hot summers and chilly winters. The summer temperature is up to +42C, and the average temperature in winter is up to –10C. Natural forests are concentrated primarily in the north and north-east of the Plateau, but a rich variety of fruit trees and medical herbs grows endemically throughout the entire region. There is known to be over thousand mineral springs on the territory of Armenia, most famous of them are mineral waters of Djermuk, Arzni, Bjni, etc.

§ 2. The Stone Age on the Armenian Highland

Modern archaeological data indicates that the earliest human activity on the Armenian Plateau occurred around 1 million years ago. These earliest humans were gatherers and hunters living in small groups of 20-30, who were familiar with the use of primitive instruments made of stone and wood. Choppers, tips of arrows, cutting blades, and other instruments used by these early settlers were made of obsidian – a dark-colored glass-like volcanic stone abundant on the Armenian Plateau. Much of this obsidian can be seen in the road side soils while on a ride from Yerevan to Sevan.

The arrival of the Ice Period at around 100 thousand years ago affected the climate on the Armenian Plateau dramatically, leading also to changes in its flora and fauna. Whereas the Great Glacier did not reach the Caucasus, ice nevertheless did cover pockets of the Armenian Plateau, such as mountains and other elevated terrain, spearing just the river ravines and lower-lying valleys. Only those groups of humans survived who managed to adapt to the severing climate by developing the old, and acquiring new skills. It is in this period that humans inhabiting the Armenian Plateau discovered fire, and learned to use body- and foot-ware. Armed with fire, they drew wild animals out of the mountain caves, turning these into shelters and eventually, into primitive residences. A number of such early human camping sites have been discovered and studied on the territory of the Republic of Armenia, the largest and best known of which is Cave Satani Dar.

Given the relatively modest coverage in plantation and vegetation of the Armenian Plateau, gathering did not evolve into a leading form of human activity, and was pushed back instead by big-mammal hunting such as on mammoths, rhinos, bulls, bears, and deer.

Mt. Aragats

Approximately 10 thousand years ago, with the end of the Ice Period, the Armenian Plateau stepped into the New Stone Age, as global climate acquired its current characteristics, and basic conditions improved for human life. Humans began using elastic plants to make bows and arrows, and weave baskets, and discovered clay as material for making various house ware. Stone instruments continued to improve in sophistication and variety. Stone axe could now be used to carve boats, build carts, and put up cabins. By the end of the New

Stone Age humans domesticated the dog, the sheep, the goat and the cow. Bulls were used in heavy traction, and hoes with stone endings in plowing the soil for farming. During this period, humans learned about spinning plant fiber and animal hair to weave fabric, and building a pottery wheel to produce finer and more stylish cutlery.

3. The Bronze and Iron Ages on the Armenian Highland

Through a multi-millennial journey of continuous social and economic emancipation, and all the way straight through Paleolith and Neolith, the population of the Armenian Plateau achieved the stage of decline of its primitive tribal order by the end of the 4th millennium B.C.

Ceramic container (karas) from Metsamor

The ensuing 3rd and 2nd millennia B.C. delivered the Bronze Age. Bronze phased out stone as the primary material of instruments of labor, and helped speed up social development significantly. Plows with bronze ends replaced hoes with ends made of stone. This enabled a rapid expansion of the areas under farming, and increased food productivity. During this period humans domesticated the horse, completing a pivotal process in early human achievement -- the domestication of wild animals. Of the Bronze Age settlements on the territory of Armenia, two are particularly well studied – those in Lchashen and Vanadzor. Artifacts from these sites are now on display at the National Museum of History of Armenia. In areas better suited for settled productive activity, fortified urban settlements began to form. Farming and cattle breeding developed further.

More and more common became tribal wars for control over fertile territory, food stock and cattle. Related tribes engaged in alliances to defend their territorial and material assets against the encroachment of others.

Starting from the mid-2nd millennium BC the inhabitants of the Armenian Plateau learned to make instruments from iron. Throughout the Armenian Plateau and eastern Asia Minor, iron minerals can often be found right on the surface: so, mining required a relatively easy effort. Therefore, the processing and use of instruments made of iron occurred on the Armenian Plateau much earlier than elsewhere in the world – an incidence owing the fortunate combination of both availability and accessibility of iron-rich minerals in this particular geographic area.

Natterjack figurine from onyx, which served as a weight measurement. From excavations at Metsamor

Studies on the site of a settlement as old as the middle of the 2nd millennium BC located at Metsamor near Echmiatsin authenticate this idea. The site at Metsamor represents a small hill, dominating over the surrounding flat terrain. The hill served as the center of a fortified settlement that was home to a population settled at the site for at least several generations. This population engaged in both farming and crafts. Remnants of furnaces, scraps of iron ore and the presence of items made of iron leave no doubt in that instruments from iron were already of common use. In addition, some of the items discovered at this site were found to be of Mesopotamian origin – an evidence of established trade relationships between ancient civilizations.

Thus, toward the beginning of the 1st millennium BC, the population of the Armenian Plateau stepped confidently into the Iron Age.

CHAPTER 2

FORMATION OF THE ARMENIAN PEOPLE

§ 1. Settlement of Proto-Armenian Tribes and the Earliest State Entities on the Armenian Plateau.

By the start of the 2nd millennium BC the population of the Armenian Plateau reached the stage of state formation. Around that period, numerous State entities began to emerge on the territory of the Armenian Plateau, such as the tribal unions Hayasa, Isuwa, Arme, Sukhmu, Daya, Nairi, Uruatri, among others. These entities had mixed ethnic profile, and populations speaking in both Indo-European, as well as non-Indo-European languages. Their emergence was the result of not only general socio-economic development, but also the critical need for self-defense against the aggressive expansionist policies of powerful neighboring states – the Hittite Kingdom and Assyria.

Hittite sources of the 14th-13th cc. BC and Assyrian sources of 13th-11th cc. BC convey important knowledge about the geography, social order, and material capacity of these early State formations. For instance, these proto-states often comprised several dozen tribes, and were run by elected military leaders, who carried the title 'King'.

Hittite and Assyrian Kings waged numerous wars against Armenian states, and made agreements with or against them. Often, the name of one of these states would be used in reference to the entire proto-Armenian world. Thus, Hittite sources employed the name 'Hayasa' to refer to the same country that Assyrian sources referred to as 'Nairi' or 'Uruatri'.

§ 2. Formation of the Armenian People. The Armenian Language

Armenian language belongs to the Indo-European family of languages. The same family also includes the Slavic, the majority of European, as well as the Iranian and Indian languages.

THE INDO-EUROPEAN FAMILY OF LANGUAGES

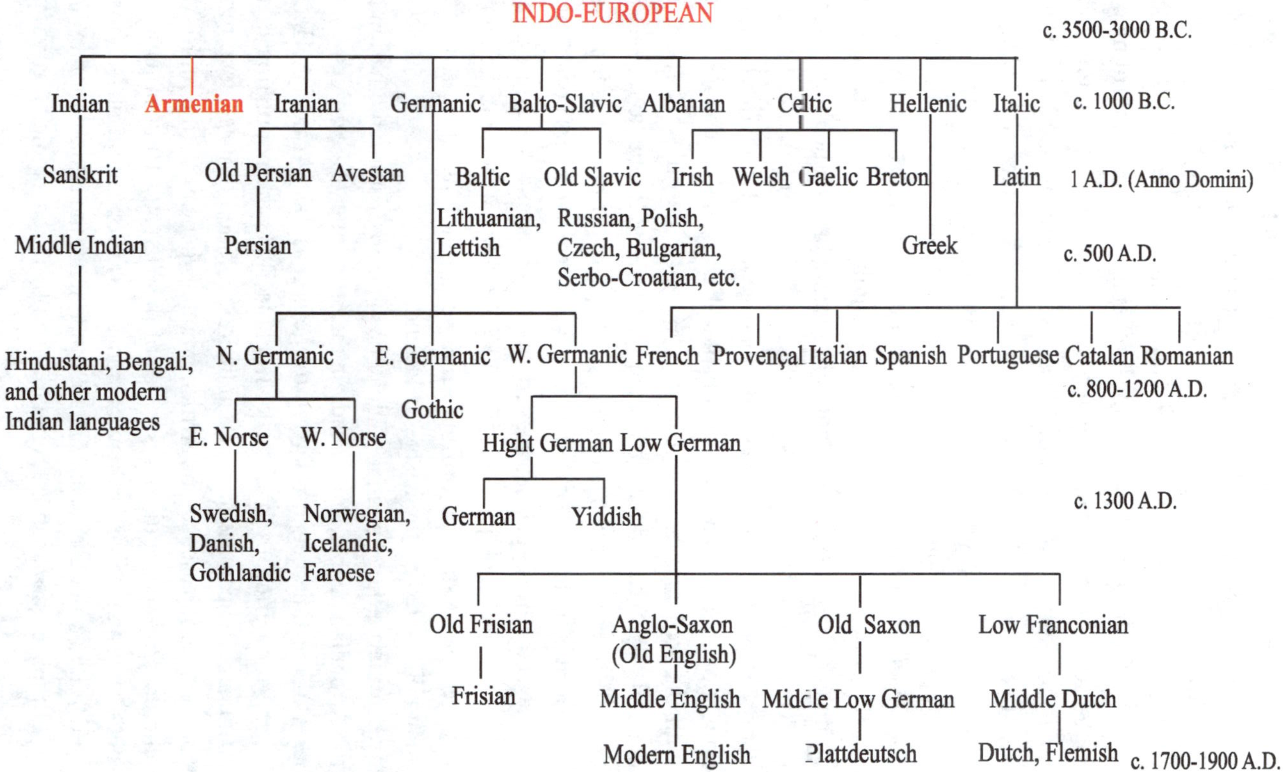

Modern linguistics traces the homeland of Indo-European languages to the Near East, specifically to the area that includes central and eastern Asia Minor, western part of the Armenian Plateau, and northern parts of contemporary Syria and Iraq. The most commonly accepted theory suggests that in the period from IV to II millennia B.C. ancestors of modern Indo-Europeans sustained several waves of migration, departing native lands and spreading across the vast expanse of new territory, in more than one direction. In transit, they came upon and intermixed with various local tribes, many of them non-Indo-European origin, and absorbed patterns of their ethnic and linguistic characteristics.

Depending on the migrant group, the process lasted between several centuries and well around a millennium. It concluded with the communities on the move eventually settling on a particular territory – an event of a significant catalytic effect on their formation and consolidation as people. The process of ethno-genesis also involved indigenous populations, including non-Indo-Europeans, who assimilated with the settlers, whether peacefully or not, tilting the matrix of the emerging cultures and societies with patterns of linguistic residue noticeable in the grammar and colloquial speech of many modern Indo-European languages. Territories settled by the newcomers became their mother countries, getting named after predominant ethnic groups. Thus, the southern part of the Balkan Peninsula became known as Greece, the western part of the same peninsula – as Albania, and the island populated by the Irish – as Ireland.

Similarly, the Armenian Plateau became the historic motherland of the Armenian people, and already in the 6th century BC, official chronicles of the time began referring to the country as 'Armenia'. Hence, during the period from III to I Millennia B.C., the population of the Armenian Plateau sustained a landmark evolution of its societal mold, completing, in essence, the Armenian ethno-genesis by the mid-I Millennium B.C. The indigenous tribes of the Plateau - Hurrian, Urartian, and Caucasian, some of them of non-Indo-European origin – contributed to this process as well. On the other hand, the assimilation of lesser groups of new settler population with mixed ethnicity continued throughout the following centuries.

The Armenian ethno-genesis resulted in promoting the Armenian language to the fore, as the winner language. Being itself of Indo-European origin, the Armenian language, nevertheless, contains noticeable patterns of non-Indo-European linguistic heritage – the input of non-Indo-European tribes populating the Armenian plateau too.

The tribal union, around which the final unification of Armenian tribes took place, was Hayasa: hence, 'Hay' – the name by which Armenians identify themselves, and 'Hayastan' – as they call the country. Neighbors of Armenians to the South, who interfaced with them primarily through the tribe Arme named the country 'Armenia', and its inhabitants – 'Armenians'.

§ 3. The Legend on the Genesis of the Armenian People

Movses Khorenatsi (late-5th century AD), founder of the Armenian Historiography, recorded the following legend on the origins of the Armenian people, based on his account of various verbal sources through which the story had been transmitted over the preceding centuries and generations.

Patriarch Hayk. Modern sculpture.

In the ancient times, one of the powerful titans named Bel subordinated the other titans to his will, and declared himself the ruler of Babylon. Only one titan by the name Hayk defied him. This powerful hero with splendid curls gathered his sons, grandsons, and the rest of his folk numbering 300, and led them to the north – to the "Country of Ararat", whereupon they settled. The few people of that land welcomed his rule, and thus the country took the name 'Hayk' after him. The sons and grandsons of Hayk multiplied, and spread all over the country, giving their names to its provinces, mountains, valleys and rivers. Thus, Mt. Aragats got its name from Aramaniak, Mt. Masis – from Amasia, Lake Geghama (modern Sevan) – from Gegham, the county of Garni – from Garnik, the Shirak highland – from Shara, the province of Korduk – from Kadmos, the province of Syunik – from Sisak, and so it goes on.

Bel got worried. He sent messengers to Hayk demanding loyalty. Being the proud and freedom-loving hero that he was, Hayk declined. So, Bel furnished a large fighting force, and went to war against Hayk. In the face of this impending danger, Hayk too gathered his fighters and every single man of his folk who could hold a spear, and hit the road to engage Bel half-way. The two armies met near a lake, where the battle took place. Hayk called upon his men to fight fearlessly to defend their land and freedom, and to not waiver, and not retreat before the enemy's overwhelming force. So, a ruthless battle began, claiming the lives of many heroes on both sides. Bel saw this, and dread captured his spirit. He decided to re-position, and wait until additional troops arrive. Conscious of Bel's plot, Hayk cut through the fighting crowd, strained his bow, and shot aiming at Bel. Launched by the mighty hand of the hero, the projectile pierced Bel's body armor, and knocked him down dead. Seeing their leader fall, Bel's fighters fled in panic. As for Hayk and his folk, they held up and celebrated victory.

Hayk is revered as the Patriarch of Armenians, and Eponymous - the hero who gave his name to the country and its people. The year of the battle is considered the beginning of the Armenian calendar. Armenian chroniclers of the early medieval period have studied the lives of Hayk and his off-springs, and concluded that these events might have taken place in the year 2292 BC – almost 4.5 thousand ago.

As any other legend, this story on the Armenian Genesis combines the mythical with the real, echoing true events that took place in immemorial times when the Indo-European Armenian tribes spread over the entire Armenian Plateau, assimilating all other tribes.

4. The geographic and political shape of Ancient Armenia

Historical Armenia covers an area of about 300,000 sq. km that is congruent geographically with the Armenian Plateau. Mountainous terrain and climatic variations in different zones of the Plateau conditioned the evolution of Armenia in its earliest stages as a less then sufficiently integrated commonwealth of over a dozen semi-autonomous provinces with different types, levels, and pace of socio-economic development. Populations in these provinces differed considerably from one another in lifestyle, outfit, and even spoken language. Armenians called these provinces 'Ashkharh' or 'World' in English. In the early 4th c. A.D., in the wake of the feudalist period, Ashkharhs were institutionalized in Armenia by a royal decree, becoming the nation's principal territorial and administrative units. A full description of the 15 Ashkharhs comprising Armenia Major is contained in 'Ashkharhatsuyts' – the famous treatise of Anania Shirakatsi, a prominent Armenian author and mathematician of the early Medieval period.

These 15 Ashkharhs were: Bardzr Hayk (High Armenia), Tsopk (Sophene), Tayk, Gugark, Artsakh, Utik, Paytakaran, Syunik, Vaspurakan, Parskahayk, Rshtunik, Mokk, Taron, Aghdznik, and Ayrarat.

Historical Armenia consisted of two principal ethnic and territorial components: Armenia Major and Armenia Minor, the latter including provinces west of the upper Euphrates River, and south of the Eastern Pontic Mountains. Armenia Minor, originally populated by Armenian tribes, participated in the Armenian ethno-genesis fully. Later, in the Hellenistic period, however, Armenia Minor got considerably disengaged from Armenia Major politically, as well as ethnically, due to historical circumstances that will be discussed later in this book, and more diverse demographics. Armenia Minor never again joined the Armenian state, although a sizeable Armenian population continued to live there until 1915.

Modern Republic of Armenia includes only a few of the original provinces: Ayrarat, Syunik and Gugark. It occupies a territory of 30,000 sq. km -- just one-tenth of Armenia Major.

CHAPTER 3

THE FIRST UNIFIED ARMENAN STATE: THE VAN KINGDOM

§ 1. The emergence of the Van Kingdom (Urartu)

The weakening and demise of the Hittite Kingdom by the end of the 13th c. B.C. relieved the Armenian states of the external pressures they were facing from the west, and resulted in somewhat of a slow-down in the process of state formation in the western part of the Armenian Plateau. The same period, however, also brought new pressures – this time in the south, along the frontier with Assyria, incursions from which into neighboring Armenian states for purposes of property- and slave-taking had become more frequent. The growing threat from Assyria facilitated the process of consolidation of Armenian states and their eventual merging within a single unified state. Centripetal trends achieved a greater momentum in states that shared a border with Assyria, and were thus more vulnerable to threat it posed, such as Nairi, Shupria, and Uruatri. Naturally, these states formed the core of the emerging pan-Armenian alliance around which the final consolidation and formation of the unified Armenian state occurred.

The leading force behind this alignment was the Kingdom of Biaina, which succeeded in bringing together all other 'kingdoms' of the Armenian Plateau to build defense against a common enemy. Assyrian sources chronicling the mid-9th c. B.C. already refer to the existence of a unified state on the Armenian Plateau that by 860 B.C. controlled territories south and west of the Lake Van.

Known as the Kingdom of Van, this first unified state on the territory of the Armenian Plateau existed from the 9th to the 6th centuries B.C. In the inscriptions of its kings it was referred to as 'BIAINA', although the Assyrian sources called the kingdom 'URARTU'. The capital of Biaina (Urartu) was located on the south-eastern shore of Lake Van, and was called Tushpa (Van - in modern Turkey).

The name 'Urartu' gained common recognition in the 19th century, following a series of extensive site excavations on the territory of ancient Assyria, and the deciphering of Assyrian cuneiform texts uncovered during these projects. Only toward the beginning of the 20th century was the name 'Biaina' deciphered and read for the first time, owing the successful compilation, study and translation of the cuneiform texts left by the rulers of the Van Kingdom itself.

The earliest among these rulers were **Arame (860-845 B.C.) and Sarduri I (845-825 B.C.).** These rulers not only successfully contained and neutralized threats posed by the powerful Assyrian state, but also managed to significantly expand the frontiers of their state eastward, unifying all provinces around Lake Van. Areas on the lake's eastern shore emerged as the economic and political powerhouse of the Kingdom. Here, on a remote slope of an imposing rock that defines the lake's eastern horizon, Sarduri I built a superior fortress around which the capital of his state – the town of Tushpa rose before long.

Kings **Ishpuini (825-810 B.C.) and Menua (810-786 B.C.)** further extended the borders of the state toward West and North reaching River Arax. Here, King Menua built the city-fortress Menuakhinili. City-fortresses were built on all recently acquired territories.

King Argishti's helmet

The unification of numerous small, scattered kingdoms within a single consolidated Armenian state helped facilitate the country's economic progress. All over the land irrigation canals began being built, arable grounds expanded, and gardens and vineyards set. Even today, a 72 km canal built by King Menua continues to supply water to the city of Van.

2. The strengthening and expansion of the Van Kingdom. The Struggle with Assyria

Under Kings **Argishti I (786-764 B.C.)** and **Sarduri II (764-735 B.C.)** the Van Kingdom reached the zenith of its power and prosperity. Through a series of military campaigns, the Kingdom absorbed an additional number of smaller State entities, and by the 8th century B.C. established control over most of the territory of the Armenian Plateau, extending from River Euphrates in the West to Lake Sevan in the North-East.

Expansion, however, did not always proceed smoothly, but was often met with fierce resistance locally. To counter this, the Van Kings practiced massive relocations of conquered populations to other provinces of the state, thereby contributing to the Kingdom's demographic and linguistic emancipation, and its subsequent graduation as a more homogeneous society.

Cuneiform "passport" of Yerevan

In 782 B.C. King Argishti I founded the city-fortress Erebuni – an elaborate urban and administrative project now contained within the limits of Armenia's capital city Yerevan, and viewed indisputably as its first 'town plan'. Archaeological excavations on the site in the 1950s helped recover, among many precious artifacts, a cuneiform tablet containing Argishti's original record on the founding of the fortress Erebuni. Viewed as the 'birth certificate' of Yerevan, the tablet is a spectacular testimony on stone to the aproximate 2,800 years of history of the Armenian capital. It is now on display at the National Museum of History of Armenia.

Several years later, at location in the central part of the Ararat Valley, King Argishti I also founded fortress Argishtikhinili that would become, several centuries later, one of Armenia's twelve historical capital cities – Armavir.

Taking advantage of growing crisis in Assyria the Van Kings also launched a series of military incursions into the Assyrian territory, seizing large amounts of material assets. Driven by the need to establish control over the ancient trade routes crisscrossing the region, these incursions generally served the pursuit of economic and commercial interests of the Kingdom.

Over 500 cuneiform texts left by the Van Kings are identified today on the territory of modern Armenia, as well as in Turkey and Azerbaijan. Mostly, these are records of conquests of provinces and peoples, founding of towns, fortresses and temples, planting of gardens and vineyards, horse and other domestic animal breeding, and production of various items and objects in iron, bronze or gold.

3. The Government and Economy of the Van Kingdom

The head of state in the Van Kingdom was the King who possess absolute power. He was the sole decision-maker on important matters of the state, in pursuit of which he would rely on a close circle of advisors. The state was divided into provinces headed by members of loyal aristocracy appointed by the King. Vassal 'kingdoms', nevertheless, were often allowed to preserve their existing ruling houses, with the condition that they paid regular duties to the King.

The ultimate source of the King's power was his military, consisting of infantry, cavalry, and charioteer force. Warriors were armed with iron swords, spears and javelins, bows and arrows, and carried bronze helmets and shields. The latter accessories, particularly among the aristocracy, were often decorated with lavish ornaments. The military was organized into corps of 3 thousand warriors each that in turn divided into 50-warrior battalions. The entire male population of the Kingdom was subject to military duty.

The Van Kingdom was a slavery state. It launched military campaigns to get the spoil, and assert control over international trade routes that brought enormous profit. Slave labor was mainly used in the construction of palaces, fortresses, temples, irrigation canals, as well as in crafts. Artificial irrigation was widely used, leading to the carving of irrigation tunnels in solid rock.

The 72 km-long canal built by King Menua has survived to nowdays. It delivered water to Tushpa, while another 25 km-long canal built by Rusa I near Tushpa was designated specifically to deliver water to the reservoir for seasonal irrigation. The canal built by Rusa II in the River Hrazdan canyon near Yerevan functions even today.

Free members of the community were engaged in farming and cattle breeding. Gardening and vineyards were also well developed. The population cultivated grain and oil-yielding crops, and bred cattle. Rock inscriptions left by the Van Kings contain numerous references to the large number of cattle in the kingdom -- in hundreds and thousands, and rich reserves of grain, oil and wine, used in ceremonies of sacrifices to the local Gods.

4. The demise and breakup of the Van Kingdom

In the second half of the 8th century, the Assyrian state that had reached the zenith of its power, delivered the Van Kingdom a series of powerful blows. In battles in 743 and 735 BC, Sarduri II was defeated by Assyria and lost control of the southern and south-western provinces and important trade routes. His successor **Rusa I (735-713)** launched an extensive campaign to restore the shaking power and authority of the Van Kingdom.

But in 714 BC King Sargon II of Assyria launched a new devastating campaign, invading the Van Kingdom with a large army. Gardens and vineyards were destroyed, irrigation canals clogged, towns and temples looted, and the population taken into slavery. Although the Assyrians failed to conquer the capital city Tushpa, they seized the holy city of **Musasir**, where the temples of the main deities of the state were located, along with an enormous amount of jewelry and other treasures.

Despite the devastating campaign of 714 BC, Kings **Argishti II (713-685)** and **Rusa II (685-645)** continued to pursue active external policies. They conducted many campaigns, reasserting control over former vassals, and building new fortresses instead of the older ones.

Rusa II built the town-fortress of Teishebaini on the opposite hill overlooking the fortress of Erebuni on the outskirts of modern-day Yerevan. Teishebaini was a major economic and military center, and a provincial capital with large storage facilities where wine, oil and other food items were kept for military needs.

By the late 7th century, it had become harder and harder for the

Van Kingdom to defend itself against the incursions by Scythes and Cymmerians. The territory of the Van Kingdom gradually shrank, and its power challenged by vassal "kings" and tribes more often. The power of the Van Kings extended only as far as the territories adjacent to the Eastern shore of the Lake Van.

In 585 BC the terminally weakened Van Kingdom fell under the blow of a rising new power – the Median Kingdom.

§ 5. The Culture of the Van Kingdom. Cuneiforms

The Van Kingdom left a rich cultural heritage. Urban planning reached a high level of development. Fortress-towns were built that became territorial, regional or provincial administrative and military-political centers. A fortress-town had a citadel, which served as a residence for the head of the provincial administration. Here, in huge 1,000 liter clay vessels, they stored large amounts of food supplies for military and public needs. The city, where regular people lived, was spread around the citadel. Many fortress-towns from the Van Kingdom period

Citadel of Van

were excavated on the territory of the Republic of Armenia, including Erebuni, Teishebaini, Argishtikhinili, among others.

Construction materials, commonly, used included stone, clay, and less often – brick. Palaces and houses had simple architecture -- one-floor buildings with roofs were made of wood or reed, covered by clay. The interior space in residential quarters was decorated by frescos and wall paintings, with stone statues of gods and mythical creatures placed near entrances. Temples were built using polished stone blocs. A Stela found in the palace of the Assyrian King Sargon II depicts a scene of the capture and looting of the temple of the god Khaldi in Musasir. The architectural design of the temple in Musasir reminds of the well-known Hellenistic temple in Garni.

Excavations of fortresses from the Van Kingdom period have led to the discovery of many different types of armor, beautiful pieces of pottery, clay and bronze statuettes – all serving as evidence of the existence of highly developed arts and craft.

A large part of our knowledge about the history and culture of the Van Kingdom comes from cuneiform inscriptions of Van and well as Assyrian Kings.

At present, there are over 500 large and brief cuneiform inscriptions known to be left by the rulers of the Van Kingdom. Cuneiform is a syllabic script, created in Ancient Mesopotamia. The inscriptions of Assyrian kings were made in cuneiform. The Assyrian cuneiform was quickly adopted in the Van Kingdom, and adapted to the local language.

Depiction of God Khaldi

The language of the Van inscriptions, known as "Urartian", is not of Indo-European origin. It was deciphered long ago, and all of the inscriptions in that language have been read. It probably was the language spoken by the ruling elite – the population of the province of Biainili, located to the east of Lake Van. After the formation of a unified state, that language became the official state language of the Van Kingdom. It was used to record history, make construction records, and write letters. But throughout the entire territory of this huge country, comprising many state formations and tribal unions, Armenian – a language of Indo-European origin – was the spoken language. The two languages co-existed in parallel. They have many loan words – an evidence of their lasting contact and mutual enrichment. After the fall of the Van Kingdom, the "Urartian" language no longer held the status of an official state language, its script was forgotten, its speakers fully assimilated, and absorbed by the Indo-European-speaking majority population of the Armenian Plateau. The non Indo-European-speaking population fully participated in the completion of the formation of the Armenian people and the Armenian language.

From excavations of the Erebuni Fortress

Temple of Musasir: Reconstruction

The religion of the Van Kingdom was polytheistic. Its peoples worshiped the forces of nature. The cuneiform inscriptions refer to several hundred gods and goddesses. Under the rules of the existing polytheistic faith system, all local deities of conquered tribes and territories were included in the Pantheon, which explains their great variety. The main gods in the Pantheon were: Khaldi, God of Heavens, War and Victory; Varubane, Khaldi's wife and the Goddess of Fertility; and Teisheba, God of the Lightning and Forces of nature; Shivini, God of the Sun, Creator of Life. The main temple of God Khaldi was in Ardini-Musasir, in the southeast of the country.

CHAPTER 4

ARMENIA IN THE 6TH-3RD CENTURIES BC

§ 1. Formation of the Yervanduni Kingdom

The disintegration of the Van Kingdom in the late 7th century B.C. again resulted in the emergence of several competing kingdoms on the territory of the Armenian Plateau. One of the former tributaries of the Van Kingdom emerged under its ruler named Paruyr in south-western part of the country. According to Movses Khorenatsi, Paruyr joined the coalition of the kings of Media and Babylon against Assyria. In 612, the allies besieged, captured and ruined the capital of Assyria Nineveh. For his assistance, Paruyr was granted by them the title of the King of Armenia.

By the mid-6th century B.C., one other kingdom rose to prominence in the central part of the Armenian Plateau. Its ruler Yervand succeeded in re-uniting other minor “kingdoms” in a single state. The new ruling family is called Yervanduni, after its founder. In the newly united Armenian state, Indo-European tribes who made the predominant ethnic majority of the population took the leading position. As a result, the Indo-European Armenian language became the spoken state language. All other ethnic tribes populating the Armenian Plateau were absorbed and assimilated. The formation of the Armenian people, in general, was complete, and although in the following centuries, an additional number of small ethnic groups were absorbed, it certainly did little to alter the fundamental ethnic base of the Armenian people and its language.

The new Armenian state was immediately confronted by the power of the Median Empire then in its peak, and was forced to accept its suzerainty. According to the Greek author Xenophon, the King of Armenia maintained his power and autonomy in domestic affairs, but had to pay tribute to the Median Emperor.

In 550 B.C., Cyrus, the ruler of Persia from the Achaemenid dynasty, overthrew the Median Emperor and established his own rule in Iran. According to Xenophon, Cyrus was actively assisted in that effort by his childhood friend, the Armenian Crown Prince Tigran, son of Yervand. After long wars, Cyrus succeeded in extending his power over almost every country and state in the Near East, bringing them under the supremacy of a vast empire. The Armenian Yervanduni Kingdom too was subordinated to the supreme power of the Persian Emperor, and paid tribute, while maintaining its autonomy in domestic affairs.

2. Armenian Kingdom within the Achaemenid Empire

Early on during the reign of Darius I (522-486) the Achaemenid power found itself on the verge of a decline. Almost every subordinate people in the Empire rose up against the Persian rule. Darius I, however, was able to suppress these rebellions, and preserve the Achaemenid Empire. He marked his victories by commissioning the Behistun Inscription.

The cuneiform text, engraved in three languages – Old Persian, Akkadian, and Elamite, on a towering rock near the city of Hamadan, Iran, describes the deeds of Darius I aimed at asserting his power and suppressing the rebellions of nations subdued to the Persian rule. Among others, the inscription also describes the success of the Persian army in containing the insurgency in Armenia only in a matter of five field battles.

The Behistun Inscription makes the first official reference to the name "ARMENIA."

Interestingly, the name "Armenia" appears only in the Old Persian text of the Inscription, while the Akkadian and Elamite texts refer to the same as "Urartu." That leads to suggest that these names are identical, and each neighboring nation had a name for the same country according to its linguistic rules and tradition.

To strengthen the Achaemenid Empire, Darius carried out a series of administrative and financial reforms. The territory of the vast Empire was divided into 20 satrapies (provinces), with specific amounts and procedures of taxation determined for each of them.

Stella from excavations in Persepolis. Armenians offering tribute to the Persian King.

The territory of Armenia was assigned to two satrapies: western provinces of the country were included in the 13th satrapy, and eastern – in the 18th. Satrapies were ruled by satraps appointed by the Persian King from among the members of the Orontid (Yervanduni) dynasty. Armenian satrapies paid their taxes in silver, as well as Armenia's famed wine and purebred horses. Depictions of Armenians, as well as other subdued nations paying tribute to Darius were found in archaeological excavations in Persepolis, the capital of Persia.

Thanks to the Greek historian Xenophon, who was with the 10,000-member Greek army as it was retreating through Armenia to the Black Sea, a wealth of information has reached us regarding the economy and daily life of the Armenians in 5th-4th centuries B.C.

The 10,000-strong corps of Greek mercenaries had been hired to serve Crown Prince Cyrus Junior who sought the Persian Throne. Cyrus was killed in the Battle of Kunaxa in 401 B.C., and the Greek mercenaries, with Xenophon as one of their commanders, were forced to retreat towards the Black Sea, moving across the Armenian territory.

Xenophon describes Armenia as a large and prosperous country. Retreating up the stream of the river Tigris, the Greeks first moved across the territory of the 18th satrapy. The ruler Orontes (King Yervand) observed the movement of the Greeks with a small armed force, but did not risk confronting them. Greek troops found plenty of food, wine and beer in the Armenian villages. The Greek historian de-

scribes the village dwellings as somewhat two-floored structures, with separate entrances for people and the cattle. Food consisted primarily of meat and dairy products, as well as wheat and rye bread. There were huge vessels in one of the corners of the dwelling, half-buried in the ground, from which wine and beer could be drained through long cane pipes. The Greeks, avoiding cities and crowded roads, gradually moved toward north-west, and finally reached the frontiers of the 13th satrapy, ruled by Tiribaz. The latter permitted the Greeks to pass through his country on the condition that they cause no damage or destruction in population centers along their route.

3. The Campaign of Alexander the Great and Armenia

In 334 B.C., the army of Alexander the Great invaded Asia Minor, marking the beginning of the famous Eastern Expedition to conquer the Achaemenid Empire. Following a series of victories, Alexander conquered the western part of the Persian state. The decisive battle took place in 331 B.C. near the village of Gaugamela, not far from the ruins of Nineveh, the ancient capital of Assyria (territory of modern-day Iraq).

According to ancient authors, Armenians, among other peoples subordinate to the Persians, participated in that battle. The rulers of both Armenian satrapies headed their troops into battle, fighting alongside the Persian army, on its right flank. The right flank pushed back the enemy, and even broke into the Macedonians' rear positions. However, the Persian King Darius III fled the battlefield, and it sealed its outcome in favor of Alexander.

Having conquered the Persian state, Alexander established a new Empire, where Greco-Macedonian settlers became the new ruling elite, and founded Greek-style autonomous cities that provided for the economic and political foundations of the Empire. The Greek language became the lingua franca of the era, and Greek art, religion, and philosophy, fused with the art and faith systems of the peoples of the Near East, gained universal following. The Hellenistic Era began.

Armenia, which was of no strategic value to Alexander, was spared his conquest. Following the Battle of Gaugamela, Armenia de facto freed itself of the Persian rule, and gained independence. Satraps from the Yervanduni family became bona fide kings of 3 Armenian Kingdoms. Armavir became the capital of Armenia Major. Restoring independence helped the country achieve economic development. The use of Greek language and Hellenistic culture in the area gained in prominence.

4. The Seleucids and the Armenian Kingdoms

After the death of Alexander in 323 B.C., a long power struggle broke out among his top lieutenants. As a result, several Hellenistic kingdoms emerged on the ruins of Alexander's Empire, the largest of which was Seleucid state, extending from Asia Minor to Syria and to India.

The Seleucid state shared a common border with Armenia, and made several attempt to assert its rule over the Armenian kingdoms. The Seleucids spared no effort in flaring up centrifugal tendencies in Armenia, attempting to divide the country. As a result, Armenia Minor, as well as Sophene-Commagene, also ruled by members of the Yervanduni family, separated from Armenia Major.

In 201 B.C., Seleucid King Antiochus III succeeded in conquering the divided Armenian kingdoms, and turned them into satrapies of the Seleucid state. Antiochus III appointed Artashes as the ruler of Armenia Major, and Zareh – the ruler of Sophene (a south-western part of Armenia), both members of Yervanduni family. Commagene and Armenia Minor were conquered by the Seleucids even earlier. Thus, after almost a century of independence, Armenia, for a certain period of time, came under the Seleucid rule.

CHAPTER 5

ARMENIAN STATE AT THE HEIGHT OF ITS POWER. THE EMPIRE OF TIGRAN THE GREAT

§ 1. Artashes I: reunification of Armenian Territories

In 190 B.C., Roman legions devastated the army of King Antiochus III in a decisive battle at Magnesia (modern-day Turkey), thereby crushing the power of the Seleucid state.

That battle was of crucial importance to Armenia. Taking advantage of the weakening of the Seleucids, the ruler of Armenia Major Artashes and the ruler of Sophene Zareh declared sovereignty, thereby restoring the independence of Armenia.

Artashes I (189-160 B.C.), in a series of raids, gained control of, and annexed to Armenia all Armenian-populated territories, with the exception of Sophene and Armenia Minor. "Everyone in his state speaks the same language," wrote 1st-century Greek geographer and historian Strabo.

Thanks to the 5th-century Armenian historiographer Movses Khorenatsi, many legends describing the reign and deeds of King Artashes were recorded, and preserved to our days. Having defeated the mountainous tribes of the Alans (ancestors of modern-day Ossetians), Artashes took the Prince of the Alans prisoner. The sister of the latter, Satenik, went up to the bank of the river, and pleaded Artashes to grant her brother his freedom, since "kings do not destroy the progeny of other rulers." Artashes liked the beautiful princess. According to the custom, he kidnapped, and married her, establishing a lasting friendship between the two nations.

Artashes I carried out an administrative and land reform, demarcated private and community lands, erecting stone marks with inscriptions. Throughout many centuries, historians doubted the veracity of that assertion by Movses Khorenatsi, until a number of these stone marks were found during archaeological excavations a few decades ago.

Hannibal

Artashes I encouraged trades and agriculture, patronized commerce, built roads and cities. According to Strabo, "no square inch of uncultured land" remained in Armenia under the reign of Artashes. **In 188 B.C., he founded the new capital of Armenia in the Ararat Valley, and named it after himself – Artashat.** According to the ancient Greek historian Plutarch, the King founded the city of Artashat on the advice of the great *Carthaginian general Hannibal.*

Hannibal, having escaped Carthage, entered into service with Antiochus III. Following the defeat of Antiochus, when the Romans demanded that Hannibal be handed over, he found refuge in Armenia. In 189-188 B.C., while the Roman troops were in Asia Minor, Hannibal was forced to stay in Armenia, which was outside the Roman sphere of influence. It was then that he, having noted the comfortable location of the hill, surrounded by the waters of the Arax River, advised King Artashes I to found a city there. The King assigned Hannibal to personally oversee the construction. No wonder two centuries later Roman authors called Artashat the "Armenian Carthage."

2. The Early Reign of Tigran II: Armenian-Pontic alliance

Artashes was succeeded by his sons: **Artavazd I** (165-131) and **Tigran I** (130-95). The weakening Seleucid power and the smaller neighboring Hellenistic states no longer presented a threat to Armenia. However, Armenia soon confronted a new dangerous adversary. The late 2nd century B.C. saw the rise of the Parthian state in the northeastern provinces of Iran, which by the end of the 2nd century defeated the Seleucids, and conquered the whole of Iran and Mesopotamia. In the war with Parthia, the Armenian army was defeated. With a few territorial concessions, the parties concluded peace, to safeguard which the Armenian Crown Prince Tigran was taken hostage. After his father's death, and in exchange for new territorial concessions to Parthia, Tigran returned to his homeland, and inherited the Armenian throne.

During the reign of Tigran II the Great (95-55 B.C.), Armenia achieved the height of its political power.

Coin of Tigran II

Tigran was an effective ruler, and a talented general and diplomat. He sought to strengthen Armenia's international position and economy, to do that he needed to take control over international trade and transit routes between the West and the East. But first and foremost, Tigran II sought to complete the unification of the Armenian lands started earlier by Artashes I.

In 94 B.C. Tigran II captured the Armenian kingdom of Sophene, annexing it to Armenia Major. Further, he intended to annex Armenia Minor too, which was then under the rule of King Mithridates VI Eupator of Pontus. Mithridates, however, offered him an alliance against the neighboring states, which was reinforced by the marriage of Tigran II and the daughter of Mithridates Cleopatra. Armenia Minor remained under the rule of the Pontian King.

Having thus reinforced his supply lines, Tigran II launched a war against Parthia – Armenia's old competitor. Parthia was delivered a devastating defeat in 87 B.C., and its king was deprived of the title "King of Kings" in favor of Tigran II. Armenia annexed Northern Mesopotamia and a number of other territories. The rulers of neighboring Atropatene, Iberia, Albania, minor kingdoms of Commagene, Adiabene, and Osroene, pledged allegiance to Armenia.

For the peoples of the Near East, Tigran II was the most powerful of all sovereigns. In 83 B.C. Tigran seized the last remaining possessions of the Seleucids – Syria and Cilicia, extending the borders of his state to Palestine and the Mediterranean Sea.

In 77 B.C., Tigran founded his new capital Tigranakert in the central part of his state (south-west of Armenia), re-settling there over 100,000 people deported from conquered Hellenistic cities. The status of royal capital city was also granted to Antioch, the former capital of the Seleucids in Syria, and Artashat, the capital of Armenia.

Tigran's reign was accompanied by the robust development of domestic and foreign trade, to expand and support that, the state minted coins of various denomination. Many of these coins have reached our times, thanks to which we have an accurate image of the likeness of Tigran, and of the Armenian royal regalia of the era. These coins were minted according to Greek standards, and bore inscriptions in Greek.

3. Roman-Armenian War: The Invasion of Lucullus

The strengthening and expansion of the state of Tigran II ran against the interests of the Roman Empire, which sought to establish itself in the Near East. Roman general Lucullus, sent there by Rome, crushed the army of Mithridates VI Eupator, Tigran's father-in-law and ally, and captured the Pontian Kingdom. Mithridates himself found refuge in Armenia. Lucullus sent an embassy to Tigran II, demanding the handover of Mithridates, but was denied. That presented an opportunity of the Romans to launch a war against Tigran II. In the spring of 69 B.C. the army of Lucullus unexpectedly invaded Armenia and laid siege to Tigranakert.

Tigran II, who was touring the southern frontiers of his Empire, did not anticipate a Roman offensive. He promptly began assembling troops for the decisive battle. But before that, a select unit of his force, outmaneuvering the Romans, entered Tigranakert, and quietly escorted the Royal family out into safety. In the decisive battle of Tigranakert on October 6, 69 B.C. Tigran's multinational army suffered a defeat. The units of Greek mercenaries, entrusted with the defense of Tigranakert, handed the city to Lucullus. The Romans looted the city, also causing partial destruction. Lucullus moved his army deeper into the Armenian territory, with the view to capture Artashat. In 68 B.C., in a battle at River Aratsani Tigran delivered the Roman legions a blow, forcing them to leave Armenia. Tigran II also helped Mithridates Eupator to winback his kingdom from the Romans.

4. The Invasion of Pompeius: Artashat Treaty

The Roman Senate recalled Lucullus, and instead sent general Gnaeus Pompeius to the East. Pompeius defeated Mithridates Eupator and recaptured the Pontian Kingdom. After that, he made an alliance with the Parthian Empire against Armenia, and moved his troops toward it.

Tigran II appeared to face a hard confrontation. In 68 B.C. his own son Tigran Jr. rebelled against him, trying to seize the throne. Having failed, Tigran Jr. fled to the Parthian King, where he found a warm reception and even married his daughter. The following year, Tigran Jr., assisted by the Parthians, invaded Armenia again, but was defeated by his father and fled, this time to the West to Pompeius. Tigran Jr. showed the Roman troops the road to Artashat, hoping in secret that Pompeius, after defeating Tigran II, will appoint him the King of Armenia. At the same time, King of Parthia invaded Armenia with his army, to assist his son-in-law Tigran Jr.

Confronting both of his enemies simultaneously, Tigran the Great had to choose the lesser of the two evils. After preliminary negotiations, he went to Pompeius' headquarters, as the latter had approached Artashat. **In 66 B.C. Tigran II and Roman general Pompeius concluded the Treaty of Artashat.** Armenia was declared a "friend and ally" of Rome, preserving its borders, but surrendering Rome other territorial acquisitions, and assuming a massive burden of reparations. Thus, Tigran II preserved Armenia's territorial integrity and his title of King of Kings. Tigran Jr., who was very dissatisfied with such a turn of events, was arrested by Pompeius and taken to Rome as a hostage.

§ 5. The Reign of Artavazd II

Under the reign of Artavazd II (55-34 B.C.), the son and successor of Tigran the Great, Armenia still maintained its status as a great power. But its position between two powerful neighbors Rome and Parthia remained vulnerable.

In 53 B.C. Roman general Marcus Crassus launched an expedition against Parthia. He demanded that Artavazd, as a "friend and ally" of Rome, join his effort with the Roman army. Artavazd, having met with Crassus personally, realized that the latter had chosen the shortest, but most dangerous route for his expedition. The Armenian King advised him to move to Parthia through the territory of allied Armenia, but having found that Crassus was not disposed to take advice, left him and returned to Armenia. Crassus threatened to deal with the disobeying King of Armenia after his victory. At the same time, the Parthian King invaded Armenia, forcing Artavazd II to direct all of his resources to his country's defense, instead of assisting the Romans.

Coins of Artavazd II

Artavazd, foreseeing the failure of Crassus' expedition, chose to establish an alliance with Parthia, thereby breaking his "friendship" with Rome. The new alliance with Parthia was strengthened with the dynastic marriage of the Parthian Crown Prince and the sister of Artavazd II.

In the Battle of Carrhae, the Romans suffered a total defeat by the Parthians. The severed head of Crassus was brought to the capital of Armenia Artashat, where the new allies were celebrating the wedding.

The alliance with Parthia allowed Armenia to successfully withstand the Roman expansion for a considerable period of time. However, dynastic succession in Parthia resulted in the collapse of the Armenian-Parthian alliance by 38 B.C.

Rome did not give up its hopes for the conquest of both Armenia and Parthia. In 36 B.C. Mark Anthony, ruler of the eastern provinces of the Roman Empire launched a new campaign against Parthia across the territory of Armenia. Artavazd II assumed neutrality, since the Armenian-Parthian alliance had ended, and Armenia was not in a position to confront Rome.

The Parthians again crushed the Roman army. Anthony pulled together whatever remained of his troops, and with the aid of Artavazd II, managed to retreat through Armenia.

Anthony blamed his defeat on the neutrality of Artavazd II. In 34 B.C. Anthony led an unexpected large-scale military invasion of Armenia, detaining Artavazd II and his family through deception, and taking them with him to Egypt, declaring their country a Roman province.

The elder son of Artavazd II, Artashes, escaped to Parthia.

While in detention, Artavazd II was offered physical safety and return of his liberty and power in exchange for pledging loyalty to Cleopatra, Queen of Egypt. Artavazd II rejected that choice and preferred death to humiliation. Artavazd II was executed on the order of Cleopatra. His family was later taken to Rome.

6. Fall of the Artashesian Dynasty

The struggle for single leadership of the Roman Empire between Mark Anthony and Octavian ended with the defeat and death of Anthony. Taking advantage of the situation, the eldest son of Artavazd II, Artashes II, ousted the Roman troops with the help of Parthia in 30 B.C., and restored Armenia's independence.

Having become the sole ruler of the Roman Empire, Octavian Augustus focused for some time on the strengthening and consolidation of his power. In 20 B.C. he led a massive army to the East, forcing Parthia to conclude a peace treaty, complete with the return of captured Roman standards and prisoners of war from the legions of Crassus and Anthony, and the annulment of alliance with Armenia.

Under Rome's military and diplomatic pressure, Artashes II (30-20 B.C.) was killed by conspirators. On the "request of the Armenians," the stepson of Emperor Augustus Tiberius held a public coronation in Artashat for Tigran III (20-6 B.C.), another son of Artavazd II, who had been taken prisoner along with his father, and later brought up in Rome. After that, Armenia turned into a client kingdom of Rome.

Coins of Tigran IV and Erato

The last representative of the Artashesian dynasty was **Tigran IV** (6 B.C – 1 AD), who ruled jointly with his sister Queen Erato. In 1 AD, Tigran IV fell in a battle against invading mountainous tribes. His death marked the end of the Artashesian dynasty, which wrote so many wonderful pages in the history of Armenia.

CHAPTER 6

THE GOVERNMENT AND ECONOMY OF ANCIENT ARMENIA

§1. Treaty of Hrandea. The beginning of the Arshakuni Dynasty

After the end of the Artashesian dynasty, the struggle between Rome and Parthia for control over Armenia escalated to a new level. Armenia held strategic importance for both powers. An alliance between Armenia and Parthia represented a threat to the eastern provinces of Rome, whereas Roman control over Armenia minimized any potential Parthian threat to Roman possessions.

For almost a century, the struggle between Parthia and Rome for control over Armenia revealed no victors. Neither side was able to decisively overpower the other, for the designs of both were undermined by the struggle of the Armenian people for independence. No Roman or Parthian puppet in Armenia stayed in office for any significant term – they either were expelled or "deceased unexpectedly." Finally, Parthia was the first to abandon its designs for the conquest of Armenia, adopting instead a policy that was more sensitive to the Armenian interests. In 52 AD Trdat I, brother of the King of Parthia was declared the sovereign King of Armenia. The Roman Empire, however, did not give up its sights on Armenia as easily. On the orders of Emperor Nero, Roman troops under the command of Corbulo captured the capital of Armenia Artashat, causing heavy destruction in the city. At the end of the 10-year war, the Roman army was surrounded by the Armenian and Parthian troops at a place called Hrandea, and surrendered.

In 64 AD the Treaty of Hrandea was signed, under which Rome recognized Trdat I as the sovereign King of Armenia, provided that he be crowned by the Emperor in Rome. Thus, both Rome and Parthia, having failed to conquer Armenia, recognized it as an independent state and provided joint assurances of its sovereignty. The ascension of Trdat I to the throne marked the beginning of the Arshakuni royal dynasty in Armenia.

In 66 AD, Trdat I headed a 3,000-member entourage to Rome, where he was crowned in a public ceremony by Nero. The Emperor received Trdat with honors, holding celebrations and gladiator games. Trdat presented the Emperor with expensive gifts, and demonstrated his fine archery skills by targeting wild animals in the arena. Having crowned Trdat as the King of Armenia, and providing him with presents, Nero also dispatched with him to Armenia a team of experienced master masons, to help rebuild Artashat from the ruins. Beside many buildings constructed the capital, these masters also built a small but magnificent temple at the Royal summer residence at the fortress of Garni.

Pre-Christian Temple of Garni

§ 2. Government of Ancient Armenia

The King was the Head of State, carrying the title "Great King," and since the reign of Tigran the Great – "King of Kings." Often, the royal title was amended by elements as "God," "Kind," "Gracious,"

The Kingdom of Urartu, Ninth–Sixth Centuries B.C.

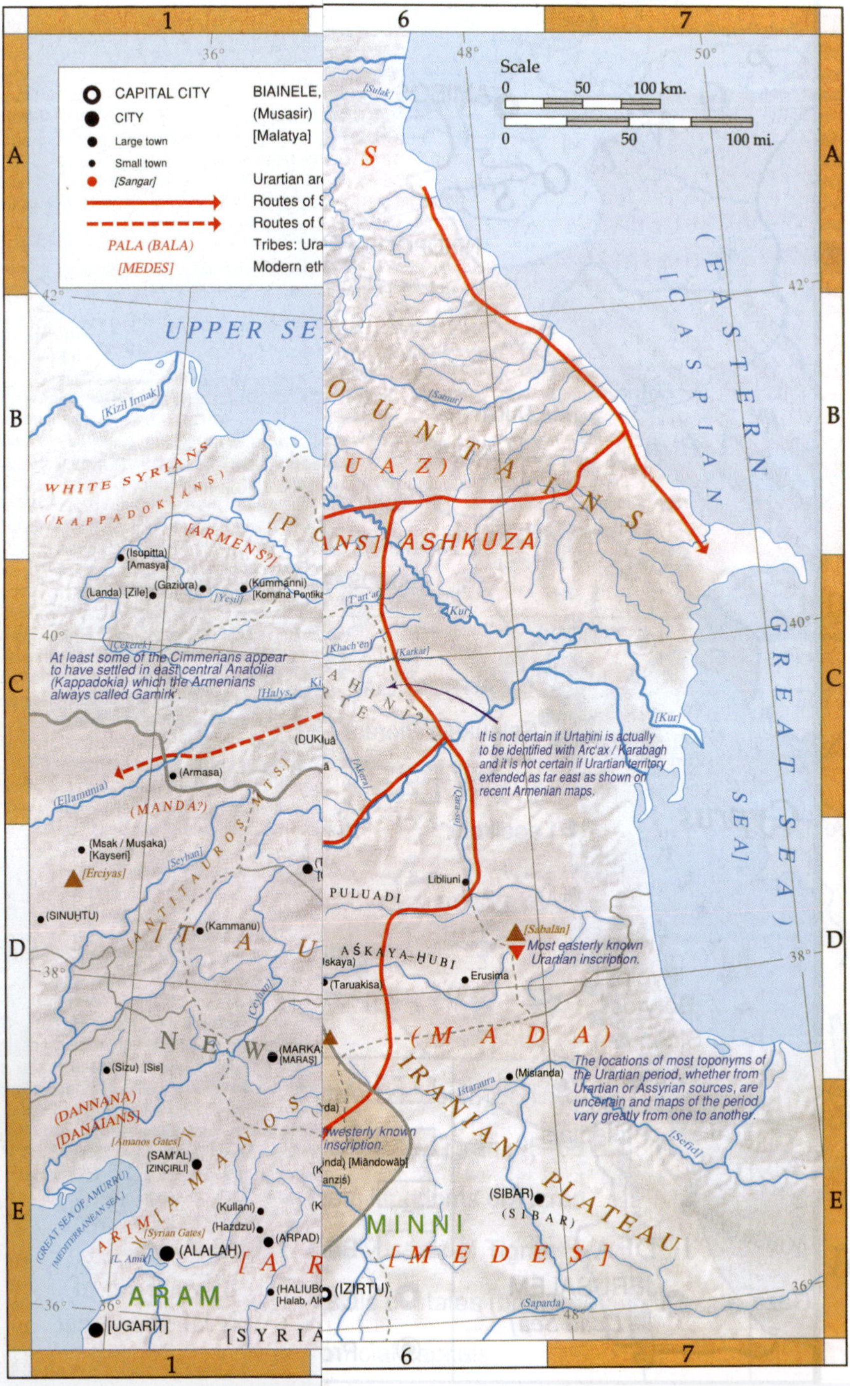

Silver coin of
Tigran the Great

etc. All of that aimed at elevating the institute of royal power. These and other titles often appear on coins and in royal inscriptions attributed to members of the Yervanduni and Artashesian families. Royal power was unlimited. The King and only the King could found cities and fortresses, declare war and make peace.

The King ruled the country with the help of the Court, comprised of sons and brothers of the King, and members of aristocracy close to the King. From among them, the King appointed heads of various public services. Some of the more important of these positions were the following:

Hazarapet: headed the economic affairs of the state, tax collection, urban development, defense construction, construction of roads, bridges, canals, and the Mint;

Sparapet: commanded the Armed Forces of the state and other military commanders;

Tagadir Aspet: conducted the ceremony of royal coronation, diplomatic affairs with other states;

Senekapet: headed the Royal Chancery, and ran the judicial affairs;

Krmapet: the Supreme Priest; headed the college of priests and ran the country's religious affairs.

Issues of special importance to the state, such as succession or adoption of new laws, were brought before the **Ashkharhazhoghov** – a forum of delegates representing all segments of the population. Ashkharhajoghov was convened near Mount Npat, not far from the religious center of Bagavan.

The territory of Armenia was divided into 120 political-military units called strategies. Royal appointees from among the King's close advisers or local aristocracy headed them.

The number of the Armenian military personnel during the reign of Tigran the Great reached as high as 300,000. Of these, one-third included Armenians, and the rest – troops contributed by dependent kings and other rulers.

3. The Economy of Ancient Armenia: Agriculture, Trades, Commerce

Agriculture was the foundation of the economy of Ancient Armenia. Farming and cattle breeding were highly developed. Winemaking and horticulture were developing as well. Horse breeding was one of the more developed fields of activity. Armenian horses were famous in the region since the times of the Achaemenid Empire, and were mainly bred for military purposes. Even ancient authors noted the high combat training and readiness of the Armenian cavalry.

Rural population was free, and was organized in communities. Communities formed a statistical unit, and were the basic administrative constituent of the state. An elected elder headed the community, and its most important issues were addressed at the general meeting of the members of the community. The community land was regularly reassigned among its large patriarchal families. Communities provided troops for service in the military.

During the Artashesian period, Armenia also saw the emergence of private economic enterprises – **dastakerts** and **agaraks**, along with its rural communities. Dastakerts were the property of the King, members of the aristocracy, priest class and military leadership. Agaraks were significantly smaller in size, and were granted to members of the military and civil servants. These farms used enslaved POW labor, and grew grains, vegetables, fruits, as well as breeding cattle.

Private landowners sought to expand their plots by seizing communal property. The state, acting in its own best interests, protected the possessions of rural communities. As early as under Artashes I, special stone signs were introduced to demarcate community and private land.

Cities and urban population played an important role in the Armenian economy. Traders and craftsmen living in these cities were also organized in communities, and had a system of local self-government. The urban population had more advantages than those in the rural communities, paid lower taxes and enjoyed greater protection from the state.

4. The Culture of Ancient Armenia

In the Hellenistic period, the Armenian culture experienced a remarkable progress. The period of reign of the last kings of the Yervanduni dynasty was marked by a continuous growth in one of Armenia's traditional activities – urban development. This included the founding of new cities as Bagavan, Yervandakert, Yervandashat, and others. The reign of Artashes I was marked by the founding of the cities of Artashat, Zarishat, Zarehavan, Nakhijevan, and others. Tigran the Great founded the new capital of Tigranakert in the south-west of the country, on the crossroads of ancient trade routes.

Tigranakert and Artashat boasted magnificent palaces and gardens. There were special theater halls for performances by local and visiting theater troops. Plutarch describes how Artavazd II and King Orodes II of Parthia celebrated the wedding of Artavazd's sister and Crown Prince Pakor of Parthia in Artashat in 53 B.C. The guests at the wedding were enjoying the performance of Euripides' famous tragedy "Bacchae", when the severed head of Marcus Crassus, the Roman general defeated by the Parthians, was brought into the room.

King Artavazd II himself, according to Plutarch, wrote tragedies in Greek. This not only testifies to his education, but it also indicates the popularity of the Greek language among large segments of the Armenian population. The Courts of Tigran II and Artavazd II were known for the large number of philosophers, poets, and historians of Hellenistic culture who lived and worked there.

The kings also built powerful fortresses in strategic locations around the country. Some of the most impenetrable of these fortresses, such as Artagers, Olane, Babiursa and others, played an important role in the country's defense against its enemies.

One of the best known of these fortresses is Garni, where the Royal summer residence was located. The walls of the fortress were built of basalt blocs attached to each other by copper brackets. Walls were 10 meters high and 2 meters deep. Inside the fortress, near the royal palace, there was a bathhouse with a beautiful mosaic floor. But the most magnificent structure was the pagan temple.

Temple of Garni: General View

The temple of Garni (now restored), built in the form of an almost perfect equilateral Greek peripteral from white limestone on the edge of a deep canyon, sharply stands out in contrast with its darker backdrop of surrounding mountains. It is the only architectural monument from the Hellenistic period, preserved in the entire Caucasus region.

Oral folk art tradition gained importance during the period. Traveling singers, artists and dancers performed pieces from epic sagas, songs and legends. Only a small portion of this has reached us through the works of Movses Khorenatsi.

The legend of "Ara the Beautiful" tells how Queen Semiramis of Assyria was smitten by passion for the Armenian King Ara the Beautiful. Ara rejected her, and she went to war against him. In the decisive battle, Ara the Beautiful was killed. Semiramis placed Ara's body on the summit of a mountain, hoping that she could return him to life with the help of her magic. Unsuccessful, and remorseful of her actions, she put Ara's son on the throne of Armenia.

The legend of "Artashes and Satenik" recalls the war that King Artashes I fought against the Alans (Ossetians) who had invaded Armenia from the north. Artashes defeated them in a battle on the River Kur, and took their Prince prisoner. His sister, Princess Satenik of the Alans asked the King for his release. The King liked her, and crossing the river on back of his black stallion in a rapid maneuver, kidnapped the Princess. The marriage of Artashes and Satenik brought an end to the enmity between the two peoples.

Khorenatsi also recorded the ancient ceremonial hymn about the birth of God Vahagn.

In a ringing musical rhythm, the hymn describes the birth of the God, as the Earth, the Heavens and the Golden Sea come together in pains of contraction, and the Golden Cane within the Sea goes into labor. As its vent breathes out smolder and flame, a golden-haired youngster leaps out of the blaze. He has golden hair, his stubble is aglow, and his eyes were like two radiating Suns.

§ 5. The Pagan (pre-Christian) Religion

Already during the Stone Age (7th-4th Millennia B.C.) the ancient Armenians had developed basic elements of religious thinking. Rock drawings from 7th – 4th millennia B.C. discovered in the mountains of the Armenian plateau help understand the lifestyle of pre-historic hunters, and the emergence of early thinking about super-natural forces. An ancient observatory discovered near the village Karahunj (early 2nd millennium), similar to Stonehenge in England, and a rock-drawn map of the stellar sky discovered in the Metsamor settlement (mid-2nd millennium) indicate that, even as early as period described, there already was a certain understanding regarding the influence of celestial bodies on terrestrial life.

One of the stone blocs in Karahunj, adjusted for observation of celestial bodies

Even in the pre-historic period, there was the worship of "vishaps" (dragons), related to the marine origins of life. Their likenesses in the form of large stone-fish figures were placed near water springs and canals.

"Vishap"

As early as in the pre-historic era, tribal societies worshiped the forces of nature. Every tribe had its deities. With the emergence of tribal unions, separate tribal deities began to be identified as members of a single pantheon.

The original supreme deity in the ancient Armenian pantheon was **Hayk, the god of hunting.** His name lies in the origins of the word "Hay," by which Armenians self-identify their ethnicity. In later periods, when ancient Armenian tribes adopted a sedentary lifestyle, the status of the supreme deity was conveyed to **Aregak-Ararich,** symbolizing the Sun, the Creator of Life.

God **Tork Angegh** was the symbol of the forces of nature. God **Ara** represented the cycle of life and rebirth.

In the Yervanduni period, with Armenia under a prolonged Achaemenid rule, the Armenian pantheon evolved significantly under the influence of Iranian beliefs. The status of the supreme deity was conveyed to **Aramazd**, the God of the Heavens, and of the good forces helping the humans.

Goddess **Anahit** was the Guardian Mother of the Land of the Armenians, the Goddess of Fertility and Motherhood, and the Inspirer of Good Deeds. **Vahagn** was worshiped as the God of War, Thunder and Lightning. He was the Protector of the Land of the Armenians, who fought the Vishaps, killing them with his lightning strikes. **Astghik** the Goddess of Love was his Sweetheart, to whose embrace Vahagn returned after his victorious battles. **Mihr** (Mithra) was the God of the Sun, **Vanatur** – the God of Hospitality, **Tir** – the God of Knowledge and Script, and **Naneh** – the Goddess of Wisdom and Guardian of the Family Hearth.

In the Hellenistic period, the Armenian pre-Christian pantheon developed a strong identical connection to the Greek Olympic pantheon: Aramazd-Zeus, Vahagn-Heracles, Astghik-Aphrodite, and Anahit-Hera, among others.

The feast of Navasard was dedicated to Goddess Anahit, the Guardian of the Land of the Armenians. The King, the aristocracy, representatives of urban and rural communities from around the country celebrated the feast of harvest and ripening of grapes near the religious center of Bagavan. The feast lasted about two weeks, during which the public enjoyed athletic competitions and horse races. Winners received awards and gifts. August 11 was celebrated as Amanor – the New Year's Eve in the Armenian Calendar. The King conducted a ceremonial hunt, and concluded the celebrations with a royal banquet.

Head and left hand of the original bronze statue of Goddess Anahit. British Museum, London

CHAPTER 7

THE ESTABLISHMENT OF FEUDALISM IN ARMENIA. ADOPTION OF CHRISTIANITY AS STATE RELIGION

§1. Armenia in the 2nd-3rd Centuries. Development of the Hereditary Reign of the Arshakuni Royal Family

The almost century-long competition between Rome and Parthia for control over Armenia revealed no victors. Under the Treaty of Hrandea in 64 both powers were forced to recognize Armenia's state sovereignty, and act as its joint guarantors. In order to stay loyal to both powers, the King of Armenia was to be selected from among the members of the Arshakuni royal family, and the selection confirmed by the Roman Emperor.

The first Arshakuni to ascend to the Armenian throne was **Trdat I Arshakuni (64-88).** He rebuilt the country's devastated economy, restored the city of Artashat, and developed domestic and foreign trade. In popular memory, his image is merged with that of Artashes I – a leader who restored Armenia's independence.

Trdat was succeeded on the Armenian throne by **Sanatruk Arshakuni (88-110)**, during whose rule Christianity began to penetrate Armenia, preached by Apostles **Thaddeus** (late 1st century) and **Bartholomew (early 2nd century)**. Sanatruk was followed on the Armenian throne by his son **Vagharsh I (117-140)** under whom the new capital of Armenia **Vagharshapat** (present-day Echmiadzin) was built. Following the death of Vagharsh, the Roman Empire, then at the height of its power, appointed **Soemos-Tigran (141-215)** as the king of Armenia, who was probably remotely related to the previous Armenian royal family. There is a record of a rebellion by the Armenian aristocracy, which was defeated, resulting in yet another destruction of Artashat, and the deployment of Roman garrisons in Armenia.

After the death of Soemos, the Armenian throne, with the consent of Rome, passed on to **Vagharsh II (185-198).** Roman garrisons were withdrawn from the country. Rome even provided financial aid to Vagharsh II, to help strengthen the Armenian military, as it sought to protect the country and the Empire's eastern provinces from recurring invasions by mountainous tribes.

Following the death of Vagharsh II in the war against one of these tribes, his son **Khosrov I (198-215)** ascended to the Armenian throne. Thus, Armenia came under the de-facto hereditary rule of the Arshakuni royal family. The weakening Parthian state could no longer object to it, but the Roman Empire had certain initial reservations. King Khosrov was summoned to Rome, arrested and not too much later deceased in Roman custody. His son **Trdat II (216-252)** was declared King of Armenia.

In the meantime, Iran had a royal dynastic succession. The ruler of Fars Province Artashir, son of Sassan, rebelled against Parthia's ruling Arshakuni family. In 226 he overthrew King Artavan V Arshakuni. Iran entered the period of reign of the Sassanid dynasty (226-650).

Parthian princes and many members of the nobility moved to Armenia, being granted hereditary land possessions by the King Trdat. Trdat II actively supported the attempts by Parthian Arshakuni to restore their power in Iran. Because of that, the Sassanids saw the Armenian Arshakuni as their sworn enemy.

Under Shahpur I the Sassanid power reached the peak of its might. The Roman army was crushed, and Emperor Valentinian taken prisoner. Taking advantage of the situation, Shahpur I occupied Armenia and appointed as its ruler his son Vormizd-Artashir, who attempted to introduce Zoroastrianism to Armenia.

Soon, with the help of the Roman Empire, **Khosrov II,** son of Trdat II, was declared King of Armenia. Joint Roman and Armenian troops delivered the Persians a series of serious military defeats. The Armenian army invaded Iran.

Khosrov II fell victim of a conspiracy organized against him by the Sassanids. Pretending to be fleeing Sassanid persecution, a prince named Anak Partev arrived in Armenia with his family. The Persian king had promised him the possessions of the Suren family, along with major privileges. Khosrov II received Anak as his relative, and granted him land possessions. At an opportune moment, Anak did not hesitate to assassinate Khosrov II, although he was killed as well, as he tried to escape. Anak Partev's entire family was executed with the exception of baby Gregory, saved by his nanny. Gregory was to become the Baptist of the Land of the Armenians.

Persian troops conquered Armenia. Devout loyalists helped the son of Khosrov II escape to Rome for his safety.

2. Transition to Feudalism

As early as in the 2nd-3rd centuries, feudal system began to develop in Armenia. Slavery that was not particularly widespread disappeared altogether. Monetary tax was replaced by in kind. Domestic trade sharply declined. Production of goods was increasingly replaced by subsistence economy. Minting of Armenian money ceased, and instead, Roman and Parthian money began to be used in foreign trade transactions.

As early as in the late 3rd century, temporary land possessions that had once been granted in recognition of civil or military service began to turn into hereditary fiefdoms (feuds). Civil service positions became hereditary as well. A ruling class of feudal landlords emerges, consisting of large, mid-size and minor landlords, who had the power to exercise administrative and judicial authority within their possessions. They collected taxes from the population, and carried out jurisprudence. Large feudal landlords in Armenia were called **ishkhan or nakharar,** and their fiefdom – **ishkhanutiun or nakhararutiun.** Only the head of the family held the title ishkhan or nakharar, all other members of the family held the title **sepuh.**

All members of the feudal class were **free people.** Free people did not pay taxes, but as vassals of the King were obliged to enroll in military or civil service. The free class also included the clergy, since the Christian Church was itself one of the largest landowners.

The exploited class consisted of the **unfree** that included the rural, as well as in a later period the urban population. The unfree paid the feudal tribute, and performed various duties.

3. Royal Power and Nakharars. "Gahnamak"

The development and strengthening of the feudal system was accompanied by the gradual weakening of the power of the King. If in the past the Royal Treasury was able to raise a significant amount of tax revenue from across the country, over time the Kings started increasingly to rely on revenues raised from their direct possessions only. The King was the largest landlord, and his hereditary possessions included Armenia's largest and most fertile province – Ayrarat. He also owned all key and border fortresses in Armenia.

King's appointees called **shahabs** ran all major Armenian cities within the royal domain. The city population was involved in trades and commerce, and paid significant amounts in revenue to the treasury. Cities, although unevenly concentrated throughout the territory of Armenia, represented the base of the Royal power. There was a unique, mutually beneficial alliance of sorts between the King and the cities, which provided for the economic links between the country's various provinces.

While the economic and legal power of the feudal landowners was still in the process of formation, they supported the central power of the King. Relations between the King and nakharars were regulated by a specially adopted document called **"Gahnamak".**

"Gahnamak" was a list of all feudal owners in Armenia, arranged in the order precedence based on political weight and influence. The first ten entries included nakharar families, members of which occupied all of the high-level public service positions in the country on a hereditary basis. They were regarded as "senior nakharars," exercised enormous authority, and held significant political influence. The remaining nakharar positions were regarded as "junior," since their placeholders occupied lower-tier positions in public service, and correspondingly enjoyed lesser political weight. According to the order of precedence under Gahnamak, nakharars were entitled to a seat at royal conferences and banquets.

4. Armenian Military: "Zoranamak"

The fame of the Armenian military was well known throughout the Near East. It was admired, and its services coveted by both the Byzantine Emperors and Persian Kings. The military consisted of the Royal Guard and the Armed Forces, raised by nakharars. The size of the wartime military personnel was 100,000 members.

"Zoranamak" provided the list of all feudal landowners of Armenia, and established the terms of their vassal military service, as well as the number of fighters each nakharar was required to arm, equip and contribute on Royal orders. Required contributions ranged from just a few dozen fighters for some to several hundreds or thousands for others, and up to a maximum of 10 thousand fighters.

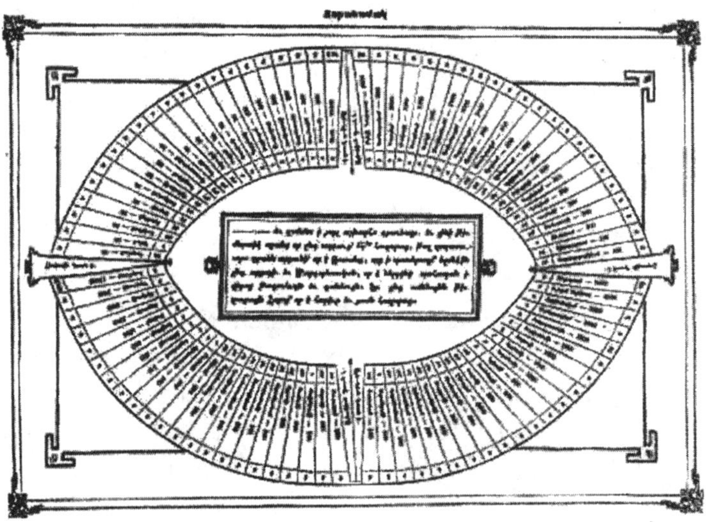

The commander-in-chief of the military was called **sparapet**. The Armed Forces were divided into 4 wings, per directions of the horizon. Each wing had a commander called **bdeshkh**, who was also one of the four deputies to sparapet. Under Zoranamak, all nakharars clearly realized what wing they were assigned to, and where to report, and in what timeframe, if there was an order. The Royal Guard was placed under the special military command of a **maghkhaz**.

The famed Armenian Cavalry provided the principal combat power of the Armenian military. In wartime, enlisting from among the urban and rural population enhanced the size of the military.

5. Armenia in the Late 3rd Century. The Reign of Trdat III

Trdat, the son of Khosrov II and the legitimate heir to the Armenian throne, was taken to Rome following the assassination of his father, and brought up by a well-known Roman family. He grew up to become a strong, tall and well-built young man, took the Olympic Championship in wrestling, and earned fame in combat against the Gothic tribes. With help from the Romans, Trdat began the re-conquest of Armenia.

In the late 3rd century, Roman Army, aided by Armenian troops, delivered the Sassanids a series of devastating defeats. In 298, the two powers concluded a 40-year peace treaty. Both parties recognized **Trdat III (298-330)** as King of Armenia.

Armenia entered a prolonged period of peaceful development and the Armenian people was afforded the opportunity to rebuild their country again.

Grigor, whose father was the assassin of Khosrov II, grew up in Caesarea, Cappadocia, where he adopted Christianity and later admitted to service for Trdat III, in order to repent for the sins committed by his family. When it was found that he was a Christian, Trdat III offered him to renounce the "false faith" and worship the pagan gods. When Grigor declined, he was brutally tortured, and thrown into Khor Virap (an underground chamber for those sentenced to death), from where no one had ever emerged alive. Forgotten by all, St. Gregory lived in that chamber, amid snakes and scorpions, for 13 years.

6. Adoption of Christianity as State Religion

Christianity was preached in Armenia as early as in the 1st century by Apostle Thaddeus, and the 2nd century by Apostle Bartholomew. Although they had numerous followers, the Armenian public, as a whole, was not mature enough then to have embraced Christianity.

Holy virgins Hripsime, Gayane and their disciples, also preached Christianity in Armenia. All of them were stoned to death by the orders of the King, as defectors from the official pagan faith. For that, the God brought upon Trdat and his advisers an incurable disease.

The sister of the King saw a dream, whereupon the Lord said that only St. Gregory could cure Trdat. The King was convinced that Gregory had long been deceased, however, he sent after him, and how surprised every one of the pagans was to find out that St. Gregory was still alive! St. Gregory cured King Trdat, who finally placed his faith in God, and adopted Christianity. On his orders, St. Gregory toured the entire country of Armenia, making sure that pagan temples everywhere were destroyed, and the population converted to the Christian faith.

St. Echmiadzin

In 301, Christianity was declared the official religion of Armenia.

For his lifetime of work, St. Gregory was called the Illuminator. He was elevated as the First Catholicos (Supreme Patriarch) of the Armenian Apostolic Church.

Armenia became the first Christian state in the world. Only in 313 did Roman Emperor Constantine the Great end the persecution of Christians, authorizing them to practice their faith. In 325 he also convened the 1st Universal Council in Nicaea, which adopted the "Symbol of Faith." Yet only in 381, following the 2nd Universal Council in Ephesus, did Christianity become the official religion of the Roman Empire.

7. Armenia in the 4th Century. Weakening of the Central Power

During the 4th century, Armenia entered a period of feudal fragmentation. Large feudal landlords acquired greater independence, and often rebelled against the central power, seeking help from neighboring rulers. Armenian kings often were forced to confront both domestic centrifugal forces, and foreign enemies, such as the Roman Empire and the Sassanid Persia, long known to have sought the conquest of Armenia.

King **Khosrov III (331-338)** was able to assert control over his senior nakharars. In order to prevent any insubordination by them, he insisted that their families permanently resided in the capital, as hostages. The King built the city of **Dvin**, moving his capital there from Artashat. He ordered the planning of a new forest near the city, and populated it with various wild animals for royal hunting and entertainment. The Khosrov Nature Preserve exists to this day.

Under King **Ti(g)ran (338-350)**, the army of King Shahpur II of Persia, having defeated the Romans, invaded Armenia, which was an ally of Rome, and brought devastation to the southern provinces of the country. King Shahpur II then summoned Tiran to his palace, pretending to be preparing a peace treaty, and blinded him.

Tiran's son **Arshak II (350-364)** was able to successfully contain centrifugal forces for a certain period of time. To strengthen central power, he envisaged the building of new urban centers. The nakharars, however, unhappy with the policy of strengthening of the central power, openly rebelled, and ruined one of the cities under construction. Nakharars Meruzhan Artsruni and Vahan Mamikonian switched loyalties, entering the service of Shahpur II, and assuming command of Persian military contingent, invaded Armenia, causing great devastation. Arshak II was able to curb the rebellion, and expel the Persian troops. Shahpur II then lured him to his palace, and instead of signing a peace treaty, imprisoned him.

5th century historian Faustus Byuzand provides a unique and enlightening account of these events. Before receiving the Armenian King, Shahpur II ordered to cover part of the ground in his Royal garden with soil specially imported from Armenia. While giving Arshak II a walking tour of his garden, he noticed that when Arshak walked on Persian soil, he was regretful for insubordination, and made every ef-

fort to assure his loyalty to Shahpur, but whenever he stepped onto Armenian soil, his behavior changed to defiant and independent again. Shahpur was convinced that once Arshak returned to Armenia, he would again assert independence.

Shahpurs troops again devastated Armenia, destroying cities – the base of Royal power in Armenia, and deporting tens of thousands of tradesmen, as prisoners. After an 11-month siege of Fortress Artagers, the Persians took it, capturing Queen Parandzem of Armenia, and torturing her to death. For several years, Armenia remain under Persian rule, until patriotic forces united under Pap, the heir to the Armenian throne, and aided by the Romans, defeated and expelled the Persian troops out of the country.

8. The First Partition of Armenia

King **Pap (370-374)** carried out reforms aimed at strengthening the central authority and the country's defense, again causing the dissatisfaction of the nakharars and the Church. Christian Rome, pretending to act as an "ally" of Armenia, was no less interested in conquering Armenia than the Persians, and in fact, acted in pursuit of undermining Pap's authority. On the secret order of the Emperor, the Commander of Roman troops in Armenia invited the Armenian King to a banquet, and treacherously killed him. Rome immediately followed by installing its puppet **Varazdat (374-378)** on the Armenian throne. The latter was a member of a distant branch of the Arshakuni family that had long ago settled in Constantinople, and had made a name becoming an Olympic champion. Unfamiliar with anything Armenian, Varazdat was unable to establish a power base in Armenia. Patriotic-minded nakharars expelled him, and declared the underage children of Pap as Kings.

When, as a result of the events described above, central power in Armenia finally disintegrated, Persia and the Roman Empire came to an agreement, and in **387 conducted the first partition of Armenia.** One third of Armenia came under Rome, and two-third under Persia. Formally, both parts of Armenia continued to be ruled by kings from the Arshakuni family.

CHAPTER 8

ARMENIA BETWEEN PERSIA AND BYZANTIUM

§ 1. Creation of the Armenian Alphabet

Following the partition of Armenia between Rome and Byzantium in 387, it was evident that the Armenian people faced not only the threat of loss of statehood, but also physical assimilation. There was a great need in finding a way to preserve and strengthen the national and cultural identity of the Armenian people. In addition, although Christianity had been the official religion in Armenia for about 100 years, the deep-rooted centuries-old traditions of its pre-Christian faith were very strong. Lıturgy in Armenian Churches was conducted in Greek and Assyrian, which the ordinary people could not understand. The same languages were used to read the Holy Scriptures, which then were orally interpreted for the faithful. Apparently, these practices made the understanding of the Christian doctrine very difficult. There was a need to have the Holy Scriptures and Church literature in Armenian. Hence, there was a need for a national alphabet.

Sahak Parthev and Mesrop Mashtots (modern sculpture)

Mesrop Mashtots, the creator of the Armenian alphabet was a well educated man. He was fluent in Greek, Assyrian, and Persian, had served in his youth as a Secretary at the Court, and later took his monastic vows and became a preacher. Having preached in various provinces of Armenia, Mashtots became convinced that it would be impossible to eradicate paganism without a Bible written in Armenian, hence there was a need for a national alphabet. He asked help from Catholicos Sahak Partev (grandson of Gregory the Illuminator). With the help of the Catholicos, Mesrop Mashtots presented his project on the creation of the Armenian alphabet to the King of Persian Armenia **Vramshapuh**.

There had been prior attempts at creating a national alphabet, including the so-called "Danielian script". The King presented them to Mesrop Mashtots. Mashtots tried to use the Danielian script to translate a foreign text into Armenian, but the attempt was not successful. This was likely a syncretic script, not quite suitable for the phonetic structure of the Armenian language, and could not serve as a basis for the creation of an alphabet. There is no accurate historical record on them.

Armenian Alphabet

Having obtained the approval and material support of both the King and the Catholicos, Mesrop Mashtots assembled a group of young people hungry for knowledge, spent several years in pursuit of his vision, and visited libraries of many famous centers of education in the Hellenistic world, including Samosata, Nisibis, and others.

After a long, scrupulous research, Mashtots created the Armenian alphabet. It consisted of 36 letters, also used to write numerals. There was a letter corresponding to each sound in the Armenian language, which made reading and writing easier. The first phrase that Mesrop Mashtots translated into Armenian, using the newly created Armenian alphabet was the Biblical: "Hear counsel, and receive instruction, that thou mayest be wise in thy latter end."

Having also developed the cursive form of the Armenian alphabet, Mesrop Mashtots returned to Armenian in 406, where he was received with great honors and public jubilation. With the help of the King and the Catholicos, Mashtots toured the entire Armenia, opening schools and introducing the script.

Mesrop Mashtots lived a long and industrious life, tutoring many students and followers. He was buried in the village of Oshakan, near Echmiadzin, and a church was built at his grave. The Armenian Apostolic Church elevated Mesrop Mashtots to Sainthood. The alphabet that Mashtots created is in use to this day.

§ 2. National Religious Wars against Persian Rule in 450-451 and 481-484

In 428, Royal rule in the Persian-ruled part of Armenia was abolished. In the Roman-ruled part of Armenia that had occurred even earlier. Armenia became a province of the Persian Empire, governed by **marzpan**, a viceroy appointed by the King. However, neither Persia, and nor Rome had attempted yet to limit the freedom of religion in Armenia, or the rights of the nakharars, many of whom still retained their hereditary public service positions.

By mid-5th century, the Persian King presented a demand that the Armenians denounce Christianity and accept Zoroastrianism. The Persian leadership was concerned that in the event of a war against Byzantium Armenia might rebel and provide support to the Empire that shared its faith. Armenians convened a council in Artashat, attended by representatives of all segments of the Armenian society, at which the decision was made to write a letter to the Persian king, explaining the reasons for declining his demand. The Persian King then decided to introduce Zoroastrianism by force. A Persian army was sent to Armenia.

Armenians rose up in defense of their faith, and openly rebelled against the Persian rule, under the command of Sparapet (Commander-in-Chief of the Armenian Army) **Vardan Mamikonian.** Neighboring Iberia and Albania, both of which were Christian, also joined the rebellion. The insurgents conferred with the Byzantine Emperor, and received a pledge of support.

The marzpan of Armenia, **Vasak Syuni,** held a different view on the question of religious conversion. He argued that Zoroastrianism could be accepted pro forma, to assure Persia of the loyalty of the Armenians, providing a way to seek the restoration of the Royal rule within the Persian state. The majority, causing Vasak to leave the insurgency, rejected this plan.

The decisive battle took place on May 26, 451, on the Avarayr Plain. The outnumbering Persian army won the battle, which claimed the life of Sparapet Vardan Mamikonian.

The Byzantine Empire did not support the anti-Persian rebellion in Armenia. Emperor Marcianus was "busy" by ecumenical questions, and had convened the IV Universal Council in Chalcedon. The Council resolved that Jesus Christ had two natures (physes) – divine and human. Those who recognized only one nature of Jesus, were declared "monophysites," and excommunicated.

The Armenian clergy, outraged by Byzantine's deceitful policies, did not attend the Council in Chalcedon, and the Armenian Church did not recognize its decisions. Since then, the Armenian Apostolic Church separated from the Byzantine Orthodox Church, and became fully autocephalous. Later, on its Councils of 506 and 554, the Armenian Apostolic Church repudiates also the Nestorian Dyophysitic and the Eutichian utmost Monophysitic formulas too. The Christology of the Armenian Apostolic Church was formulated fundamentally in line with Alexandrian Theological School and it believes in Cyrillian formula "One Nature of the Incarnate Word".

Because of the ecumenical schism and the readiness of the Armenian rebels to fight for their faith, the Persian king no longer insisted on Armenia's conversion to Zoroastrianism. Although Armenia remained Christian, it became just as strong an adversary of the Byzantine Empire, as Persia.

In 481-484, Armenia again rebelled against Persia as the latter tried to enforce Zoroastrianism. Sparapet **Vahan Mamikonian** led the rebellion. As a result, Armenians succeeded not only in defending their faith, but also convincing Persia to recognize Armenia's self-rule.

Since then, all civil service positions were filled by Armenian nakharars, with the right of inheritance. Nakharars also gained the right to elect the **Tanuter** (Governer of the Country) whose nomination was subject to confirmation or rejection by the Persian monarch.

§ 3. Armenia in the 6th Century under the Persian and Byzantine Rule

In the 6th century, Armenia remained partitioned between the Byzantine Empire and the Sassanid Persia.

Feudalism continued to develop in the eastern part of Armenia under Persian rule. Armenia maintained internal autonomy, and state institutions continued to function. The country was governed by Tanuter – appointed by the Persian King from among the Armenian nakharars, or sometimes members of the Persian ruling family. The Armenian Apostolic Church retained its privileges, and was the country's largest landowner. Civil service positions were generally filled by Armenian nakharars, on hereditary basis, and were passed on to first-born successors, along with corresponding titles. Just like in the past under the Armenian kings, nakharars were required to perform vassal military service, now of course for the Persian monarch. Persian kings made periodic attempts to undermine the positions of the nakharars, seeking a tightening of the rules of autonomy, and the introduction of Zoroastrianism. Nakharars usually resisted attempts, triggering the next insurgency against the Persians. The rebellion in 571 by Armenian nakharars under **Vardan Mamikonian** (Vardan the Handsome) turned into a war of liberation that lasted 20 years.

In the western part of Armenia, under Byzantine since the partition of 387, the situation was somewhat different. Byzantine ruled not only one-third of Armenia Major, but also the whole of Armenia Minor, which had a significant Armenian population. In the early 6th century, after a series of prolonged wars, Emperor Justinian I (527-565) restored the former borders of the Empire and reintroduced slavery. To finally incorporate the Armenian territories into the empire, he needed to abolish the feudal system, and weaken the economic and political autonomy of the nakharars.

Justinian divided the Armenian-populated territories of the empire into 4 administrative areas: Armenia I, Armenia II, Armenia III and Armenia IV. If in the past the nakharars exercised military, judicial and administrative authority within their possessions, now they no longer had it, being turned into ordinary landowners. On imperial orders, the first-born succession rule for land inheritance was abolished, and all the sons and daughters of the nakharar were granted the right of inheritance. That facilitated the fragmentation of nakharar estates, undermining the economic and political bases of the feudal system.

Byzantium had not given up its desire for the conquest of all of Armenia, and therefore it supported the new Armenian rebellion against Persia in 571-572. Persia and Byzantium engaged in a 20-year war, with ended with the victory of Byzantium. Military activities took place on the territory of Armenia, which was again subjected to devastation and destruction. As described below, Emperor Mauricius (582-602), in exchange for helping King Khosrov II of Persia restore his throne, gained territorial concessions from him at the expense of Armenia.

In 591 the second partition of Armenia took place. This time, the country was divided almost equally between the Byzantine Empire and the Sassanid Persia. Both sides conducted a policy that encouraged the deployment of Armenian troops outside the country. 6th century Armenian historian Sebeos has preserved the content of Emperor Mauricius' letter to Khosrov II of Persia, in which he advises to use Armenian troops on the remote borders of his kingdom. "If they win, they will have defeated our enemies, and if they die, it's our enemies that will die."

4. Early Medieval Culture of Armenia

In the preceding era, Armenia had a great need in written word, and had accumulated an enormous literary potential. All of that splashed out with the creation of the Armenian alphabet. That period was marked by the rise of a whole galaxy of talented Armenian authors – writers, translators, hagiographers, historians, philosophers, etc. Classical translations of many canonical works of the Church's "founding fathers" were performed. The Armenian translation of the Holy Bible from Greek and Arameian came to be known as one of the best. Certain spiritual treatises reached modern times only in their Armenian translation. Some of the more famous authors and their notable works include the following:

Faustus Byuzand, History of Armenia: describes events of the 4th century, when the Armenian kings were engaged in an uneven struggle with Persia and the Roman Empire, to preserve central power and the country's territorial integrity;

Aghathangelos, History of Armenia: describes events related to the adoption of Christianity in Armenia as state religion; contains the record of historical events of the late 3rd and early 4th centuries in Armenia, Rome and Persia;

Koryun: Life of Mashtots: contains a detailed description of the life and work of Mesrop Mashtots, creator of the Armenian alphabet;

Movses Khorenatsi, History of Armenia: a complete history of Armenia from pre-historic times to the author's era, based on a critical review of multi-language sources, many of which are presently lost; represents one of the most comprehensive records of not only events related to the history of Armenia, but also to those of neighboring nations, as well as of ancient Armenian epic chronicles and legends. Khorenatsi is rightfully regarded as the Father of the Armenian Historiography, and his works are translated to many foreign languages;

Yeghishe, History of Vardanants: describes events of the mid-5th century, as the Armenian people fought an uneven struggle against the Persian power, to preserve its national identity and Christian faith;

Page from the manuscript The History of Armenia by Movses Khorenatsi

Ghazar Parpetsi, History of Armenia: contains a detailed account of the events of the second half of the 5th century, and the Armenian rebellion against Persia under Vahan Mamikonian; provides a brief account of the history of ancient Armenia as well;

Yeznik Koghbatsi, Denial of Heresies: a detailed analysis of various pre-Christian, heretical and other faith schools from the standpoint of the Christian doctrine;

David Anhaght, Frontiers of Wisdom: a masterful adaptation of classical philosophical ideas to the Christian doctrine, to resolve Christological disputes; the famous philosopher, known for his encyclopedic knowledge, lived and taught in Alexandria, Rome and Athens, and always emerged as the winner in philosophical debates, having earned the title "Anhaght" – "Invincible."

The works of these, as well as other authors from the 5th century are of enormous historical and cultural value as examples of the early Christian civilization, and many of them have been translated into various European languages.

In the 6th-9th centuries, the rich traditions of the Armenian historiography were further developed by historians Hovhan Mamikonian, Movses Kaghankatvatsi and others.

Bishop **Sebeos** (7th century) dedicated his efforts to the study of ancient history and events pertaining to his own era. His work draws many parallels with the History by Movses Khorenatsi, but the factual material he operates on often differs from that of Khorenatsi, indicating that he might have used sources that were unknown to Khorenatsi.

The History by **Ghevond** (8th century author) discusses events of the period of foreign invasions and Arab rule in Armenia. It also contains a detailed description of taxes levied by the Caliphate in Armenia.

The historical period was marked by the development of exact sciences in Armenia. **Anania Shirakatsi,** a world-famous scientist of the 7th century, made valuable contributions to the study of mathematics, physics, astronomy and the calendar.

Shirakatsi argued that the Earth has the shape of a ball, and offered scientific hypotheses to Solar and Lunar eclipses that are similar to the modern explanations of these phenomena. His tables of four mathematical actions are regarded as particularly valuable.

Temple Zvartnots. Restored columns

The period was also marked by the early development of the Armenian Christian architecture. The 4th-5th centuries saw the construction of the first Christian churches on the spots where once pre-Christian temples stood. One of the best monuments of Armenia's early Christian architecture, built on the spot of a pre-Christian temple is the Cathedral of the Only Begotten, constructed in 303 in Vagharshapat (present-day Echmiadzin) -- the oldest continually active church in Armenia and the world.

Initially, simple Roman oblong buildings were the prevailing

Ruins of Zvartsnots Temple

architectural style. The 5th century was marked by the development of the basilica – arched buildings with supporting columns. This style was followed in the churches built in Ashtishat, Yereruyk, and elsewhere. A very typical example of a domed temple built in this era and preserved to this day is the temple of St. Hripsime (618).

Model of Zvartnots Temple

A unique example of central dome structure is the famous temple of Zvartsnots, the ruins of which are located on the road from Yerevan to Echmiadzin. Zvartsnots was built in the mid-7th century, and represented a three-story pyramidal structure resting on powerful, circularly arranged internal columns. The temple had many round windows that allowed the light to penetrate the interior, and its exterior walls were covered by rich decorative art.

CHAPTER 9

ARMENIA UNDER ARAB DOMINATION. REIGN OF THE BAGRATUNI DYNASTY

§ 1. Establishment of Arab Rule in Armenia

Soon after its establishment in early VII century, the Arab Caliphate embarked on a policy of conquest against its neighboring countries. The Persian state was destroyed, and Byzantium lost its Near Eastern provinces.

The first Arabs invasion into Armenia took place in 640, resulting in the destruction of Dvin. Arab invasions also occurred in 642/643 and 650. Since Armenia was not powerful enough, and the Byzantine Empire, itself trying hard to fight off the Arabs, was unable to provide any meaningful assistance, Armenian Sparapet Theodoros Rshtuni determined that, in order to save the country from future invasions, he needed to negotiate with the Arabs.

In **652, Theodoros Rshtuni** traveled to Damascus and concluded a treaty with the Arab viceroy of Syria Emir Muawia. Armenia recognized the supremacy of the Caliph and agreed to pay a tribute - a certain amount within its ability, and was allowed to maintain 15,000 troops. The Caliphate agreed to provide military assistance to Armenia if an enemy attacked it. The treaty was directed against Byzantium, and served the interests of both parties. The treaty allowed Armenia to retain de facto independence until the late 7th century. The brief period of peace afforded the Armenian people the opportunity to develop and prosper. It was in the 7th century that the two masterpieces of the Armenian architecture – the temple of St. Hripsime and the temple of Zvartnots were built. The temple of St. Hripsime has remained active throughout the centuries, and up to the present. The temple of Zvartnots was a unique architectural marvel, with a circular shape, and a height of 50 meters.

2. Armenia within the Arab Caliphate

In the late 7th century, when the Arab Caliphate finally prevailed over Byzantium, it no longer needed a semi-independent Armenia. In 703, the powerful Arab army invaded Armenia spreading devastation along its way. Prosperous cities were reduced to rubble, churches destroyed, fortresses taken, the population killed or enslaved and deported. Having conquered Armenia and the rest of the South Caucasus, the Arabs established a Caliphate-dependent governorate called Armina, with the administrative center in the capital of Armenia Dvin.

In 725 the Arabs conducted a population and land census. The population, including the nobility and clergy, was required to pay property and individual taxes. The Armenian population was being driven out of fertile lands and forced to into the mountainous areas. To consolidate their power, the Arabs began to resettle Muslim tribes in Armenia, causing changes in the ethnic makeup of the population. The newly settled tribes formed self-governing emirates and caused the Armenian population considerable troubles by mounting insistent attacks against them. As a result of continuous persecution and economic hardship many Armenians began leaving the country and re-settling within the borders of the Byzantine Empire. Many nakharar families ceased to exist, while some moved to Byzantium.

3. Struggle of the Armenian People Against the Arabs

The Armenian people did not simply accept submission, but in fact mounted a series of rebellions against the Arab yoke. The first anti-Arab rebellion in **703** was led by **Smbat Bagratuni,** who succeeded in completely destroying the enemy's forces in the Battle of Vardanakert. The rebellion subsided only after the Arab authorities were forced to recognize the hereditary rights of the Armenian nakharars. Several years later, the Arab governor invited the Armenian nakharars to Nakhijevan, enticing them with promises to expand their hereditary rights, and burned several hundred people alive enclosed in church. But even these atrocities failed to break the spirit and momentum of the Armenian liberation movement.

As a civil war broke out in the Caliphate in **748-750** between the Omayyad and Abbasid families, Armenians, led by **Grigor Mamikonian,** launched a liberation struggle. After the civil war, the new Caliph moved to brutally suppress the Armenian rebellion.

The largest Armenian rebellion occurred in **774-775,** and was led by **Mushegh Mamikonian and Smbat Bagratuni.** The insurgents struck and defeated the Arab garrisons, captured many fortresses and towns, and laid siege of the city of Karin. The Caliph sent a 30,000-strong retaliatory army to Armenia. In the decisive battle, the rebels fought bravely, but were outnumbered by the Arabs, which determined the outcome of the battle due to their number. The rebellion was crushed mercilessly.

A large anti-Arab uprising took place in 850-855. By the mid-9th century, the Armenian nakharars, taking advantage of the weakening of the Caliphate, had achieved significant domestic autonomy. The nakharars collected taxes from the population themselves, and then sent the Caliph that revenue. To undermine the position of the nakharars, and push the country to bankruptcy, the Caliph sent Emir Abuseth to Armenia in 850, under the pretense of collecting the revenue. Princes Bagratuni, Artsruni and others met the Emir at the border of their possessions, and paid him the revenue, without letting him into the country. Besides, they also subdued a number of Arab tribes that had been repeatedly looting and pillaging the Armenian countryside. That was an act of outright insubordination, and the following year, the Caliph sent Emir Yusuf to Armenia, along with troops. By deception, Yusuf captured a group of nakharars, looted the provinces of Taron and Vaspurakan, and decided to spend the winter in the city of Mush. Units under the command of the insurgent nakharars, joint by militia from the population of the mountainous areas, mounted an unexpected attack against the Arab troops, and killed Yusuf.

In 852, the Caliph sent to Armenia a large armed contingent under the command of general Bughay, who in the course of the following several years managed to devastate many provinces, and arrest many nakharars, but failed to suppress the rebellion completely nonetheless. Despite their brutality, the Arabs were unable to stop the country's social and economic development, and kill the liberation movement. The period was marked by a number of nakharar families, including Bagratuni, Syuni, Artsruni, and others, gaining considerable strength and power, while families as Mamikionian, Kamsarakan, and others left the scene and disappeared.

4. Reestablishment of Armenia's Independence. The Rise of the Bagratuni Dynasty

By the end of the 9th century, the Arab Caliphate had weakened and was on the verge of decline. In order to keep Armenia under control, the Caliph began to appoint the country's governors from among the Armenian nakharars. In 855, **Ashot Bagratuni** was appointed the Great Prince (governor) of Armenia. During his long and peaceful reign, Armenia gained considerable economic and political power. Universally respected and admired, Ashot Bagratuni was declared the King of Armenia in 869, in a congress of Armenian nakharars. The congress appealed to the Caliph, asking him to recognize that act. Only 16 years later, having realized the futility of his attempts to restore full control over the country, and fearful that otherwise Armenia would ally itself with Byzantium, did **the Caliph finally recognize Ashot Bagratuni as the King of Armenia.** Although formally Armenia remained as part of the Caliphate, it managed to restore its independence.

In 885, Ashot I was officially crowned as the King of Armenia, marking the **beginning of the Bagratuni Royal Family (885-1045).** The Caliph sent Ashot Bagratuni a royal crown and regalia. Ashot I was also recognized as King by Byzantine Emperor of Armenian origine Basil I, who sent him a royal crown as well.

§ 5. Strengthening of the Bagratuni Kingdom

Ashot I (885-890) was an outstanding statesman and diplomat. Through dynastic marriages and concessions, he succeeded in uniting independent Armenian principalities and even Arab emirates into a single state. He visited Constantinople and made a trade alliance with Byuzantium. On his way back to Armenia, he dies unexpectedly.

Fortress Amberd

His son and successor **Smbat I (890-914)** continued his father's policy, strengthening and expanding the Armenian state. In 893 he also visited Constantinople and reinforced the alliance with Byzantium.

The strengthening power of the Bagratuni kings caused the dissatisfaction of the Caliph and neighboring Arab emirates, as well as senior Armenian nakharars, who sought to maintain their independence. Emir Yusuf of the neighboring Atropatene conducted a series of incursions into Armenia, but each time suffered a defeat. Yusuf took advantage of dissatisfaction of the ruler of Vaspurakan **Gagik Artsruni,** and with the consent of the Caliph, crowned him as the King in 908, granting him the right to collect Armenia's taxes. The troops of Yusuf and Gagik Artsruni entered the possessions of the Bagratuni family. Misleading Smbat I with promises of peace, Yusuf arrested him and ordered to be crucified on the wall of the Dvin Fortress. Armenia was looted, and once again pushed to the brink of losing its independence.

Smbat's son and successor **Ashot II (914-928)** headed the struggle against foreign occupiers. With a small force, he managed to score impressive victories, earning the popular nickname Ashot Yerkat –

"Steel." In 921 at a battle near Lake Sevan he completely wiped out the outnumbering Arab forces. Gevorg Marzpetuni, a nakharar loyal to Ashot, scored a similarly impressive victory over the Arabs. Watching the country's devastation, many Armenian nakharars united behind the idea of a central power. Ashot Yerkat travelled to Constantinople and signed a treaty of alliance against the Caliphate. The Caliph, concerned with that development, not only sent Ashot Yerkat a royal crown in 922, but also bestowed upon him the title Shah of Shahs – King of Kings, which amounted to the recognition of the Bagratuni as sovereign rulers of Armenia, and all local kings, princes and emirs as his vassals.

6. Armenian Kingdom of Bagratuni at the Height of its Power. Structure of Government.

During the reign of kings Abas I (928-953), Ashot III (953-977), Smbat II (977-990), Gagik I (990-1021) Armenia enjoyed a period of political, economic and cultural ascent. The country focused on restoring the economy, destroyed in the preceding period.

Abas I moved his residence to the city of Kars, which for a brief period became the capital of Armenia. The core of the Armenian armed forces was 10,000-strong royal guard, called Azatagund. It was a professional army formed from members of nobility. In wartime, it was joined by the Marzpan Corps - armed forces under the command of vassal kings, princes and emirs. The size of the army, comprised of infantry and cavalry, reached up to 100,000. Their commander in chief was Sparapet, appointed from among the nakharars known as the most loyal to the throne.

The Great Prince administered the royal estates and the Treasury, and supervised all other state officials, while reporting directly to the King. Over time, that position became hereditary for the Pahlavuni family. The highest judicial authority traditionally belonged to the Head of Church – the Catholicos.

Large-scale construction projects were launched. Queen Khosrovanush oversaw the construction of monastic centers in Sanahin and

Haghpat, as well as numerous schools and hospitals.

The city of Ani was built and declared the new capital of Armenia in 961. The official coronation of Ashot III as King of Kings of Armenia was attended by the kings of Georgia and Albania, as well as kings and emirs of a number of Armenian provinces.

Grand Cathedral of Ani

The city was located on an elevated plateau near river Akhurian, and surrounded by a circle of powerful fortifications. Over time, Ani became a major commercial and tradecraft center, with a system of urban self-government.

The city had numerous manufacturing shops and guilds. Over time it also built many convenient markets, hotels, paved streets and churches. The city began to grow so rapidly, that 20 years later Smbat II built the second ring of fortified walls around it, with a length of 2,500 meters and a height of 10 meters. In 987, Smbat II recaptured Armenia's former capital Dvin from the Arabs. Other major cities in Armenia included Van, Kars, Artsn, Nakhijevan, Manazkert.

King Gagik I won a number of victories against neighboring Arab emirates, and further expanded the territory of the Bagratuni family possessions. Old fortresses were restored and new ones built, including Bjni, Amberd, and others, in addition to churches and monasteries.

7. Armenia's Economic Development in the 9th-11th Centuries

The reign of the Bagratuni family was marked by the rapid development of Armenia's economy. In agriculture, the three-field system was widely adopted, along with artificial irrigation and enrichment of plough-land. Heavy plough with metal share was used to cultivate virgin soil. Agricultural products included green beans, cucumber, cabbage, carrot, watermelon, etc. Grape cultivation was an important area of activity.

The natural abundance of valley and highland pastures in Armenia ensured the widespread development of cattle breeding, both large and small. Cattle breeding not only helped supply the country's growing population with meat and dairy products, but also provided the country's tradesmen with raw materials such as skin and wool. Urban life was actively developed. Instead of the ancient cities destroyed by the Persians, new cities emerged, serving as medieval centers of trades and commerce. Large cities enjoyed self-government, and elected their officials. Tradesmen were organized in shops with elected leadership. Some of the better-developed professions included smithcraft, armor making, pottery and leather processing. Major and small towns had permanent markets where agricultural and manufactured production was sold. Trade fairs were often held on major crossroads and places of pilgrimage.

Traders, moneychangers and jewelers were organized in guilds, and elected elders for themselfs. Armenian traders actively participated in the international transit trade between the West and the East. Caravans to the Black Sea or Mediterranean ports transported Chinese silk and Indian spices, gems and gold jewelry, and Russian furs were exported to Baghdad and Cairo. Special money exchange guild in any major Armenian city ensured the availability of a large amount of foreign and domestic currency in different denominations. Armenian manufactured products enjoyed a consumer demand both within and outside the country. Armenia exported horses, cochineal (red paint), salt, copper, wines, silk and wool fabric, gold and silver jewelry.

§ 8. The decline of the Bagratuni Kingdom.

In the 9th century, the central power of the Bagratuni family began to decline, setting off a dynastic competition for the Armenian throne. A number of provinces in the country began to distance themselves economically, with their rulers striving to assert independence from the kings in Ani. Some of the major provinces among these included Vaspurakan, Syunik, Tashir and Vanand kingdoms and the Tayk, Taron and Artsakh principalities.

The Byzantine Empire, which was at the height of its power, began absorbing them one by one. In exchange for transfer of these minor provinces to Byzantine rule, Emperor Basil II provided their rulers possessions in Asia Minor, and honorable Byzantine titles. Part of the Armenian nobility, under the pressure of Byzantium, supported a treacherous policy of Armenia's unification with Byzantium. Acting along this line, King Hovhannes-Smbat left a will, in which he bequeathed Armenia's capital Ani to Byzantium.

Ani: City Walls

The attempts by Byzantium to capture Ani by force were unsuccessful. Sparapet Vahram Pahlavuni repelled all attacks, and with popular support, declared **Gagik II (1042-1045)**, the nephew of the previous king, as King of Armenia. Following that, Emperor Constantine Monomachus invited Gagik II to Constantinople pretending to be interested in concluding a treaty of alliance. **In 1045, having deceitfully taken King Gagik II prisoner, Byzantium overthrew the Bagratuni Dynasty, and soon after captured Armenia's capital Ani.**

§ 9. Armenia's Conquest by the Seljuks. The Battle of Manazkert.

In the early 11th century, nomadic Turkic Seljuk tribes from Central Asia streamed westward, and conquered Iran. In 1055, the Seljuks conquered the capital of the Caliphate Baghdad, and the Caliph granted their leader Tughril the title of the Sultan (king). The Seljuks conducted regular incursions into Armenia (1047, 1048, 1054, and 1064), causing the destruction of cities as Artsn, Kars, Ani, Dvin, and taking more than 100,000 people away into slavery.

Cathedral of Kars. Citadel in the background

In **1071**, a decisive battle took place near the Armenian city of **Manazkert** between the armies of the Seljuk Turks and the Byzantine Empire. The Byzantine army was crushed, and the rule of the Seljuk Turks descended upon the Near East.

Following the battle of Manazkert, the Seljuks captured Asia Minor, and created a vast empire the frontiers of which extended from the Bosporus to Central Asia. Armenia was included in the Seljuk state, and subjected to new destruction. In separate provinces, however, semi-independent local Armenian kingdoms and principalities continued to survive.

CHAPTER 10

THE ARMENIAN STATE IN CILICIA

§ 1. Armenians in Cilicia. The Formation of Armenian Principalities in the 11th Century

Cilicia is a province in the southeast of the Asia Minor peninsula. On three sides, it is surrounded by the rugged mountains of the Taurus Range, and in the South – by the waters of the Mediterranean Sea. It is divided into mountainous and lowland parts. Cilicia has been known for its rich natural resources, moderate climate, fertile soil and green pastures. The country was crisscrossed with full-flowing rivers, and its coast was blessed with convenient harbors.

Armenians inhabited this area, along with Greeks and Assyrians, since antiquity. The Armenian population in Cilicia increased rapidly in the mid-11th century due to immigration from Armenia, and Armenians soon became the ethnic majority.

The unassailable Fortress Lambron

The resettlement of Armenians in Cilicia was the result of the policy of the Byzantine Empire to force Armenians out of their historical homeland, to retain control over Armenia. With the fall of the Bagratuni Dynasty, and as a result of the devastating invasions of the Seljuk Turks, the number of Armenians resettling in Cilicia grew larger and larger. Many noble families resettled there as well.

One of the Armenian princes, **Ruben (1080-1095),** captured several fortresses in the mountainous part of Cilicia and declared himself a ruler, independent of Byzantine. This event, taken place **in 1080, marked the beginning of the independent Armenian principality of Rubinians in Cilicia, which was destined to become the second homeland for the Armenians.**

Levon's fortress – Odzaberd

All attempts by Byzantium and the Sultanate of Iconia to subdue the principality founded by Ruben were unsuccessful. The ensuring crusader campaigns further weakened the Sultanate of Iconia and contributed to the strengthening of the newly-born Cilician Armenian state, the capital of which became the city of **Sis**.

§ 2. Unification of the Armenian Principalities under the Leadership of the Rubinian Princes

In 1096-1099, the first Crusader campaign took place. The Sultanate of Iconia and other Seljuk emirates suffered a defeat. Several Crusader states were formed in the Near East. An opportunity emerged to liberate the Armenian lands.

Ruben's successors were able to take advantage of that opportunity. **Toros I (1095-1128)** captured the cities of Sis and Anarzaba from Byzantium, and repelled the Seljuks' attempts to invade Cilicia. **Levon I (1129-1137),** aided by the Armenian population, took control of the lowland Cilicia, driving out the Byzantine and Crusader troops. That already constituted an open challenge to the Byzantium; therefore the Emperor personally led a punitive expedition. The powerful Byzantine army captured first the lowland Cilicia, and then undertook an offensive against the fortresses in mountainous Cilicia. Levon I, together with his two sons, was taken prisoner and escorted to Constantinople. Cilicia once again fell under the control of Byzantium.

A few years later, one of Levon's sons, Toros, escaped Byzantine captivity, and took leadership of the liberation movement in Cilicia. **Toros II (1145-1169)** quickly took control of mountainous Cilicia, driving out the Byzantine garrisons. His younger brothers **Mleh** and **Stephane**, who also had escaped Byzantine captivity, assisted him. Having assembled a 30,000-strong army, Toros soon established control over lowland Cilicia as well. Only a handful of major cities remained under Byzantine control. All attempts by the Byzantine troops to reestablish control over Cilicia were unsuccessful. Also unsuccessful were attempts by the Seljuks and Crusaders to capture Cilicia's frontier territories.

Toros's brothers and successors **Mleh (1169-1176)** and **Stephane (1176-1187)** completed the unification, with the Armenian principality, of lowland Cilicia, with its convenient harbors of **Adana, Ayas and Tarsus,** which were major centers of international transit trade in the Near East.

3. Reign of Levon II. International recognition of the Cilician Armenian Kingdom

Levon II Rubinian (1187-1219) was a talented general and smart politician. He achieved victories over his neighboring Muslim countries and expanded the borders of his state, bringing major feudals under central power. To develop foreign trade, Levon II minted gold, silver and copper coins with the image of his likeness and an Armenian inscription on them, and established trade relations with Venice and Genoa. He smartly took advantage of the capabilities of the Crusaders, using them in the interests of his state.

Coins of Levon II

In 1190, during the Third Crusade, German Emperor Friedrich Barbarossa tragically died during the passage through the Cilician mountains. The German army of Crusaders found itself in a difficult position. Friedrich's successor needed to not only promptly ensure the material supply of the troops, and lead them to Palestine, but also to organize the transportation of his father's remains to Germany. Levon II extended to him the help he needed. In appreciation Heinrich VI, having become the Emperor, fulfilled his promise to crown Levon as King.

At the Christmas holidays in 1197, the Archbishop of Mainz, acting in his capacity as the envoy of the Holy Roman Emperor, crowned Levon II as the King of Cilician Armenia, in an official and public ceremony, under the Catholic rite. Levon II also received a crown from Emperor Alexius III of Byzantine.

On January 6, 1198, the day on which the Armenian Church celebrates Christmas, Levon II was elevated to the throne under the Armenian rite in a large public ceremony in Tarsus.

4. Establishment of the Rule of Zakarian Princes in Armenia Major. Armenian-Georgian Union

In the early 12th century the Seljuk Empire disintegrated. Several independent Muslim emirates emerged on the territory of Armenia. At the same time, the period was marked by the rise of the Georgian state, which had overthrown the Seljuk rule. Many Armenian principalities sought Georgian protection, combining forces in the struggle against Muslim emirates.

One of the highly positioned families in the Georgian Court was the Armenian noble Zakarian (Mkhargrdzeli-Arghutinsky) family: **Zakare Zakarian** was the **Amirspasalar** (commander in chief), and his brother **Ivane – Atabek** (head of palace services, mentor to the crown prince). They jointly headed the movement for the liberation of Armenian territories.

In the late 12th century, during the reign of **Queen Tamar of Georgia (1184-1207)**, Armenian-Georgian cooperation helped liberate the entire northeastern part of Armenia, the cities of Ani, Kars, Dvin, etc. **By 1207, Armenia's northeastern provinces were liberated from the Seljuks and united under the rule of the Zakarian noble family.**

Zakare Zakarian was the ruler of all liberated Armenian territories, while also serving as the Amirspasalar of Georgia. Other Armenian noble families, such as Proshian, Orbelian, Dopian, Vachutian, and others, served as his vassals. Zakarians had their capital in Ani. During the peaceful reign of Zakarians, Armenia again achieved economic and cultural progress. Cities, fortresses and roads were restored, and foreign and domestic trade increased.

§ 5. Reign of the Hetumian Dynasty in Cilicia. Armenian-Mongol Alliance

In 1236-1244, Mongol Tartars conquered Armenia. Ani, Karin, Kars, Dvin and other cities were reduced to rubble, the population either killed or taken to slavery. Nomadic Turkic tribes that had accompanied the Mongols seized some of Armenia's best lands and settled there.

The Mongol rule took a very heavy toll on Armenia. Size of the arable land shrank, crafts and domestic trade declined, urban life came to halt, mass exodus of the population from the country continued.

The Cilician Armenian Kingdom, surrounded by hostile Muslim states, was oriented towards an alliance with the Mongols. King **Hetum I (1226-1270)** personally traveled to the capital of Mongolia Karakorum, where he was received with great honors by Great Khan Mangu, and concluded a mutually beneficial political-military and trade alliance with him. With the help of the Cilician army, the Mongols took Baghdad in 1258, delivering a final blow to the Arab Caliphate.

Genghis Khan, founder of the Mongol state

Coin of Hetum I

Cilicia became the main transit hub on the Great Silk Road. Armenian traders used their own vessels to conduct an active trade with Western Europe. Venice, Genoa, Marseille and other cities ran trade warehouses and factories in Cilician ports.

6. Government and Economy in Cilician Armenia

The Armenian state in Cilicia represented a case of a successful combination of Armenia's tested and time-honored experience in statehood, and Western European feudalism. The state's principal ruling class included major and minor feudal. Possessions of major feudal landlords were hereditary. Minor landlords were granted possessions for their service, or received a monetary retainer.

As the head of state, the King enjoyed significant power. He had the power to make decisions on all domestic and foreign policy matters, declare war and make peace, and held the exclusive power to mint golden and silver money, built fortresses found cities.

The King governed the country with the help of the court. The apparatus consisted of various services, some of which were traditional, while others adopted under the Western European influence, and had European names. Sparapet in Cilicia was called **Connetable**. He commanded the Army, and was responsible for the protection of borders. **Payl** was the mentor of the Heir Apparent, and served as the Regent in case the Heir was underage.

The **Chancellor**, who had a large Secretariat and a staff of interpreters, conducted foreign relations. The **Steward** was responsible for management and logistics at the Palace, and its expenditures. The **Head of the Customs** oversaw the state revenues. On issues of national importance, the King consulted with the **State Council**, comprised of major landlords only.

The number of military personnel reached 60,000. Its core was the cavalry, armed in accordance with the European custom. These units were formed from the nobility, and were in professional service. In war, the popular militia joined them.

Cilicia's mild Mediterranean climate enabled the cultivation of grains, as well as melons and gourds. Citruses and olives were also cultivated, as a new area of agricultural activity. Grape growing was a major traditional activity. Mountain pastures contributed to the development of cattle breeding. Cilicia exported purebred horses, wool items, wines. Cilician ports served as transit hubs for the transportation of silk, spices, precious stones, etc. to Western Europe.

7. The decline of the Cilician Armenian State

In the 13th century, the Mameluk Kingdom in Egypt began to conquer the Crusader states in Palestine one after the other. The Cilician Kingdom found itself to be only Christian state remaining in the Near East.

Throughout the 14th century Mameluks conducted regular attacks against Cilicia. For a certain period of time, that pressure was successfully contained with the help of the Mongols.

The position of the Cilician Armenian Kingdom rapidly deteriorated by the mid-14th century, as the declining Mongol Empire, itself defeated by the Mameluks, could no longer provide assistance.

The situation was exacerbated by the absence of unity within the Armenian nobility, some of who suggested negotiating with the Egyptian Sultan, and recognizing his rule, while others sought help from the West, and vowed in exchange to subordinate the Armenian Church to the Roman Pope.

Armenian manuscript from Cilicia

Step by step, the Mameluks captured and annexed the coastal provinces of Cilicia, and in 1374 laid siege of its capital Sis. The city was taken following a prolonged siege, and the last Armenian King Levon VI Lusignan taken prisoner. **In 1375 the Cilician Armenian Kingdom fell under assail from the Egyptian Mameluks, and the Armenian people lost their statehood for the next 500 years.**

CHAPTER 11

ARMENIA UNDER THE YOKE OF NOMADIC TRIBES IN THE 13TH TO 15TH CENTURIES

1. Armenia under the Mongol Rule in the 13th to 14th Centuries

In 1221, a 20,000 strong Mongol army under the command of Subedey and Jebe undertook a reconnaissance mission in the South Caucasus. Having looted Armenia and Albania, the Mongol army moved in the direction of Tiflis. In the decisive battle, joint Armenian-Georgian forces led by King Georgi Lasha of Georgia and the ruler of Armenia Ivané Zakarian suffered a defeat. Marching across the South Caucasus, the Mongols moved further toward the North Caucasus, defeated the Kipchaks, and in the battle of Kalka in 1223 beat the troops of Russian princes. Having amassed enough loot and information about the countries they passed through, the Mongols then turned back.

The main Mongol campaign against the South Caucasus started in 1236. While the armies of Batu Khan were capturing Russian lands, another Mongol army was conquering Iran and the South Caucasus. In Armenia, after a prolonged siege, the Mongols captured and looted the cities of Dvin, Ani, Kars, Karin, and Van. Smaller cities were reduced to rubble. The population was ruthlessly killed or taken into slavery and sent to Mongolia. **By 1244, the Mongols had completed the conquest of Armenia,** captured Northern Iraq and Syria. The Georgian kings and Armenian princes were left with no choice but to submit to Mongols by becoming their tributaries, and were required to participate in Mongol campaigns.

The Mongol rule was devastating for Armenia. Armenia was looted, its economy completely ruined, and urban life brought to a halt. Mongols who were nomadic needed only uninhabited pastures. Cities were destroyed so they would not become centers of resistance, and Mongols were not interested in agriculture.

Mongols conducted a population census, and established heavy taxes for those who remained alive. Tax collection was accompanied with abuse and lawlessness. The Armenians and Georgians rose up in protest on a number of occasions, but these attempts were brutally suppressed. The Mongols pursued a policy of discouragement and destruction of the local ruling class, and succeeded in pushing many noble families to extinction.

While the Mongols adhered to their original pagan belief system, the Christian church and clergy enjoyed a privileged position. Mongols allowed the restoration of churches and practice of religion. But starting from the late 13th century, when the Mongol elite began adopting Islam, the Church and the Christian faith came under persecution. The situation in Armenia further deteriorated in the 14th century, as the united Mongol state disintegrated into independent khanates, and constant internecine struggle among Mongol khans exposed the country to new waves of violence and destruction.

In the late 14th century, the state of Tamerlane emerged in Central Asia, with its brutality surpassing even the Mongols. Tamerlane's armies devastated Armenia in a series of invasions in 1386, 1394, 1398 and 1403. The urban life came to a complete halt. The population was once again massacred or taken to slavery. Armenia was almost depopulated, and the exodus from the country took on a mass character.

2. Armenia under the Rule of Turkic Nomadic Tribes in the 14th Century

After the fall of the Mongols, Turkic tribes that had resettled in some of Armenia's best lands during the Mongol rule, asserted independence and sought to impose their rule throughout the country. A group of tribes named Karakoyunlu settled in central Armenia, and another group named Akkoyunlu in the south-western provinces. Constant wars between them in the late 14th and early 15th centuries led to the complete destruction of the country.

Initially, the Karakoyunlu prevailed in that struggle, succeeding to establish its state on the territory of Armenia. Their leader named Kara Yusuf assumed the title Shah-i-Armen – the Ruler of Armenia. A brief period of peace arrived. The Armenian people again returned to peaceful life and work, restoring churches, and cities. Small Armenian principalities survived in Syunik, Artsakh, Sassoun, Khlat, Gugark, and Vaspurakan. To establish a good rapport with, and test the loyalty of the Armenian population, Kara Yusuf and his successors favored the Armenian Church and began to appoint Armenian princes as rulers in the provinces.

By the mid-15th century, the economic center of the country again moved to the Ayrarat province, with Yerevan becoming its new administrative center. In these circumstances, the need arose to return the Mother See to Armenia. Earlier during the Seljuk invasions, the See had moved from Ani to Cilicia – the new center of Armenian statehood. After the fall of the Cilician Armenian kingdom, however, Cilicia no longer held that role. The Karakoyunlu rulers supported the move of the Mother See into their territory. When Catholicos Grigor I refused to leave Sis for Ayrarat, a representative clerical assembly with delegates from all of the provinces of Armenia convened in Echmiadzin **in 1441, and elected a new Catholicos. Since then, and to this day, the Supreme Catholicos-Patriarch of All Armenians resides in Echmiadzin.** The move of the Mother See to Echmiadzin further elevated the national and political importance of the Ayrarat Province.

Catholicos Grigor and his elected successors continue to remain in Sis and bore the title "Catholicos of Cilicia". Part of the Armenian parishes in the world till now continue to remain under the ecclesiastic jurisdiction of Catolicos of Cilicia.

In 1468, the leader of the Akkoyunlu Uzun Hassan conquered Armenia, and for a brief period, the country was annexed to his state. Uzun Hassan conducted a population census, and streamlined taxation. He entrusted local tax collection largely to the Armenians. The Akkoyunlu rule also lasted only a brief period, because of inter-dynastic disputes that escalated in the late 15th century.

3. Turko-Persian Wars. Partitions of Armenia between the Ottoman Turkey and Safavid Iran

During the Mongol invasions, one of the Turkic tribes settled in the north-western part of Asia Minor. In 1299, the leader of that tribe by the name Othman declared independence and founded a state which came to be known after him, as Ottoman Turkey. In 1453 the Ottoman Turks seized Constantinople and destroyed the Byzantine Empire. Ottoman Turkey rose to become the most powerful nation in the Middle East, conquering the Balkans and the entire Asia Minor.

In 1502 Shah Ismail of the Safavid family founded a new Persian state in Western Iran. Having defeated the Akkoyunlu, Shah Ismail conquered Transcaucasia, Iraq and soon established his rule over the entire Iran. He made Tebriz the capital of the new state.

The unification of Iran alarmed the Ottoman Turkey, leading Sultan Selim I to send a major army against Iran. In 1512 he crashed Shah Ismail in a battle, and conquered Tebriz. Soon he also conquered Iraq, Syria, Arabia and Egypt. The entire Transcaucasia came under the Ottoman rule, which, as a result of conquests by Selim I turned into a vast empire.

Shah Ismail did not just accept defeat. He assembled a new combat force, and soon succeeded in driving the Turks out of Iran and Transcaucasia. The war continued with mixed success for almost half a century. Military activities were taking place mainly on the territory of Armenia, which was devastated many times by both warring parties. In 1555, tired of pointless wars, Ottoman Turkey and Iran concluded a peace treaty. Under that treaty, made in Amassia, the parties divided Armenia and the entire Transcaucasia between them. **That became the Third Partition of Armenia.**

The peace, however, did not last long. In the late 16th century, the Ottoman Empire, which was at the height of its power, launched a new war and conquered the whole Transcaucasia. In 1590, Young Shah Abbas I was forced to concede these territories. Iran was unprepared for war.

Shah Abbas began to prepare for a new war. With the help of the English, he created a powerful artillery, reorganized the Persian Army and in 1603 launched a new war against Ottoman Turkey. Persian troops occupied Armenia. When the Turkish Army moved forward, the Persian Army retreated. To deprive the Turks of supplies and cover, Shah Abbas ordered the destruction of all population centers, deporting

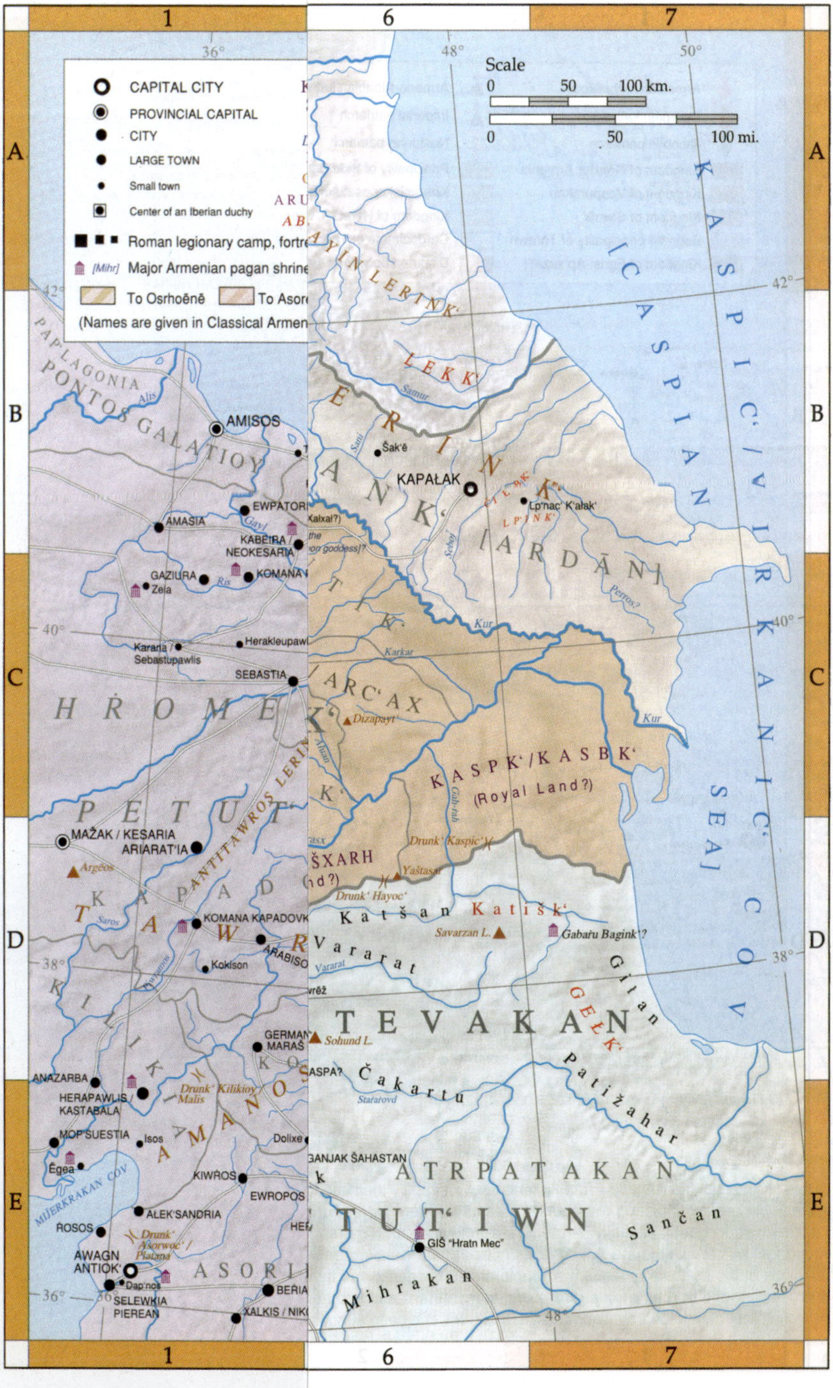
CAPITAL CITY
PROVINCIAL CAPITAL
CITY
LARGE TOWN
Small town
Center of an Iberian duchy
Roman legionary camp, fortre
[Mihr] Major Armenian pagan shrine
To Osrhoēnē
To Asor
(Names are given in Classical Armen
Scale
0 50 100 km.
0 50 100 mi.
PAPLAGONIA
PONTOS GALATIOY
AMISOS
EWPATOR
AMASIA
KABEIRA / NEOKESARIA
GAZIURA
KOMANA
Zela
Karana / Sebastupawlis
Herakleupawl
SEBASTIA
HŘOMEK'
PETUT
MAŽAK / KESARIA
ARIARAT'IA
Argēos
KAPAD
TAWR
KOMANA KAPADOVK
ARABISO
Kokison
KILIKIA
ANAZARBA
HERAPAWLIS / KASTABALA
Drunk' Kilikioy / Malis
MOP'SUESTIA
Isos
Ēgea
MIJERKRAKAN COV
AMANOS
KIWŘOS
EWROPOS
AŁEK'SANDRIA
ŘOSOS
Drunk' Asorwoc' / Platana
AWAGN ANTIOK'
Dap'nos
SELEWKIA PIEREAN
ASORI
BERIA
XALKIS / NIK
GERMAN MARAŠ
Sohund L.
ASPA?
Dolixe
GANJAK ŠAHASTAN
ANTITAWROS LERIN
Alis
Gayl
Ris
Saros
Sanr
Samur
Šak'ē
KAPAŁAK
Lp'nac' K'ałak'
ŁPINK'
ČIŁBK'
ŁEKK'
KAYIN LERINK'
ARU
AB
ANK' [ARDĀN]
Perros?
Kur
Karkar
ARC'AX
Dizapayt'
KASPK'/KASBK' (Royal Land?)
Drunk' Kaspic'
Yaštasar
ŠXARH
Drunk' Hayoc'
Katšan
Katišk'
Savarzan L.
Gabaru Bagink'?
Vararat
TEVAKAN
Gilan
GEŁK'
Patižahar
Čakartu
Stařavod
ATRPATAKAN
TUT'IWN
Sančan
GIŠ "Hratn Mec"
Mihrakan
KASPIC' / VIRKANIC' COV [CASPIAN SEA]
36°
48°
50°
42°
40°
38°
1
6
7
A
B
C
D
E

87. Armenia in the Early Bagratid Period, 884–962

the entire Armenian population of the Ayrarat Province.

Over 300,000 people were subjected to forced resettlement, many of whom drowned while trying to cross River Arax. Shah Abbas offered Armenians resettlement in various provinces across Iran, while those from the city of Jugha, many of whom were wealthy traders and craftsmen, the King resettled near his capital city of Isfahan, in a newly built suburban town called **Nor Jugha** (New Jugha). The war continued with mixed success for over 30 years, ending with a peace treaty between the parties.

Under the peace treaty of **1639**, Armenia and the entire Transcaucasia were once again divided between Ottoman Turkey and Iran. The line of partition extended along River Akhurian, then in a straight line, splitting Armenia into two. **This was the fourth partition of Armenia.**

§4. Armenian Culture in the 10th-14th Centuries

The peaceful period of development and national independence for Armenia under the reign of Bagratuni in Armenia Major, and later in the Cilician Armenian Kingdom facilitated a robust growth of science and culture in the country.

The adoption of Christianity in Armenia resulted in the opening of religious schools, which prepared generations of public and religious servants. Elementary schools subsidized by the state and the Church functioned in almost all cities and major rural population centers. Young people were sent abroad to study in some of the most prestigious educational institutions of the era.

In the 9-10th centuries, institutions of higher education called **Vardapetarans** were established in large cities and monasteries. Vardapetarans tought a curriculum known as "Seven Liberal Arts." The period of study was 7-8 years. Graduates received a Vardapet's (Bachelor's) Degree, and a teacher's qualification. Vardapetarans also included a number of special medical schools.

In the early 13th century, several Western European church schools with well-known faculty developed into universities. The University of Paris, one of the oldest in Europe, was founded in 1200. A similar

Church in Gladzor. Walls of the university auditoriums are on the left

process occurred in Armenia. **In 1280, the famous Vardapetaran in Gladzor was reorganized into a University** with two schools – Theology and Law. It admitted students only with a Vardapet's degree. The period of study was 3-4 years. Faculty at the Gladzor Univeristy included many of the most famous scholars of the era – Nerses Mshetsi, Yesayi Nchetsi, Hovhan Vorotnetsi, and others. In the late 14th century, in an attempt to avoid regular attacks by nomadic tribes, the university moved to the better protected Tatev Monastery, where it existed until 1444. The last rector of the Tatev University was famous philosopher **Grigor Tatevatsi.** Until the mid-14th century, another university functioned in Sis, the capital of the Cilician Armenian Kingdom.

Universities and Vardapetarans helped advance science. One of the most famous scholars of the era was **Grigor Magistros Pahlavuni,** who translated into Armenian and critiqued the work "Geometry" by Euclid. Another scholar – **Mkhitar Heratsi,** was a famous physician. His medical treatise was written in a simple language that regular people could understand, and was widely popular in the general public.

Another area of rapid progress was legal thought. In the 13th century, Vardapet **Mkhitar Gosh** wrote the first Armenian Code – a set of civil laws developed on the basis of the traditional law then in effect in Armenia, and church rules. In a similar, but independent effort, Constantine Connetable created a Code for Cilician Armenia.

Traditional Armenian historiography was enriched by many new scholarly works. **Hovhannes Draskhanakertsi,** in his treatise "History" described the events of the 9-10th centuries. **Tovma Artsruni** wrote the History of the Artsruni Family, and **Stephanos Orbelian** created the History of Syunik. In the 11th century, **Aristakes Lastivertsi** provided a description of the events in the 10-11th centuries, accompanied by detours into the history of Byzantine and the Seljuks. Another author of the same period – **Stephanos Taronatsi,** nicknamed Asoghik, first in the Armenian historiography, offered a narrative of the history of Armenia in the context of world history. Thanks to the treatise called History by **Kirakos Gandzaketsi,** we now have a fairly complete understanding of the events of the 12-13th centuries taken place not only in Armenia and Cilicia, but also in the entire Near East

Tatev Monastery

The 10-14th centuries marked a period of rebirth for the Armenian literature. The Armenian national epos **"Sassountsi Davit"** was created in reflection of the centuries-long struggle of the Armenian people against the Arab conquerors. Despite the fact that its epistemology dates as far back in time as when the Van Kingdom confronted Assyria, the main set of events reflected in the epos concerns Armenia's resistance against the Caliphate, with the right of each people to liberty being its fundamental premise. That is exactly what the characters of the epos stand and fight for.

Monument in Yerevan to David of Sassoon, hero of the Armenian national epos

The most venerable and celebrated representative of the Armenian Renaissance was **Grigor Narekatsi.** His famous poem – Book of Lamentations – is known around the world, and has been translated to many world languages. He also wrote beautiful poems about love and happiness. A major figure of national and literary acclaim was **Nerses Shnorhali,** who wrote not only **sharakans** – spiritual music, but also poems and verses reflecting on everyday life. He created puzzles that were very popular among the general public. Another famous intellectual – **Vardan Aygektsi,** was known for his fables, in which he bashed greed, treason, and cruelty, and extolled the virtues of honesty and loyalty. Fables written by another famous intellectual – Mkhitar Gosh, were particularly popular among the public.

Popular poets of the period included **Frik** and **Nahapet Kuchak,** who wrote in a simple language that the regular folk could understand, praising friendship, loyalty to fatherland, and speaking up against injustice in life, and against foreign domination.

The period under review was marked by the robust development of the Armenian music, including the creation of many masterpieces of religious choral music, and the invention of **"khazes"**, a special system of music notation. Popular music was developed as well. Travelling bards called **gusans** performed music that was close to the hearts of the average people, singing about love, heroism, good and evil, and presenting epical songs in musical arrangements.

The Armenian theatrical tradition continued to develop. On town squares and markets, and during big fairs travelling artists offered masked performances, animal trainers demonstrated their skills, as did clowns, musicians, and rope walkers.

In the 9-14th centuries, the Armenian architecture thrived as well. Many masterpieces of medieval Armenian architecture were built in that period, including the monastery complexes of **Sanahin, Haghpat, Kecharis, Haghartsin, and Goshavank.** One of the most unique architectural complexes built in that period is the Monastery of **Geghard**, part of which is carved in solid rock, while its remaining structures organically blend with the surrounding landscape.

Monastic complex of Geghard

Wonderful churches were built in many large cities and royal residences, with rich exteriors and beautiful interiors decorated with frescos. The Mother Cathedral of the capital city of Ani particularly stood

Surb Khach (Holly Cross) Church on Akhtamar Island

out for its grandeur. Its architect, named **Trdat**, also built a church in Ani – an exact replica of the famous three-storied temple of Zvartnots that laid in ruins already. Trdat also undertook the restoration of the dome of the famous St. Sophia Cathedral in Constantinople, destroyed in an earthquake, when Greek architects failed to perform it. The dome of the St Sophia Cathedral, restored by Trdat, still stands to this day.

Architect **Manuel** built another masterpiece of Armenian architecture – the temple of Surb Khach (Holly Cross) on the Akhtamar Island. The temple had a separate Royal stairway to the second floor, was richly decorated on the outside, with frescoes covering its interior walls. In addition, Manuel also built a Royal palace on the island, and a port to accommodate multiple ships.

Bas-relief of Madonna, Surb Khach Church of Akhtamar

Another architect named **Momik** built the magnificent church of Noravank, successfully blending

Noravank

the structure with the mountainous terrain surrounding it, and richly decorating it with images of the Our Lord, and the angels, which was a new element in the Armenian architecture. Momik also is the author of numerous khachkars.

Khachkar in Sanahin, 12th c.

Khachkars, or cross-stones, are a special, entirely indigenous Armenian form of decorative-functional stone art. Its origins go back to the early pre-Christian period, when guard stones were being placed on crossroads, near water springs, or at sacred sites. A cross is a mandatory attribute of the khachkar. It was sometimes carved in great detail, and generally represented the Tree of Life. Khachkars were decorated with other ornaments as well. All of that was covered by a web of fine lines and patterns. None of the khachkars resembles another, even if both are made by the same Master. Each khachkar is unique. During the middle ages, khachkars came to be used as gravestones as well.

Khachkars in Geghard

The period between the 10th and 14th centuries was marked by the rise of the Armenian miniature illustrative art. One of the greatest miniature artists of his time was **Toros Rosslin**, who lived in the Cilician Armenia. His preserved works reveal images of saints, portraits of commissioners of artwork, and their entire family. Some of his better known and well-preserved works include Gospels with illustrations depicting King Levon and his family.

Medieval miniature

CHAPTER 12

ARMENIA UNDER TURISH AND PERSIAN RULE. THE BEGINNING OF THE LIBERATION MOVEMENT

1. Armenia under Turkish and Persian Rule in the 17-18th centuries

Armenia once again found itself partitioned into Western and Eastern parts. Both the Ottoman Turkey and Persia established new administrative divisions in the Armenian territories under their control, and determined the forms and sizes of taxes and duties.

In Turkish-ruled Armenia, the country was divided into provinces – **vilayets**, governed by pashas appointed by the Sultan. Within a vilayet, the pasha held the highest administrative, financial and military authority. Judges were called kadis, and were appointed from among the Muslim clergy. Vilayets consisted of sanjaks, governed by beys.

In Persian-ruled Armenia, the administrative units were called **khanates**. The khan held the highest administrative, financial and military authority with the boundaries of his khanate, and was appointed by the Shah. Unlike pashas, khans also held a judicial authority.

The Christian Armenian population was required to pay land and personal duties. Only the clergy was exempt from personal duty. In addition, the population was required to do various labor duties, such as work on construction of monasteries, roads, channels, etc. Revenue collection was carried out with great arbitrariness and abuse of power. A Christian's witness in Court against a Muslim was not admissible.

Despite the national and religious discrimination, the establishment of a durable peace between Ottoman Turkey and Iran had a favorable impact on the Armenian population, leading to the gradual rebuilding of agriculture, and as a result, the rebirth of trade and craftsmanship.

Durable peace also stimulated international commerce. Armenian merchants once again established transit trade with neighboring countries. From the East, they imported silk, cotton, spices and precious stones to Europe. Armenian merchants had their own ships in both the Mediterranean Sea and the Indian Ocean, and successfully competed with European trades. Armenian merchants long held the monopoly over commerce with Russia through the Caspian Sea. In 1667, the Russian government granted Nor Jugha Trade Company a trade monopoly.

2. The Beginning of the Liberation Movement in Armenia.

Despite all the efforts of the occupiers, pockets of small Armenian principalities continued to exist in some of the most remote, hard to reach corners of Armenia. In Western Armenia, such principalities survived in the provinces of Zeytun, Sassoun, Mokq, Shatakh, Khnus, and Taron. These principalities enjoyed internal autonomy, but paid tribute to the government of the Sultan. Although nominally under Turkish rule, these princes in reality held no obligations before the Turkish court.

In Eastern Armenia, independent principalities survived in Artsakh, Syunik, Gardman. Rulers of these principalities under Persian rule were called **meliks**. Melik's power was hereditary, based on the first-born right. On his territory, the melik represented the highest administrative, judicial and military authority. He collected taxes and duties from the population, kept an armed force, and contributed to the border defense. Meliks paid a flat tax to the Royal Treasury, and in the case of war were required to join, along with their armed force, the Shah's army.

The survival of these pockets of independent entities across Armenia against all odds gave hope that the country would be able to restore its independence. Armenians however were not powerful enough to overthrow the Persian and Turkish yoke without external help. Armenian political leaders naively assumed that the European countries who regarded the Ottoman Empire as an enemy would assist Armenia in its liberation struggle against the Empire for the sake of defeating Turkey.

In **1547** Catholicos Stephanos Salmastetsi convened a secret meeting in Echmiadzin, at which it was resolved to send a delegation to Europe to raise support for Armenia. During a two-year tour, the delegation, headed by the Catholicos, visited Rome, Venice, Germany, Poland, and returned without any results.

In **1562**, Catholicos of Cilicia Michael Sebastatsi convened a secret meeting. The participants decided to send Abgar Tokhatetsi and his son named Sultanshah to Venice with a proposal to form an alliance. That was a period when European powers were engaged in forming an anti-Turkish coalition under the leadership of Spain. In 1571, the Turkish fleet was defeated in the Battle of Lepanto. Abgar did not receive any help from Europe, but he established a publishing press in Venice and resumed the publication of Armenian books.

By the mid-17th century, France had established itself as the powerful country in Europe. Another Armenian envoy, named Murad Baghishetsi, was sent to France, to find a support there. Murad was granted an audience with the King Louis XIV, and asked for his help against Turkey.

In **1677**, Catholicos Hakob Jughayetsi convened a secret meeting in Echmiadzin, which resolved to send a mission to Europe to raise support. The delegation was en route, when the Catholicos unexpectedly died in Constantinople, forcing the mission to return home.

None of these attempts by Armenians to obtain help were successful, for European powers had their own interests and did not wish to spend effort or money in pursuit of someone else's.

3. Origins of the Russian Orientation in the Armenian National Liberation Movement. Israel Ori

By the early 18th century, Ottoman Turkey and Iran had entered a stage of economic and political decline. In the absence of wars of conquest, the profits of the ruling class had dried down, resulting in the escalating exploitation of the conquered peoples. Population censuses were conducted in both Turkey and Iran, leading to multi-fold tax hikes. Armenians populating the rural areas sought refuge from heavy taxes and duties, as well as regular looting by nomadic Muslim tribes by resettling in larger urban centers, were they could be safer from arbitrary power abuse, and have better job opportunities. The growth of the urban Armenian population strengthened the base of the Armenian national liberation movement, stimulating it further.

One of the most prominent leaders of the Armenian national liberation movement of that era was Israel Ori (1659-1711). He was a member of the delegation that was forced to return home following the death of Catholicos Hakob Jughayetsi in 1679. Ori was determined to continue these efforts despite initial failure. He spent over 20 years in Italy, France, and Germany, served in the military and received the rank of an officer. Wherever he were, he tried to convince the European rulers to consider supporting the cause of Armenia's liberation, but received no serious help.

His plans, however, caught the attention of a German prince – Elector Johan Wilhelm of Pfaltz. Generally in favor of Ori's ideas, the prince asked him to provide assurances that Armenians would be able to contribute troops to the liberation of their country. Ori headed to Armenia, met with the Catholicos, and consulted the Armenian meliks. In 1699, a secret meeting of the Armenian nobility was held in the village of Angeghakot, where the participants offered Israel Ori written assurances, and a mandate to negotiate on their behalf. Ori returned to Pfaltz, and met with the Elector, but was soon to find out that the initial enthusiasm had died.

Disappointed with the futility of the efforts to find allies in Europe, Israel Ori turned to Russia. In 1701, he presented his project of liberation of Armenia with Russian help to Tzar Peter I. Ori assured that if the Russian army enters Transcaucasia, Georgians and Armenians will raise a 15,000-strong militia. Peter I promised to consider the plan after the end of the Nordic War, but decided to send a reconnaissance mission to the region, in the form of an embassy to Persia. Israel Ori was appointed head of the mission, in the rank of Colonel. In 1708-1709, the Embassy visited Iran, enabling Ori to meet with the King of Georgia and the Armenian meliks while on transit through the region, assuring them in Russia's support. On his return trip from Iran, Ori unexpectedly died in Astrakhan in 1711.

4. Liberation Movement in Syunik and Artsakh in the early 18th Century

In the beginning of the 18th century, Safavid Persia was in decline, and Afghan tribes had even seized its capital Isfahan. Peter I decided to take advantage of Persia's vulnerability, and annex Transcaucasia to Russia. In 1722, Russian Expeditionary Force under the Tzar's command moved towards the South, and captured Derbend.

The Derbend campaign inspired Armenians and Georgians, who recognized the opportunity of an impending liberation from the Persian yoke. Georgian troops under the command of King Vakhtang VI, joined by the troops of Armenian Meliks headed by Catholicos Yesayi Hasan-Jalalian of Gandzasar moved to greet arriving Russian army, and set camp at the city of Gandzak. After several months of wait, and learning that the Tzar had postponed the campaign to the following year, the Armenian and Georgian troops dispersed, and headed back home.

The Meliks of Syunik, ready for an insurgency, sent a mission to the King of Georgia, requesting help. In response, the King sent a group of Armenian officers of the Georgian Army to Syunik, under the command of Davit Bek. **Davit Bek** was able to unite the forces of the Meliks of Syunik, and in the fall of 1772, defeated the joint forces of the region's Muslim rulers. In a series of battles, Davit Bek asserted his rule over the entire region of Syunik, expelling the Muslim tribes and establishing a united Armenian principality. The Shah of Persia recognized the rule of Davit Bek over Syunik. The Fortress of **Halidzor** became the center of the principality. Military leaders as Mkhitar, Ter-Avetis, Toros, Parsadan, and others were put in command of the units of the Armed Forces under the new administration.

The expectations of the Armenians and Georgians for a help from Russia did not materialize. Peter I was defeated by the Turks in Bessarabia, and conceded the entire Transcaucasia to Turkey under a peace

Halidzor Fortress

treaty. In 1723 the Turkish Army captured Tiflis and Gandzak. Another Turkish Army laid siege of the **Fort of Yerevan in 1724.** After a heroic defense lasting three months, in which the Armenian population participated as well, the fort was captured by the Turks, who seized the city at the human cost of 20,000 soldiers dead.

In 1727 the Turkish Army invaded Syunik and laid siege of the Fort of Halidzor, where Davit Bek had set up his headquarters. The Armenian troops successfully repelled the Turkish offensive. Units under the command of Mkhitar Sparapet and Ter-Avetis were able to leave the fortress unnoticed, and attack the enemy from its rear, sawing panic and ultimately defeating the Turkish troops. Turks made an attempt to set up a base in Meghri, but were expelled from there as well in 1728.

In the meantime, the Turkish Army used its base in Gandzak to launch an invasion of Artsakh in 1725. Armenians deceived the ever-alert enemy and destroyed a significant number of Turkish troops under the guise of the dark in a night-time operation. In 1726, the Turks made a failed attempt to lay siege of Fortress of Shushi – the center of Artsakh. It soon became known, however, that Russia and Turkey have signed a peace treaty, and that the Russians will not be providing military assistance against the latter, causing the insurgency in Artsakh to wind down. In 1729, the leader of the Armenian liberation movement Catholicos Yesayi Hasan-Jalalian of Gandzasar passed away.

Following the death of Davit Bek in 1728, the Armenian liberation movement continued under the leadership of Mkhitar Sparapet. He repelled a series of Turkish offensives against Syunik, but internal strife had undermined the Armenian resistance, and soon the Turks were able to seize Fort Halidzor. Mkhitar Sparapet was assassinated, and the liberation movement in Syunik descended.

Turkish rule over Eastern Armenia did not last long. Nadir Khan, a talented military commander and diplomat, took leadership of the patriotic forces in Iran, and expelled Afghan tribes from the country. He also successfully leveraged the collective desire and efforts of the Armenian people to overthrow Turkish rule. In 1735, Nadir Khan defeated the Turkish troops in a decisive battle, restored the integrity of the Persian state, and returned Eastern Transcaucasia to Persian rule. In **1736, Nadir was declared Shah of Persia. In the same year, he also confirmed in writing the hereditary rights and privileges of the 5 Meliks of Karabakh,** a number of whom in later years held senior positions in service of Nadir Shah and participated in his military campaigns.

5. Armenian Culture in the 15-18th Centuries

Endless destructive wars and continuous foreign domination resulted in a decline in Armenia's cultural life. But even under the most challenging of circumstances, it continued to develop, albeit mostly in the Armenian communities in Europe and Asia.

Although the Tatev University closed in 1444, a number of schools of higher education continued to exist in monasteries around the country – in Syunik, Hovhannavank, Metsop and elsewhere. Their alumni tought at the country's various institutions.

Scientific thought developed as well. **Hakob Ghrimetsi** authored treatises titled Interpretations of the Calendar and On Nature that served as textbooks in the Armenian schools.

One of the famous physicians of the time was **Amirdovlat** of Amassia (1420-1496). For a certain period of time, he was the personal physician of the Turkish Sultan. In his works, he provided full descriptions of all medicines and medical herbs known at the time, and offered instructions on their preparation and use. Armenian historiography continued to develop on the basis of its proud tradition of the previous centuries.

In the 15th century, historian **Tovma Metsopetsi** recorded an eyewitness account of the events of his period – the campaigns of Tamerlane and Turkmen tribes against Armenia and its neighbors.

Arakel Davrizhetsi in his work titled History provided an account of political events of the first half of the 17th century in Armenia and neighboring countries, also providing a description of daily life in the Armenian colonies.

Zakaria Kanakertsi offered a brief history of Armenia starting with the establishment of the Arshakuni Dynasty, offering a detailed eyewitness account of the events of the second half of the 17th century.

In the 14-17th centuries, a new type of literary work was developed – **Travel books**, representing historical, geographic and cultural surveys of various countries. Widely used by merchants, these travel books provided descriptions of many different countries from India to Europe, and Russia to Ethiopia.

In 1445 German Johan Guttenberg invented the printing press, which was shortly spread throughout Europe. One of the leading centers of book publishing was Venice, which had traditionally strong ties with the Armenian merchants. It is by no accident that the first Armenian printing press was founded in Venice.

In **1512 in Venice, Armenian publisher Hakob Meghapart** published the first Armenian printed book titled **Urbatagirk**.

In the mid-16th century, the Armenian printing tradition in Venice was continued by **Abgar Tokhatetsi.** In 1565 he moved his press to Constantinople, where his son Sultanshah continued the publication of Armenian books in great number. Another center of Armenian publishing in the 17th century was **Amsterdam**, where the fist Armenian-language Bible and World Map were published.

In 1638, Armenian masters of Nor Jugha built and launched the first local press in Persia.

The technology of printing press enabled the publication of books in large numbers, making them available to the general public at a larger scale. Books like **Tagharan** and **Aghvesagirk**, containing a collection of folk tales, fables, puzzles, poems, dream reviews, calendars of religious holidays, medical tips, etc. enjoyed a particularly high popularity.

"Urbatagirk", the first printed book in Armenian

Armenian literature continued to develop. One of the prominent poets of the 15th century was **Mkrtich Naghash**, who wrote about love, nature, and his life journey. He also was a painter, that is how he mainly made his living.

Another famous poet was **Nahapet Kuchak,** who wrote about love, compassion, and philosophy of life. Many of his writings became songs, music for which he wrote himself.

A famous poet was **Grigoris Akhtamartsi,** who was the Catholicos of Akhtamar in Vaspurakan, and a member of the Artsruni family. He wrote about love and grief, the suffering of his people, and the foreign domination of his homeland. Many of his poems were written in reaction to the political events of his time.

Armenian architecture suffered a period of certain decline during the era. Practically a very small number of churches were built in the war-torn Armenia. The best architectural ensembles of the time were built in the Armenian colonies outside the homeland. In Armenia proper, a number of bridges were built, some of the best examples of which have survived and are in use to this day. Fortified walls were erected around churches and monasteries to defend against frequent nomadic incursions, and underground passages were built.

Many Armenian architects worked abroad. **Sinan** was a famous court architect in Turkey. He built the Palace of Selim I, the Mosque of the Successor, the New Palace, and other buildings. Beginning from the 17th century, the position of the court architect of the Ottoman Empire belonged to a member of the **Balian** family.

Vishapagorg

In Armenia proper, the main art form to develop in this period was functional art, particularly exquisite hand-woven carpets known as **Vishapagorgs** that had rich ornaments, including not only straight line patterns but also serpent-like figures – vishaps.

The period was marked by the continuous development of Armenian **illustrative art**, the best examples of which are preserved in the Matenadaran – depository of ancient manuscripts. Famous illustrative arts schools existed in Nor Jugha, Crimea, Karin and Vaspurakan.

CHAPTER 13

ADJUNCTION OF EASTERN ARMENIA TO RUSSIA. ARMENIA WITHIN THE RUSSIAN EMPIRE

1. New Projects for the Liberation of Armenia

In the second half of the 18th century the struggle for the restoration of Armenia's statehood and independence was given a new stimulus. In Armenian communities scattered all around the world, a process of formation of Armenian bourgeoisie was well underway. This newborn bourgeoisie was interested in the establishment of its own independent state for to get involved in free economic activity in their homeland. This was particularly the case among Armenian communities in India and Russia.

Hovsep Emin

Thoughts of national liberation came to the forefront influenced by the activities of **Joseph Emin** (1726-1809), who having spent ten years in Armenia and the Caucasus, tried to organize a liberation movement.

Joseph Emin was a prominent representative of Armenian liberation movement from India. Having received his education in England, Emin visited Armenia in 1759.Upon examining the domestic situation he came to the conclusion that external assistance was necessary to liberate Armenia from the Turkish-Persian yoke. It was in 1761 that Emin came to Russia to present his plan of Armenia's liberation to Chancellor Vorontzov and having obtained necessary credentials from him, he took them to the court of Irakly II, the king of Georgia. Emin stayed in Armenia, Georgia, Karabagh and the North Caucasus for over ten years, trying to organize a liberation movement. Coming across a multitude of obsta-

cles, and losing all hope, Emin returned to India. His book "The Life and Adventures of Joseph Emin" published in Madras (India) in 1770 inspired people to never abandon attempts to liberate Armenia.

Shahamir S'hahamirian

In 1771, in the Indian city of Madras, a prominent representative of Armenian liberation movement **Shahamir Shahamirian** established an Armenian publishing house. It was there that the book authored by Movses Bagramian, Emin's brother-in-arms, titled **"The New Notebook, meaning A Notice",** was published. It described the rich history of the Armenian people and inspired the young generation to embark upon the struggle for the homeland's liberation. The book was translated into Russian and soon published in St. Petersburg.

Various new plans to liberate Armenia, mainly based upon hopes for Russia's military assistance, were in the pipeline. The Armenian dream was further boosted and kept alive by the Russian-Turkish wars in the second half of the XVIII century.

In 1769, a merchant from Astrakhan, **Movses Sarafian** submitted a plan of Armenia's liberation to the Russian government. It was conceived to be carried out by Armenian and Georgian volunteers supported by Russian military regiments. The liberated Armenia was supposed to be established as independent kingdom under Russia's mandate.

In 1773, in Madras **Shahamir Shahamirian** put together and published a paper titled **"Vorogayt Paratz"** (''Vanity Trap")-a project on the liberation and state structure of independent Armenia.

The project envisaged the liberation of Armenia with the help of the Russian army and establishment of the state of law in the form of parliamentary republic. Members of Parliament were to be elected by national vote. The Parliament was to appoint the cabinet of ministers from among its members. A 6000-strong Russian contingent, fully financed by the Armenian authorities, was to be deployed in Armenia for the period of 20 years. The plan also envisaged the establishment of free trade and travel between Russia and Armenia.

After 1783, when in accordance with the Georgevski Treate Georgia was brought under Russia's mandate, the hopes for Russia's support to Armenia became even stronger. Archbishop **Joseph Argutinsky**, the spiritual confessarius of Armenians in Russia, presented his plan on Armenia's liberation to Empress Yekaterina II.

Joseph Argutinsky (Hovsep Arghutian)

According to that project, the liberated Armenia, with the capital in the city of Ani, was to become Russia's ally. Armenian king was to be appointed by Empress Yekaterina. The two states were to establish strong economic ties.

2.The 19th Century Russo-Persian Wars. Adjunction of Eastern Armenia to Russia

Since Peter the Great times Russia has been trying to strengthen its influence in the South-Caucasus. Russia's expansionist plans coincided with the aspiration of the Armenian people to get rid of the Turkish-Persian yoke and re-establish independent statehood.

In 1801, by the special decree Georgia and the regions of Lori, Shamshadin and Kazakh populated by Armenians were annexed by Russia. The establishment of Russia's presence in the South-Caucasus soon led to the military collisions with Persia and Turkey.

In the course of the **first Russo-Persian war (1804-1813)** the Russian forces under the command of General Tzitzianov defeated the Persian army on several occasions, conquering the Khanate of Gyanja in 1805, but failing to seize the Yerevan fortress. The Armenian regions of **Shirak, Karabagh and Zangezur** voluntarily came under Russia's jurisdiction. The Armenian population provided all kinds of support to the Russian forces. During the full course of the war units of Armenian volunteers fought side by side with the Russian army.

Provoked by Napoleon, Turkey waged a war against Russia in 1806-1812. Thus, in the South-Caucasus the Russian army had to fight on two fronts. There was an imminent threat of Turkey and Persia joining forces. However, General Gudovich, the new Commander-in-Chief was able to crush the Turkish army in the battle by the Akhurian River, which stopped the plan of uniting Persian and Turkish forces. Yet, Gudovich's attempt in 1808 to seize the Yerevan fortress was also unsuccessful.

In 1812, peace treaty with Turkey was signed in the city of Bucharest. However, Persia continued the war with a hope that Russia would be defeated by Napoleon. Persia asked for peace only after it had suffered new defeats by Russia. In keeping with the **Treaty of Gulistan of October 12, 1813** the northern districts of Armenia and Karabagh were included into the Russian Empire.

General Paskevich, "Comte Yerevansky"

In the course of the second **Russo-Persian war** (1827-1828) the Russian forces under the command of General Paskevich seized the territories of the Erivan and Nakhichevan khanates. On August 17, 1827 in the battle near **Oshakan**, a three thousand-strong regiment under General Krasovski crushed the Persian army, which was ten times its size, thus saving Holy Echmiadzin, the spiritual center of the Armenians. **On October 1, 1827, the Russian forces under General Paskevich laid a siege and seized the Yerevan fortress.** Later, Tsar Nickolay 1st granted the title of "the Count of Erivan" to General Paskevich for that victory.

As in the past, the Armenian population continued to provide all kinds of support to the Russian forces in the course of military activities. Catholicos Nerses Ashtaraketzi gave his blessing and encouragement to the Armenians who served the cause of the liberation of their homeland.

Units of Armenian volunteers and militia took part in all battles side by side with Russians. They provided intelligence and served as guides.

Alexander Griboyedov Memorial in Yerevan

The Persian Command would time and again initiate negotiations to get a necessary break and regroup their forces. But it was not until the Russian army had seized the city of Tabriz and moved in the direction of Tehran, the Persian capital, that the Persian Shah made a request for peace.

By the Treaty of Turkmenchay of February 10, 1828 Russia was given suzerainty over the Erivan and Nakhichevan khanates, as well the territory of the khanates in Northern Azerbaijan. The Arax River has since then been established as the common Russian-Iranian border. The Armenian population that had been taken by force to Iran before and during the last wars was given the right to resettle in the Armenian regions that came under Russia's jurisdiction. During a year and half over 40 000 Armenians from different regions of Iran were resettled in Russian Armenia. It goes without saying that a lot of credit for that should be given to **Alexander Griboyedov,** then Russian Ambassador to Iran.

3. The Russo-Turkish War of 1828-1829

The establishment of Russia's presence in the South-Caucasus alerted Ottoman Turkey, which led to the **Russo-Turkish war of 1828-1829.** On the Caucasus front, the Russian forces under the command of General Paskevich crushed the Turkish army and seized the well-defended fortresses of Kars, Akhalkalak, Akhaltskha and Baberd. The towns of Bayazet, Mush, Alashkert and Erzurum- the largest city in Eastern Turkey, were surrendered without resistance. The local Armenian population and units of volunteers made significant contribution to the victories of the Russian army. The Russian poet, Alexander Pushkin, who was traveling in the Caucasus at that time, witnessed the events in Erzurum first-hand. In his notes "Journey to Erzurum" he vividly described the feeling of elation among the Armenian population, joy, friendly attitude towards the Russian military and expectation to be liberated from the Turkish yoke.

The Turkish army suffered a devastating defeat on the Balkan front as well. On September 2, 1829 the Peace Treaty of Adrianapolis was signed between Russia and Turkey, by which the eastern coasts of the Black Sea as well as the port of Poti and the regions of Akhalkalak and Akhaltskha were ceded to Russia. To the utter disappointment of Western Armenians, under the pressure of the European powers, this was all that Russia had to be satisfied with. All other captured cities and territories were returned to the Turks. Fearing for their lives and wary of the Turkish revenge as many as 80 000 Armenians from Mush, Alashkert and Kars resettled into Eastern Armenia, Akhalkalak and Akhaltsikha.

As a result of wars with Persia, the north-eastern parts of Armenia came under Russia's jurisdiction, and around 120 000 Armenians resettled into Eastern Armenia. By doing that a portion of the Armenian population avoided the threat of physical extermination.

4. The "Armenian Province"

The Armenian people cherished hopes to gain home-rule under Russia's mandate. However, the Tsarist government, against all expectations, spared no effort to liquidate all remnants of autonomy on the territory under its jurisdiction. Realizing the impossibility of immediately changing the centuries-old way of life on the captured territories, the Tsarist government took a step-by-step approach.

In March 1828, by the decree of Tsar Nickolay I the territories of the Erivan and Nakhichevan khanates, annexed from Iran were merged into one administrative unit, named **"Armianskaya Oblast" - Armenian Province.** The Province that had its coat of arms and system of governance existed until the year of 1840. The governors of the Armenian Province were General **A. Chavchavadze** (1828-1832) and General **V. Behbutov** (1830-1838). The Province was comprised of four districts and had its local police, tax and judicial departments.

General Behbutov, Governor of the Armenian Province

The "Church Regulations " of March 11, 1836 defined the structure, rights and responsibilities of the Armenian Church. The regulations recognized all its property rights, real estate included, as well as rights in the field of education and to hold wedding ceremonies, etc.

In 1840 Armenian Province was disbanded, and in 1844 the Caucasus Vice Roi's Office was established. The new administrative and territorial division into "regions" and "districts" was carried out in line with the Russian model. In 1849 the Erivan region was established, which included five districts. The life-time dream of the Armenians about home-rule would not come true.

In 1846, the Tsar's decree recognized the right to land- ownership inheritance by local khans, meliks and beks. By doing that the Russian autocracy was strengthening the social basis of its power.

5. The Crimean War of 1853-1856

In 1853 another Russian -Turkish war was waged, better known as the **Crimean war**, because the main military activities were launched around the Crimean Peninsula. There were also military clashes on the Balkan and Caucasian fronts.

Instigated by England and France, the Ottoman forces launched offensives on the border regions of Armenia and Georgia. General Behbutov, the famous Armenian commander of the Caucasian corps, was able to stop the Ottomans attack. In the battle near village of **Bashkadiklar**, his corps of 10 000 crushed a 36 000-strong Turkish army. The Turks had to deploy an army of 60 000 on the Caucasian front. In 1854, during the battle near the village of **Kyurukdar**, the Russian regiment of 18 000 people defeated an adversary that had many more men. In November, 1855 the Kars fortress was stormed and seized. A significant portion of the territories of Western Armenia came under Russia's control. The Armenian population was actively supporting the Russian army, hoping that after the war had been over those regions would be ceded to Russia.

Meanwhile, Russia was not winning on the Crimean front. The initial success of the Russian forces alerted England and France that feared that having defeated Ottoman Turkey, Russia would capture the Black Sea straits and seize those regions of the Middle East that belonged to Turkey. In 1854, they allied Turkey in the war against Russia. The English-French troops landed in the Crimea and after a long siege captured the city of Sevastopol, which was the main base of the Russian Black Sea Navy.

Russia lost the war on the main front. By the Peace Treaty of Paris Russia had to cede the territories captured in the Balkans and South-Caucasus back to Turkey in exchange for retaining the Crimea under Russian jurisdiction. The Armenian population of Western Armenia that cherished hopes to get rid of the Ottoman rule and showed assistance to the Russian army had to abandon their homeland and resettle within the boundaries of the Russian Empire.

6. Armenia in the Middle of the 19th Century

After passing under control of Russia, Eastern Armenia developed with a much faster pace. As distinct from the Ottoman Turkey and Persia, the Armenian population of the Russian empire was protected by the law, which guaranteed their physical security and property rights. The resettlement of the large portion of the Armenian population from Western into Eastern Armenia boosted and stimulated the economy of the latter. Alexandrapole, Yerevan, Nakhichevan and Shushi developed into regional centers of crafts and trade. The Tsarist government encouraged trade development on the territories under its jurisdiction. This was done to make those territories more dependent on the Russian Empire.

In the middle of the 19th century Armenian merchants controlled a large portion of trade between the South-Caucasus and Russia. However, the Tsarist government stopped short of supporting local industries to keep up demand on exported Russian goods. It was only mining industry that continued to develop for local needs and exports to Russia. More salt was extracted from the mines in Kokhb and Nakhichevan, while almost entire amount of copper from the mines in Alaverdi and Kapan was exported to Russia.

Manufacturing of goods remained limited to crafts. Craftsmen were united in professional guilds of blacksmiths, weavers, tanners, coppersmiths, potters, etc.

Only a craftsman who owned a shop could qualify to become a member of a guild. Each guild had its bylaws, coat of arms, holidays and mutual assistance fund. A guild would elect an elder. Members of a guild would collectively protect their interests in competition with independent craftsmen. Apprentices and pupils were not given membership in guilds.

Banner of the S hoemakers Guild

Agriculture remained the main branch of the economy. Mountainous landscape, summer and winter pastures created good conditions for cattle breeding. The peasants bred cows, sheep, goats, oxen, horses and donkeys. On the flatlands, particularly in the Ararat valley, farming, gardening and bee-keeping were developed. The peasants plowed rye, oats and wheat, tilled rice, cotton and flax, and grew grapes, peaches, apricots, pomegranates, water-melons, melons, etc.

The process of forming the class of trade bourgeoisie was underway in Eastern Armenia. Failing to find necessary economic conditions in Armenia proper, the Armenian bourgeoisie launched business activities in Moscow, St. Petersburg and Tiflis.

7. Armenian Culture of the 18th and the First Half of the 19th Centuries

In the entire course of the 18th and the beginning of the 19th century the territory of Armenia was the arena for continuous wars waged between the Ottoman Empire, Persia and Russia. It is but natural, that at that time there were no conditions for cultural development on the territory of Armenia proper. That's why Armenian culture was mainly developed in Armenian colonies around the world. The main Armenian cultural centers were in Moscow, St. Petersburg, Astrakhan, Tiflis, Constantinople, Calcutta and Venice.

During the 18th century Armenian schools operated in Venice, Izmir and Madras (India). In 1810 the **Aghababian School** was opened in Astrakhan. In 1815, Ivan Lazarev, an industrialist and benefactor, used his own financial resources to establish the **Lazarevski Institute** in Moscow. In 1824, the **Nersissian School** was opened in Tiflis. To receive higher education, Armenian youngsters traveled to Europe or Russia, although not many could afford that.

Armenian publishing industry continued to develop. As in the past, publishing houses operated in Constantinople, St. Petersburg, Moscow, Venice, Calcutta and Madras. In 1771 the first publishing house in Armenia proper was established in Echmiadzin. Due to that, first Armenian periodicals were released.

In 1794, "Azdarar", the first magazine in Armenian was released by Haroutyun Shimavonian in the city of Madras (India). And as far back as in the beginning of the 19th century Armenian periodicals started to get published in Venice, Tiflis, Calcutta and Constantinople.

In 1717, due to the efforts by Mechitar of Sebastia the brotherhood of Mechitarists was founded on the island of San Lazzaro in Venice. It soon developed into the center of Armenian academic and scientific activity. Fr. Michael Chamchian, a famous Armenian historian who lived and worked there, authored a three-volume "History of Armenia", which was the first academic critique, written on the basis of Armenian and foreign sources. In 1836-1837, the Mechitarist fathers published the first **dictionary of modern Armenian language.**

The famous Armenian historians of the 18th century were **Stepanos Shahoumian**, who authored the History of David Beck, **Yessayi Hasan-Jalalian,** who wrote the Short History of Karabagh, **Abraham Yerevantsi** who gave a detailed description of the Turkish-Persian wars in the 18th century. **H.Gatrjian** in Vienna first published the two-volume World History in Armenian. In 1836, History of the Armenian People by historian **Sergey Glinka** was published in Russian.

Ivan Lazarev

The founder of modern Armenian literature was **Khachatur Abovian** (1809-1848). Having received his degree from the Dorpat University (Estonia), he returned to his homeland and embarked upon a fruitful pedagogical activity. He authored a great number of books for children. In the novel "Wounds of Armenia" he gave a first-hand description of the events of the Russian-Persian wars and unification of Eastern Armenia with Russia. The language of the book was colloquial and not literary, that was traditionally used by the Church. It laid the foundation stone for the development and secularization of the Armenian literary language. Among other writers and teachers of that period the names of Haroutyun Alamdarian and Mesrop Tagiadian should be mentioned.

Khachatur Abovian

Folk music was also developing. Folk singers were called gousans. The most famous of them was **Sayat-Nova** (1717-1795). He was a poet, singer and composer, who wrote his poetry not only in Armenian but also in Georgian and Azerbaijani.

Sayat Nova

The rich traditions of Armenian architecture were on the decline in this period, due to continuous wars and political situation. Architecture traditions find self-expression only in small architectural forms, such as khachqars, chapels, bridges, etc.

Building of the Lazarevsky Institute of Oriental Languages in Moscow

NATIONAL LIBERATION STRUGGLE OF THE ARMENIAN PEOPLE IN THE SECOND HALF OF THE 19th CENTURY. THE ARMENIAN QUESTION

1. The State of the Armenian Population in Western Armenia in the Middle of the 19th century.

By the middle of the 19th century economic stagnation in Western Armenia that remained part of the Ottoman Empire became more noticeable.

A large portion of the Armenian population was involved in agriculture. The state owned the land that was tilled by peasants. Armenian peasants had an obligation to pay a contribution to the state in the amount of 10% of the harvest. To crown it all, together with other Christians residing in the Ottoman Empire, the Armenians had to pay a per capita contribution to be able to exercise their religious worship. The state would also collect a number of illegal payments from the population. The Armenian population was unprotected from arbitrary actions of local authorities and Muslim nomandic tribes.

Armenian craftsmen played a significant role in the Ottoman Empire. With virtually non-existent industrial manufacturing, there was a great demand for the goods they produced. Craftsmen would establish professional guilds. The main centers of Armenian craft and trade were the cities of Mush, Van, Erzurum, Bitlis, Kars and Bayazet. Armenian merchants traded with European countries.

The situation with legal rights of the Armenian population in the Ottoman Empire was difficult. Like other Christian peoples, the Armenians were subjected to national discrimination and humiliation by the Muslim population and state authorities. There were no laws in Turkey that would guarantee the rights to life and property. Christian peoples of the Empire were not treated equally in courts, and their testimony did not have legal force.

It became so obvious that economically and politically the Ottoman Empire remained so much behind European countries, that the Sultans' government made an attempt to make reforms to improve the situation. In 1839, by the decree of the Sultan all residents of the Empire (Muslim and Christian) were granted equal civil rights. Declarations about free economic activity, equality in courts and softening of tax legislation were made. In reality, that system of reforms, known as Tanzimat, was never put into practice.

2. The 1862 Uprising in Zeytun

In the difficult to access mountainous regions of Western Armenia, such as Sasun and Zeytun, etc., there remained small enclaves of the Armenian population. In the second half of the 19th century the Sultans' government attempted to abolish their self-rule and subject them to taxation.

In 1862, the people of Zeytun took up arms to defend themselves against the regular Ottoman army for several months. When the army laid a siege on their city and famine started, the Zeytunians asked the European powers for protection. With the mediation of France, Zeytun retained its autonomy, but was subject to taxation. A Turkish prefect was appointed to govern the city. In exchange for that mediation, the Zeytunians had to convert into Catholicism.

The heroic self-defense of Zeytun against the Ottoman government awakened the national awareness of the Armenian people and provided a stimulus for the liberation movement.

3. The National Constitution of the Armenians in the Ottoman Empire

Like other peoples residing in the Ottoman Empire, the Armenians kept contact with the Ottoman government through their Church and community organizations. The well-to-do leadership that was in charge of community organizations and had the support of the Sultanate would deny all access to community affairs to other layers of the population

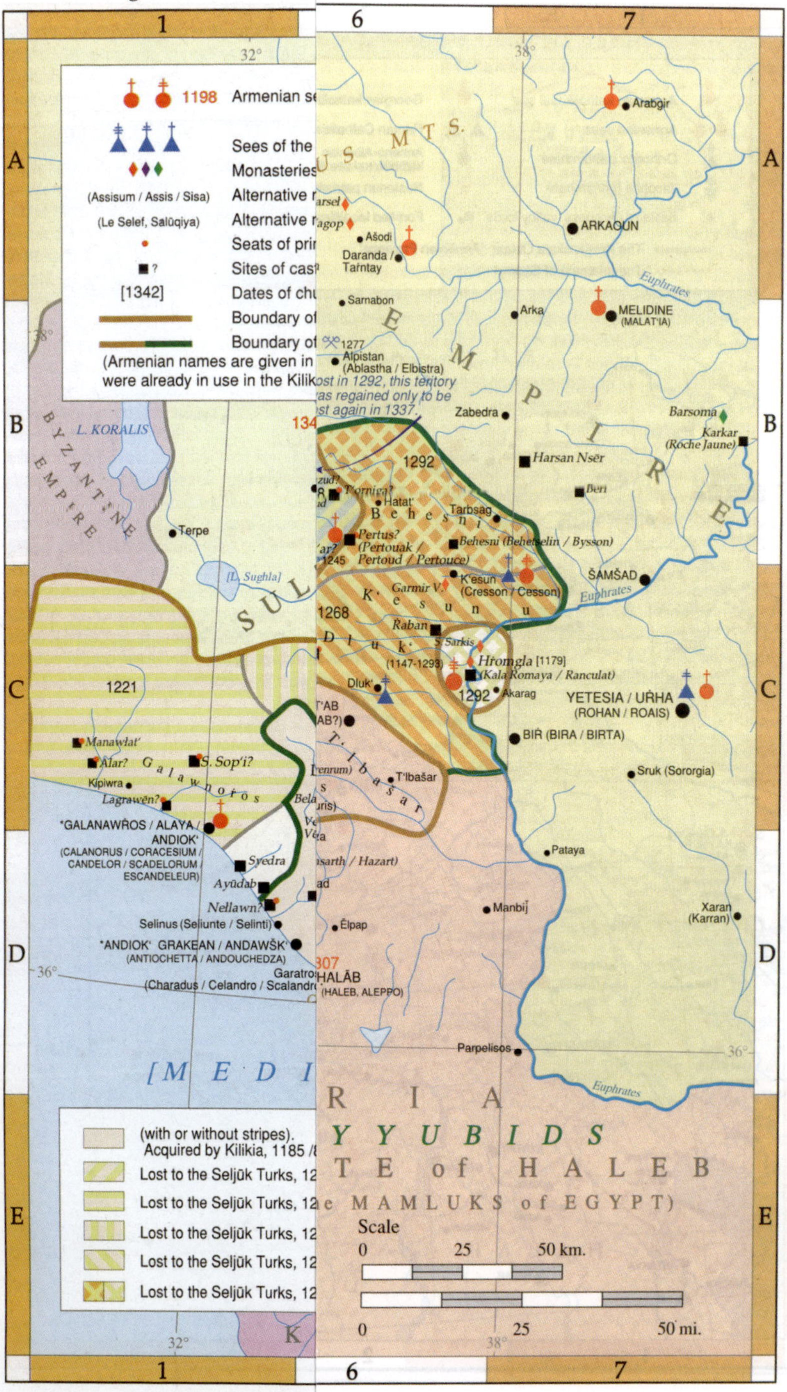

1198 Armenian se
Sees of the
Monasteries
(Assisum / Assis / Sisa) Alternative r
(Le Selef, Salūqiya) Alternative r
Seats of pri
Sites of cas
[1342] Dates of ch
Boundary of
Boundary of
(Armenian names are given in
were already in use in the Kilik
Arabgir
ARKAOUN
Euphrates
MELIDINE
(MALAT'IA)
Arka
Ašodi
Daranda / Tarntay
Sarnabon
1277
Alpistan
(Ablastha / Elbistra)
ost in 1292, this territory
as regained only to be
st again in 1337.
Zabedra
Barsoma
Karkar
(Roche Jaune)
Harsan Nsēr
Beri
1292
Tarbsag
Behesni
Pertus?
(Pertouak / Pertoud / Pertouce)
Behesni (Behetselin / Bysson)
1245
K'esun
(Cresson / Cesson)
ŠAMŠAD
Euphrates
Garmir V.
1268
Raban
S. Sarkis
Hṙomgla [1179]
(Kala Romaya / Ranculat)
(1147-1293)
Dluk'
1292
Akarag
YETESIA / UṘHA
(ROHAN / ROAIS)
BIṘ (BIRA / BIRTA)
Sruk (Sorogria)
T'ilbašar
L. KORALIS
BYZANTINE EMPIRE
Terpe
[L. Sughla]
SUL
1221
Manawłat'
Ałar?
S. Sop'i?
Galawnoros
Kipiwra
Lagrawēn?
GALANAWṘOS / ALAYA / ANDIOK'
(CALANORUS / CORACESIUM / CANDELOR / SCADELORUM / ESCANDELEUR)
Syedra
Ayūdab
Nellawn?
Selinus (Seliunte / Selinti)
ANDIOK' GRAKEAN / ANDAWŠK'
(ANTIOCHETTA / ANDOUCHEDZA)
Garatro
(Charadus / Celandro / Scalandro)
HALĀB
(HALEB, ALEPPO)
Ēlpap
Manbij
Pataya
Xaran
(Karran)
Parpelisos
Euphrates
[MEDI
RIA
YYUBIDS
TE of HALEB
e MAMLUKS of EGYPT)
(with or without stripes).
Acquired by Kilikia, 1185 /
Lost to the Seljūk Turks, 12
Lost to the Seljūk Turks, 12
Lost to the Seljūk Turks, 12
Lost to the Seljūk Turks, 12
Lost to the Seljūk Turks, 12
Scale
0 25 50 km.
0 25 50 mi.

5
6
7
A
B
C
D
E
Scale
0
50
100 km.
0
50
100 mi.
46°
48°
50°
42°
40°
38°
36°
44°
MOZDOK
Terek
Ft. Svatokrest
Aktash
Sulak
Terka
Akhlov
Fort Sundzha
Sundzha
Tatarub
Vladikavkaz
VLADIKAVKAZ
Enderi
For the Russian wars in North Caucasian wars in this period see map 157.
Veden
Dargo
Petrovsk
Tarki
Fort Daryal
Daryal Gorge
Temir-khan-shura (Buinak)
Andi
Ashilta
Himri (Gumri)
Akko
Argun
Kazbek
Botlikh
Utsunkul
Tlokh
Khunzakh
Akhvakh
Hunib (Gunib)
Salti
Kvarshi
Akusha
DERBENT
FREE TRIBES
DAGESTAN
CASPIAN SEA
Nik'ozi
KARTALINIIA
Urbnisi
Tianet
Dushet
Zhalet
Gremi
Nelkari
GORI
Ruisi
Ikalto
Telav
MTSKHET
Veliistsikhe
UDZHARMA
Ninotsminda
Bielokani
Kasumkent
Atskur
Ateni
TIFLIS
Manglisi
RUSTAVI
Bobde
Signakh
Elisu
KUBA
SABRAN
(Capuchin mission 1661-1845)
KAKHETIIA
Gish
Nukha
Khinalug
Budukh
Dmanis
Bolnisi
Vartashen
EMPIRE
Kura
Alazan
MOUNTAINS
Samur
[Kabala]
NUKHA SHEKKI
Lori
Sanain
Akhpat
Akstafinsk
Tavush
Zarishat
Marmashen
Shamkhor
GANDZHA
Aresh
SHAMAKHA
WW 1870, 1873
Aleksandropol' (Giumri)
ELIZAVETPOL' [1847-1924] (GANJA)
Kudevan
BAKU
BAKU
Kecharis
[Aragats]
Bdzhni
Sevan
Kedabek
Barda
[Ani]
Oromos
WW (1832)
Ovannavank
Gavar
Oshakan
Mazra
Sod
Gulistan
Shakhbulakh
Zardob
Rudbar
Dzhevat
As a result of these earthquakes the Russian administration was transferred to Baku.
ECHMIATSIN Since 1441
EREVAN
Garni
Kol
Oskeshen
Askeran
Agdam
Karkar
Amaras
Vagarshapat
Surmalu
Kogb
Katholikosate of Albania surpressed, 1830; became metropolitanate of Arts'akh
SHUSHI
Sal'yan
Igdir
Akori
Khor Virap
Egegis
WW 1840, 1859
Chermuk
Swiss mission, 1823-1835
Greater Ararat
Lesser Ararat
Arpa
Prindzatakh
Goris
Ktish
Goroz
Kur
Diyadin
BAYAZIT
Karababa
Vorotan
Tatev
MAKUYE
NAKHICHEVAN
Kapan
Khudaferin Bridge
Astapat
Abasabad
Karmir V.
Akulis
Ordubad
Dzhulfa
Arus
Lankaran
LANKARAN
Erjish
Bargiri
Qaraeina
Qarakilisa/ S. T'adeos
(See joined to that of S. Barduqhimeos, 1834)
S. Step'annos The Protomartyr
QARADAGH MTS
Hashtasar
Tiramayr V.
Varzharan
Astara
Astara
Ahar
Ahar
Bahlakan
Qareh
KHUY
VAN
WW (1835)
Varagavank
Kotor
Shushants'
MARAND
ARDABIL
Sabalan
Khoshab
Sufian
Barm
Salmas (Dilman)
S. Partughimeos V.
Bashkale
TABRIZ
SARAB
GILAN
Lake Ormiye (Lake Urmia)
Sahand
Hoshap
(c.1690-1915)
Jolemerik
ORMIYE
MARAGHEH
Turkmanchai
MEYANA
FUMAN
Enzeli
RASHT
Khalkhal
Kalkara
Jilo Dagh
Zab
QAJAR
PERSIAN EMPIRE
ZAGROS MTS
Kelishin Pass
Oshnuye
Seyah
MOSUL
ZANDJAN
SULTANIYEH
[Takht-i-Suleiman]
Rewandiz
Great Zab
Khabur
ERBIL
SAQQEZ

and suppressed the ordinary people.

As far back as in 1857, a group of young Armenian intellectuals, who had studied abroad, drafted new regulations for the governance of the Church and community affairs, which envisaged participation of less wealthy layers of the population in the community-related decision-making process. In **1860**, after long bureaucratic delays, under the public pressure the well-to-do leadership had to adopt the new text of regulations which was named **National Constitution.** However, the Ottoman government was not in a hurry to give its consent to the Constitution. It approved it only in 1863, after the uprising in Zeytun, wary of possible future public protests by the Armenians.

The adoption of the National Constitution was of great societal and political importance. The life of the Armenian community was significantly democratized. And although the Constitution did not provide immunity rights to life and property, or equality between the Armenian and Muslim populations, it must be viewed as a quite progressive phenomenon.

4. The Russo-Turkish War of 1877-1878. The Treaty of San-Stefano

There were several Russo-Turkish wars waged in the XIX century. The Armenian people, as well as the peoples residing in the Balkans contributed to Russia's victories and participated in those wars with a hope to get rid of the Ottoman yoke. All of them would have benefited from going under Russia's jurisdiction, where they would not have faced the threat of physical extermination, as was the case in Turkey.

Another **Russo-Turkish war took place in 1877-1878.** Russia was trying to reinstate its influence in the Middle East, which had been lost after the defeat in the Crimean war. Military activities were launched on the Balkan and Caucasian fronts.

The Commander-in-Chief of the Caucasian corps, General **M. Loris-Melikov** was of Armenian descent. Some other regiments were also commanded by Armenian generals who served in the Russian army. Suffice it to give the names of **Ter-Ghukasov and Ivan Lazarev.**

General M. Loris-Melikov, Commander in Chief of the Caucasus Front

On the Caucasian front the Russian army captured Bayazet and Alashkert and laid a siege on the city of Kars. The Ottomans, regrouping and bringing together a large force, counterattacked and laid a siege on the Bayazet fortress that remained in the rear of the Russian army. A tiny Russian garrison supported by Armenian volunteers had withstood the attacks of the far superior Turkish force until the arrival of the regiment under General Ghukasov.

The Caucasian corps would have been in predicament had the Ottomans captured Bayazet. The Russian garrison of Bayazet was under the command of Captain F. Shtokovich. The defenders of Bayazet were exhausted and ran out of ammunition, and the messengers they had sent were intercepted by the Turks. Samson Ter-Poghosyan, an Armenian volunteer, playing a madman, was able to pass through the Turkish cordons and take the message to General A. Ter-Ghukasov that hurried to the rescue of the defenders under siege. The heroic defense of Bayazet was described in literary works. A novel "Khent" (Madman) by Armenian writer Raffi and a novel "Bayazet" by Russian writer V. Picul were dedicated to it.

Having stopped the offensive of the Ottoman army on the Caucasian front, the Russian forces launched a counterattack and by 1877 stormed and seized the Kars fortress. They also captured the cities of Erzurum, Sarikamish and Ardahan. They were able to score big victories on the Balkan front as well, liberating the territory of Bulgaria and moving close to Constantinople. Under pressure by England, the **Peace Treaty of San Stefano was signed on February 19, 1878.** The Kars, Alashkert and Bayazet regions of Western Armenia were ceded to Russia. By Article 16 of the Treaty, Ottoman Empire took an obligation to implement reforms to improve the living conditions of the Armenian population in Western Armenia. Russia was to withdraw its forces from the occupied territories only after Turkey had carried out those reforms.

5. The Congress of Berlin and the "Armenian Question"

The European powers which feared that Russia would get stronger, made the interested parties review the results of the Russo-Turkish war. In June, 1878, an international congress was convened in Berlin. The Treaty of Berlin reduced the independence of the Balkan peoples, while a large portion of territories in Western Armenia captured by Russia was returned to Turkey. Only the Kars region and the port of Batum were ceded to Russia. The Russian army was to immediately withdraw from the territories of Western Armenia.

For the first time in the history of international politics the **Armenian Question** was discussed. What had once been Article 16 was transformed into Article 61 of the Peace Treaty of Berlin, which in quite vague terms advised the Ottoman government to improve the situation with the legal rights of the Armenian population and protect it from Kurdish and Circassian attacks. The Armenian delegation headed by Catholicos Khrimian was not allowed to participate in the discussion of the issue. A large number of Armenians from Western Armenia abandoned their homeland upon the withdrawal of the Russian army and resettled in Eastern Armenia.

Catholicos Mkrtich Khrimian

Since the Congress of European powers in Berlin, the Armenian Question has been included into the agenda of international politics.

6. Armenia in the second half of the 19th century. The Haiduk Movement

After the Congress of Berlin, the policy of the Ottoman Sultan Abdul-Hamid II became more anti-Armenian. There were plunders and massacres in the regions with Armenian population. During the thirty years of his reign the taxes that were collected from the Armenian population quadrupled and the cases of national discrimination became more frequent. Special militarized punitive squads "Hamidie", which drafted various outlaws and criminals, were created to oppress the Armenian population in Western Armenia.

On the other hand, by the end of the 19th century the Tsarist government radicalized its policy of national discrimination. In 1885, as many as 300 Armenian schools were shut down in the South- Caucasus and a stricter control was established upon the Armenian Church, while representatives of progressive national intellectuals were subject to oppression, many were thrown to prison or exiled to Siberia. A word about Armenian "separatism" was put into circulation. It was alleged that the quest of the Armenians to obtain self-rule in Ottoman Empire could cause a chain reaction of struggle for national liberation among the peoples under Russia's jurisdiction. Contacts between the Western Armenians and those residing in Russia were banned and severely punished. Into the Armenian regions under Russia's jurisdiction the Tsarist government brought Russian settlers.

Gevorg Chaush

Continuous persecution of Armenians in an atmosphere of impunity caused the rise of a spontaneous resistance movement. Many brave men left their homes and shelters, and went to the mountains, joining the hayduk militia, to fight against and deliver justice to the oppressors, acting alone or in groups. Famous hayduk leaders of the time included Andranik, Aghbyur Serob, Vazgen, Gevorg Chaush, Gurgen, and others. To a certain extent, the hayduk movement succeeded in deterring the Ottoman authorities and Kurdish nomadic tribes from committing more atrocities against the Armenians. Over time, their resources and methods were adopted by the Armenian political parties engaged in organizing the self-defense of the population of Western Armenia.

7. The Establishment of Armenian Political Parties

In the second half of the 19th century political groups and organizations began to emerge from the circles of Armenian intellectuals in Western and Eastern Armenia. The transformation of the Armenian Question into an issue of international politics and the establishment of the Armenian bourgeoisie awakened national awareness and revived the idea of the restoration of the Armenian statehood. In the 70s and 80s secret societies operated in Alexandrapole, Moscow, Van, Erzurum and other cities of Eastern and Western Armenia, as well as Russia. The main objective of those organizations was looking for ways for the liberation of Western Armenia and the protection of the Armenian population from the arbitrariness of the authorities.

The incessant national discrimination by the Ottoman authorities, the awakening of national awareness and the rise of the national liberation movement of the Armenian people led to the establishment of Armenian national political parties.

In 1885, Mkrtich Terlemezian founded the Armenakan party in the city of Van (Western Armenia). The ideology of that party was presented in **newspaper "Armenia"** published by Mkrtich Portugalian in Marseilles, France. The goal of the party was to awaken national awareness to embark upon liberation struggle against the Turkish yoke.

In **1887, a group of Armenian students in Geneva (Switzerland) headed by Avetis Nazarbekian and Rouben Khanazad founded the Hunchakian party.** The name of the party was picked to coincide with the name of its **newspaper -"Hunchak" (The Bell).** The short-term goal of that party's program was the liberation of the Armenians from the foreign yoke, while its long-term objective was the establishment of socialism in Armenia. After having played a major role in organizing the self-defense of the Armenian population from the Turkish plunders, the Hunchakian party split into two fractions –the nationalist and socialist, which weakened its influence and activity.

In 1890, due to the efforts of Stepan Zorian, Christaphor Mikaelian and Simon Zavarian the Dashnak party (Armenian Revolutionary Federation) was established in the city of Tiflis. The goal of the party was the liberation of Western Armenia and resolution of the Armenian Question. By the end of the 19th century the Dashnak party became the leading public and political force due to its activeness and commitment to the national-liberation movement.

CHAPTER 15

ARMENIAN COLONIES BEFORE THE 20th CENTURY

1. Armenian Settlements in the Middle Ages

According to Persian, Jewish and Greek-Roman sources individual representatives or groups of Armenian settlers had been residing in the neighboring countries since ancient times. The majority of those people immigrated to other countries of their free will in search of knowledge, jobs and for trade and business purposes.

After the Seljuk and Mongol invasions, when Armenia had to suffer for centuries under the foreign yoke, a mass exodus of Armenians from their homeland to near abroad and remote countries began, where by the 11th century Armenian colonies had been established.[1]

The **Armenian colony of Constantinopole** was established as far back as in the 7th century, when several houses of Armenian nobility immigrated to Byzantium under the Arab pressure. After the capture of Constantinople by the Turks in 1453, the Armenian colony gradually restored and restructured itself. In 1461, the Armenian Patriarchate was established. The Patriarch was the spiritual leader of the Armenian community and its representative in dealings with the Ottoman authorities. The Armenians of Constantinople were involved in trade and crafts. They owned stores, hotels, shops and warehouses. The cultural life of the community was very active. In 1567, a publishing house was opened there.

The **Armenian colonies in Bulgaria** were established yet in the early Middle ages. The Byzantine emperors forced the Armenians residing on the Armenian territories under their jurisdiction to resettle into the European provinces of the empire. Armenian military

1 Colonies were communities with significant Armenian population, where Armenians could successfully and for a long period of time preserve and develop their national identity – language, lifestyle, and traditions. A church and a national school were the key attributes of a colony.

regiments were sent to the Danube border to protect the empire against its enemies. By the 7th-8th centuries there was already a large Armenian population in Bulgaria.

After the capture of the Bagratuni Kingdom of Armenia by Byzantium, the Armenian colonies in Bulgaria became larger. In the middle of the 11th century St. Mary's Church was consecrated near the city Plovdiv, which became the spiritual center for the local Armenians. The Armenian population of Bulgaria increased in number by the 14th-15th centuries. The colony of Plovdiv became even larger, while another colony was established in Sofia along with many Armenian villages. The Bulgarian Armenians were involved in farming and crafts.

Powerful Armenian colonies were established in the Crimea as far back as in the 17th century. The Armenians settled in the urban area where they were involved in transit trade. Having established a monopoly on trade, the Crimean Armenians exported spices, furs and expensive Oriental cloths to Italy. They were involved in winegrowing and winemaking. An active trade was underway with Rech Pospolita (the Polish-Lithuanian kingdom), to where excellent Crimean wines, spices and items of Armenian jewelry were exported. Armenian churches with adjacent schools were built in many Crimean cities.

The Armenian colonies of Ukraine and Poland came into existence in the 13th-14th centuries. Numerous Armenian colonies were established in the cities of Lvov, Kamenets –Podolsk, Stanislaw, Krakow, etc. The Armenians who lived there enjoyed the freedoms of religious worship and economic activity. They also had local self-rule and independent courts. They were mainly involved in transit trade and imported rugs, silk cloths, spices and dried fruit.

The leading center among the Armenian colonies in Poland was Lvov. An Armenian Church that is still in service today was built there yet in 1363, and in the 17th century an Armenian publishing house was established in that city. The buildings of the Armenian quarter reflected the traditions of Armenian architecture.

Armenians played an important role in the political life of their country of residence. They served as Ambassadors and fulfilled diplomatic assignments. They actively participated in the Polish resistance against the Ottoman Empire. In 1683, in the battle near Vienna there were as many as 5000 Armenian soldiers in the army of the Polish King Ian Sobessky fighting against the Turks.

The Armenian colonies of Italy were established yet in the 13th century. Armenian settlers moved here from Cilicia, Crete and the Crimea. Armenian communities were established in Rome, Genoa and Florence. The largest Armenian colony was formed in the 14th-15th centuries in Venice, after the fall of the Armenian Kingdom of Cilicia. In the downtown of Venice an Armenian hotel was built that hosted Armenian merchants on their business trips to the city. There were several Armenian churches built in Venice, while stores owned by Armenian merchants could be found on the Piazza San Marco. They also used Venice as a transit point to export cotton, silk, wheat, copper and dried fruit to the rest of Europe.

The Armenian colonies of Syria were also founded in the 14th century. After the fall of the Cilician Kingdom many Armenians found shelter in Syrian cities. The larges Armenian settlement was in the city Aleppo. The colony had its elected elder, two churches and several schools. The Armenians of Aleppo were involved in trade between Europe and the countries of the Orient, exporting silk and spices from India and China to Italian cities.

It was also in the 14th century that **Armenian colonies were established in Romania.** Armenians were mainly settled in the cities of Suchava, Yassy and Fokshany. They enjoyed the freedom of worship, local self-rule, and also had elected elders and justices. All foreign trade was monopolized in the hands of Armenians. By land and sea they sent trading caravans to Russia, Poland, Bulgaria, Hungary, the Crimea, etc. New Armenian churches and schools were built.

The Armenian colonies of Iran have existed since ancient times. Those colonies became larger after the enforced immigration of Armenians during the Turkish-Persian wars. In 1604-1605, Shah Abbas I forced as many as 200 000 Armenians to resettle into Iranian cities. Armenian merchants from the city of Juga (Julfa) were settled in the suburbs of Isfahan, the Persian capital.

The settlement was named New Juga. It had local self-rule and elected elders. Armenians enjoyed the freedom of religious worship. They had their churches schools and libraries. An Armenian publishing house was established there in the 17th century.

Diamond Throne, presented by Armenians to Tsar Alexey Mikhailovich

Yet in the 16th century Armenian merchants established regular trade with Russia. By the Caspian Sea and the Volga river they imported Persian rugs, silk and spices to Russia. In the middle of the 17th century an Armenian merchant Khodja Zakar presented a throne made of diamonds to Tsar Aleksey Mikhailovich, which now belongs to the Armoury of the Kremlin. In exchange, the Tsar granted a trade monopoly on the territory of Russia to the Armenian Trade Company of New Juga. By his decree Peter the Great would confirm and extend that monopoly.

2. The Armenian Colonies of Asia and Africa in the Early Modern Time

In the 18th-19th centuries many Armenian colonies of the middle ages suffered a decline in national and cultural life. The process of assimilation became faster. Yet the tightening grip of the policy of national oppression in Western Armenian under the jurisdiction of the Ottoman Empire made more and more Armenians try their luck in foreign countries, which provided a stimulus for the rebirth of the old colonies and establishment of the new ones.

Since the 18th century the Armenian colony of Constantinople had been on the rise. A significant number of Armenian merchants and craftsmen were settled there. The colony of Constantinople grew much larger in the 18th century. Dozens of newspapers and magazines in Armenian were published there. There were 80 Armenian publishing houses, numerous educational institutions, theaters, music bands and other cultural organizations. A large class of Armenian intellectuals was formed. Many actors, writers, poets and composers lived and performed there. The Armenian community was about 200 000-strong. The colony of Constantinople became the leading economic, cultural and educational center of the Western Armenians.

A large Armenian colony was also formed in the city of Izmir, where in the beginning of the 20th century there were as many as 30 000 Armenians.

The Armenian colonies of Syria and Lebanon grew larger. By the end of the 19th century the number of the Armenian population there reached over 50 000 people. Many Armenians lived in the rural area and were involved in farming. The Armenian communities residing in the cities of Aleppo, Latakia and Beirut were involved in trade and crafts. There was a high domestic and foreign demand on the production of Armenian jewelers, weavers, tanners and rug industry. Cultural activity was somewhat slowed down by the traditional Oriental way of life. Among Armenian schools, that were not many in number, only the Nersissian School of Aleppo was famous.

It was not until the 18th century that **the Armenian colonies of Egypt** were formed, although Armenians had lived there since ancient times. The growth of Armenian colonies there coincided with the economic reforms carried out by the then ruler of Egypt Mohamed Ali. Formally, remaining under the jurisdiction of the Ottoman Empire, Egypt was, in fact, an independent state, while the intensification of economic life attracted many Armenian colonists from other parts of the empire. Small Armenian colonies were in Alexandria and Cairo. By the end of the 19th centuries the number of Armenian settlers in Egypt reached 15 000. Small as it was, the Armenian community played an important role in the economic and political life of Egypt. They monopolized the production of tobacco. In 1828, the first Armenian school was opened in Cairo, while the second one was established in Alexandria in 1851. Yet in the middle of the 19th century Armenian periodicals started to get published in Egypt. By the beginning of the 20th century there were as many as 11 Armenian schools with 1600 students in Egypt.

Nubar Pasha Nubarian

Among the statesmen of Armenian descent the name of **Nubar-pasha (Nubarian),** Egypt's long-serving Prime Minister, must be mentioned. He played an important role in the building of the Suez Canal. In 1860, he supervised the publication of the first critique of original texts from the medieval Armenian manuscripts and their translation into French. His son, **Poghos-Nubar pasha** became a famous national leader.

At the request of the Catholicos, Poghos-Nubar pasha headed the Armenian national delegation that in 1912-1914 held negotiations with the European powers on the autonomous status for Western Armenia within the Ottoman Empire. He headed the same delegation at the Paris Peace Conference in 1919 and had contacts with leaders of the world powers. His letters to President Woodrow Wilson as well as the responses of the American President that showed great respect to Poghos-Nubar are archived. Poghos-Nubar was also one of the founders of the Armenian General Benevolent Union in 1906.

In the 18th-19th centuries the Armenian colonies of Iran grew even larger. After the Russo-Persian wars many Armenians resettled into the Russian Empire, and by the middle of the 19th century there were only about 40 000 Armenians residing in Iran. But the Armenian population grew naturally and by the beginning of the **20th** century reached as many as 200 000 people. The rural Armenian population resided in its native regions of Khoy, Salmast and Urmia. Many Armenians lived in the cities of Tabriz, Tehran and Isfahan. There was a high domestic and foreign demand on the production of Armenian craftsmen. The jewelry and gold businesses, fur-coat production and winemaking were monopolized by Armenians. The businesses of weavers and blacksmiths were also on the rise. Craftsmen were united in guilds.

Iran's foreign trade with Russia and European countries was also controlled by Armenians. Dynasties of Armenian industrialists were gradually formed. The Lazarians became the main exporters of silk to Russia, while the Lianozovs were the monopolists of fishery in the South Caspian.

Armenians held diplomatic positions in Iran. They were appointed as ambassadors to the UK, France and Austria. In the second half of the 19th century Iran's Ambassador to the UK was Melkon khan, who was of Armenian descent. Another Armenian, Yeprem khan, was an active participant of the Iranian revolution of 1905-1911. Armenians had two representatives in the Mejliss –the Iranian Parliament.

Yeprem Khan

The Iranian Armenians were very successful in the fields of culture and education. Yet in 1838, an Armenian school was founded in New Juga. Later on Armenian schools were established in Tabriz and Tehran. Elementary schools operated in the rural regions of Salmast and Khoy. Armenian publishing houses functioned in Iran. Newspapers, text-books and books were being published. Since the border between Iran and Russia was open and free travel was allowed, the Armenian colony of Iran maintained permanent ties with Eastern Armenia.

The Armenian colonies of India were established in the 17th-18th centuries as a result of the immigration of a large number of Armenian colonists from Iran. Armenians settled in the coastal cities of Surkhat, Madras, Bombay, Calcutta, etc. Since the colonization of India by the English their relations with the Armenian community became quite strained. The English East-Indian trade company was sparing no effort to oust the Armenian rivals from the trade market. Having a well-armed navy, the English would often stop the ships of Armenian merchants and confiscate their cargo. Armenians actively participated in the struggle of the Indian people against the English colonization. There were many officers serving in the army of the ruler of Bengal. Gorgin khan (Grikor Haroutyunian) was Commander of the army and also held various high-ranking positions in the government.

In the 18th century the leading center of Armenian culture was in the city of **Madras.** Armenian settlers built an Armenian port, as well as several bridges and churches there. The Armenian community of Madras actively participated in the struggle for the liberation and establishment of independent Armenia. In Madras, **Shahamir Shahamirian** organized a cultural club, published books and even drafted a future Constitution for independent Armenia. It was there that published the first Armenian newspaper "Azdarar" in 1794.

In the 19th century the leading center of Armenian culture became the colony in Calcutta. It was there that the first Armenian boarding school, where Armenians students from remote regions of India and other countries could both live and study, was opened in 1821. After India had been colonized by England, the Armenian colonies there suffered a decline.

3. The Armenian Colonies of Russia in the Early Modern Period

The establishment of the Armenian colonies in Russia began in the 17th-18th centuries and chronologically coincided with Russia's aspiration to expand its southern borders towards the South-Caucasus and Balkans. The very existence of Armenian settlements in Russia had an impact on the orientation of the Armenian liberation movement, making it pro-Russian.

The unification of the Crimea with Russia in 1783 breathed new life into the Armenian colonies of the Crimea. By the emperor's decree of 1799 all the privileges of local Armenians were confirmed and extended. The Crimean Armenians preserved the freedom of religious worship, retained their independent Court (Ratusha) with proceedings held in Armenian and enjoyed free economic activity. The transit trade activity by Armenian merchants stimulated the economic development of the newly-unified territories and provided a faster pace for their integration into Russia's economy. A large class of wealthy land-owners was formed amongst the Crimean Armenians - the Spendiarovs, Aivazovskys, Seferovs, Nalbandovs and others. The Armenian churches of the Crimea also owned large sections of land. Armenian schools operated and newspapers were published in Surkhat, Karasubazar, Theodossia, Yevpatoria and other Crimean cities. The Crimean Armenians had opportunities to receive good education and were involved in fruitful cultural activity. The contribution of the Crimean Armenians to Armenian culture at large cannot be overestimated. Suffice it to give the names of a world-renowned artist Hovhaness Ayvazovsky and the founder of the Armenian Philharmonic, Alexander Spendiarov.

The Armenian colony of **Nor (new) Nakhichevan** (Rostov-on-Don) was established in 1779 after a part of the Crimean Armenians moved to Russia proper. The local government settled them in the vicinity of St. Dmitri Fortress, in the Don steppe. It was there that Armenians founded the city of Nor Nakhichevan and five villages. By the decree of Yekaterina II, the Armenians were granted self-rule and the right elect local magistrate. The population was involved in farming, cattle breeding, melon-grow and gardening. Soon Nor Nakhichevan became a well-developed city, a center of trade and crafts. In the second half of the 19th century Armenians opened factories and mills producing soap, tobacco, bricks, etc. By the beginning of the 20th century the population of Nor Nakhichevan reached 70 000 people. The colony played an important role in Armenian cultural life at large. The famous representatives of Armenian culture from Nor Nakhichevan were **Michael Nalbandian** and **Rafael Patkanian.**

Raphael Patkanian

Armenian colonies were also established in the Russian capitals. Armenians had lived in Moscow since the times of Ivan the Terrible. But the colony was formed only after 1667, when the Armenian Trade Company of Nor Juga had been granted the privilege of free trade all the way from Astrakhan to Arkhangelsk. Moscow became the center of activity for merchants, craftsmen, diplomats and artists. Among others, a well-known Armenian artist, **Bogdan (Astvatsatur) Saltanov** lived and worked in Moscow. The Lazarians, the famous dynasty of merchants and industrialists, moved to Moscow from Iran. Its representatives held high-ranking positions in the government and served the new homeland in good faith.

Michael Nalbandian

Armenians settled in St. Petersburg right after the founding of that city in 1703. Initially Armenians settled at the Vasilievsky Island where the first Armenian Church was built. The second Armenian Church was built in downtown Petersburg, at the Nevsky Avenue.

Armenian industrialists, the**, Akhverdov, Shirvanov**, **Manuilovs** and **Lazarevs** were very active there. In the outskirts of Petersburg they built factories that manufactured silk cloths. The **Isakhanovs** and **Lazarevs** retained their traditional monopoly on trade with Iran.

Among the Armenian settlements in Russia, the colony in Astrakhan stands out as a special one. It was established in the first half of the 17th century and was already on the rise in the 18th century. The Astrakhan Armenians would grow mulberry trees to produce silk and established silk industry on the territory of Russia.

In the beginning of the 19th century the majority of silk and cotton factories as well as shops and stores in Astrakhan were owned by Armenians.

By the decree of Peter the Great of 1724 the privileges of Armenians in Russia were validated and enhanced. The Astrakhan Armenians were granted self- rule and had their independent court. For court proceedings Armenians drafted the "The Law Code of the Astrakhan Armenians" in 1765, which was based on the laws described in the “Armenian Law Book” by Mkhitar Gosh as well as the traditional norms of the Armenian Law. “The Astrakhan Code” was widely used in other Armenian colonies of Russia.

The Astrakhan Armenians had a rich cultural life. They published newspapers in Armenian and Russian and established Armenian schools. The most famous of them was the Aghababian School, built in 1810 by the well-known Armenian merchant and benefactor Nicolai Aghababian.

In 1840, the Armenian court stopped operating and in 1870 after the reform of the local self-governance system in Russia the Astrakhan colony lost its autonomy. The colony continued to exist until the first quarter of the 20th century.

Tsar Peter I of Russia

After Peter the Great’s unsuccessful campaign to the Caspian many Armenians from the South-Caucasus and Iran moved to Russia and settled in the North Caucasus. Armenians settled in the vicinity of the fortresses of Kizlyar (1735) and Mozdok (1763). Like in Astrakhan, those colonies were granted the right of local self-rule by the Russian government.

By the end of the 18th century and in the beginning of the 19th Armenian colonies were established in the cities of Yekaterinodar, Maykop, Stavropol and Armavir. The Armenians of the North Caucasus were involved in farming, cattle breeding, winegrowing as well as cotton and rice growing. Huge forests of mulberry trees were used to produce silk. Armenians also founded many alcohol producing factories in that region. Due to the geographic position of the North Caucasus Armenians were able to maintain permanent ties with the homeland, and would actively follow and respond to the developments in Armenia. They opened schools, built churches, published periodicals in Armenian and had their theater troupes and music bands.

The business activity of Armenian settlers in Russia stimulated the development of economic life in the Black Sea and North Caucasus regions.

4. The Armenian Colonies of Europe in the Early Modern Period

In the modern time several Armenian colonies continued to exist in European countries. Some suffered a complete decline, but the new ones came into existence.

The life in the Armenian colonies of Bulgaria continued to be active. It was given a new stimulus after the Crimean war, when many Armenians moved to Bulgaria and settled in Sofia, Ruschuk, Yassy and Plovdiv. By the end of the 19th century the number of Armenians residing in Bulgaria reached 30 000 people. The life of the Armenian communities became more active after Bulgaria had gained independence. The Bulgarian Armenians actively participated in the liberation struggle against the Ottoman Empire. In the Balkan war of 1912, the Bulgarian Armenians established a special regiment of volunteers under the command of Andranik. Garegin Njdeh also fought under his command.

The Armenian colonies in Hungary were formed in the 18th century. In 1700, Armenians that had been scattered all around Transylvania, moved and concentrated in two cities-Armenopol and Yelizavetapol. By the decree of the King those two cities were granted a special status. They had administrative self-rule and independent courts.

An institution known as "Armenian company" responsible for tax collection, oversight of court proceedings and law and order operated there. The Armenian population was about 15-20 000 people. Among Armenians there were land owners who would eventually receive titles and be granted nobility. Several generals of Armenian descent from that colony actively participated in the struggle for the independence of Hungary and the revolution of 1848-1849. The Armenian colony of Hungary had a rich cultural life, maintained ties with the homeland and was able to bring together a large collection of Armenian manuscripts. The Armenian community of Hungary was gradually assimilated after the privileges once granted to the Armenian cities, had been taken away in the first half of the 19th century.

The Armenian colonies in Romania suffered a decline by the end of the 18th century, when the number of the Armenian population decreased due to assimilation. However, when by the middle of the 19th century Romania gained independence, the life of the Armenian colony there became much more active. Armenians continued to reside mainly in Bucharest, Yassy and Fokshany. There were given rights to hold government positions, own land and seek after nobility titles. Many of them made a career in diplomatic service. The Romanian Armenians maintained their connections with the homeland and were actively involved in charity work for their countrymen in need. The Romanian colonies became larger after the Armenian massacres in Ottoman Turkey in 1895-1896, and, particularly, after the Genocide of 1915.

The Armenian colonies in France were formed at the turn of the 18th century. The history of the Armenian-French relations can be traced back to the times of crusades and the Armenian Kingdom of Cilicia. Small groups of Armenian settlers came to France long before the 18th century. Many Armenian youngsters received their education in France. The Armenian colony of Marseilles was founded in the 19th, while it was not until the beginning of the 20th century that the Armenian communities of Lyon and Paris were established.

France was an important center for the development of Armenian culture and science. As far back as in 1811 a Chair of Armenian Studies was founded in the College de France and the critique of the original texts from the medieval Armenian manuscripts was published in Paris and translated into French. Mkrtich Portugalian began to publish his newspaper “Armenia” in Marseilles. Soon Armenian newspapers and magazines began to get published in Paris as well.

It was not until the second half of the 19th century that the **Armenian colony of England** was established. Wealthy merchants from Constantinople had their trade representations and offices in Manchester and London. At the turn of the 19th and in the beginning of the 20th century the Armenian colony in England grew larger, when many Armenians moved there after the massacres in Ottoman Turkey. In England they were involved in trade and crafts. Armenian merchants traded with countries of the Orient. Many Armenian books and magazines were published in England. The first Armenian Church was built in Manchester in 1870.

CHAPTER 16

ARMENIA AT THE TURN OF THE 19th AND THE BEGINNING OF THE 20th CENTURY

1. The Development of Capitalism

Capitalism began to develop both in Western and Eastern Armenia at the turn of the 19th and the beginning of the 20th century.

In the underdeveloped Ottoman Empire capitalism made slow progress. England, France and Germany would continue to artificially support the integrity of the collapsing empire, each of those countries trying to turn it into its own colony.

The Greek, Jewish and Armenian communities played a most active role in the economic development of the Ottoman Empire. In Constantinople, Izmir, Erzurum and other cities, Armenian industrialists established factories producing flour, vegetable oil, wine, vodka and textiles. In the cities of Western Armenia and Cilicia such as Van, Kharberd, Marash, Edessa, Ayntap and Bitlis small enterprises processing local raw materials-silk, cotton, leather and tobacco were opened. Small blacksmith shops and factories producing agricultural tools were opened in the rural regions. More sophisticated, up-to-date equipment for those regions was imported from Europe and the US by Armenian industrialists. Among most well-known entrepreneurs the names of the Kyurkchian brothers, Grikor Ipekchian and Barikian brothers should be mentioned. Those enterprises created jobs for the local Armenian population. During the repeated Armenian plunders they would often be destroyed or looted. The owners had to bribe Turkish officials to be able to restore their enterprises, each time starting from scratch.

The development of economic relations in agriculture led to the further polarization inside the rural population. The impoverished peasants would either be hired as foremen or would join the rank-and-file of the working class that was in making. Many peasants moved to the urban area in search of jobs. The existence of cheap work force stimulated the further development of capitalism. By the end of the 19th century the Armenian population in the urban regions of the Ottoman Empire increased exponentially at the cost of the decrease of the number of Armenian peasants in Western Armenia. Over 100 000 Armenians moved to cities in search of jobs. Many chose to emigrate to European countries, Russia and even as far as the US, to be rescued from constant discrimination by the Ottoman authorities and in search of a more comfortable life.

In a relatively more developed Russia capitalism progressed more quickly. The reform of 1861, by which serfdom was abolished, was implemented in the South-Caucasus and Armenia only in 1870. In 1867-1874 the administrative reform was carried out. The territory of the South-Caucasus was divided into five provinces-those of Yerevan, Tiflis, Kutaisi, Yelizavetpol and Baku. The province of Yerevan had seven districts. The province of Kars that became part of Russia in 1878 was comprised of four districts. Russians settled in the deserted lands of those territories. By this, the Tsarist government tried to change the demographic situation, weaken the Armenian liberation movement and tie the region to Russia.

The reform of 1861 and those that followed it created certain conditions for the development of capitalism in Russia. Natural resources of the region and oil-rich fields in Baku stimulated the development of capitalism in the South-Caucasus.

At the turn of the 19th century capitalism in Russia progressed with a much faster pace. Russia started the building of a strategically important Tiflis-Kars railway which was envisaged for a rapid transportation of forces in case of a new war with Turkey. **In 1899 the construction of Tiflis-Alexandrapole-Kars railway was finished and put into operation. Alexandrapole-Yerevan railway started to operate in 1901, while the construction of Yerevan-Nakhichevan-Julfa line was finished in 1908.**

The opening of that communication line gave a boost to a more active exploitation of copper mines in Alaverdi and Kapan. A concession arrangement was made for those mines to be operated by French entrepreneurs. The urban population in Eastern Armenia increased significantly. The construction of railways was another stimulus for the development of capitalism in the South-Caucasus. As there were no large industrial enterprises in Eastern Armenia, Armenian industrialists concentrated their main activity in Baku and Tiflis. The well-known industrialists were **Mantashev, Aramiants, Lianozov,** Mirzoyan, Dolukhanian and the Ghukasian brothers to name but few. They invested their capital into the oil industry in Baku. All of them were also known to be benefactors and sponsors of various representatives of Armenian culture. In agriculture new crops and cultures were cultivated such as cotton, tobacco and mulberry. The arable land was reduced at the cost of developing gardening, melon-grow and winegrowing. To meet the needs of the local market, small enterprises producing vegetable oil, tanneries, as well as cotton and silk processing factories were opened. More copper was extracted from the mines in Alaverdi and Kapan, while the salt mines in

Certificate of Gold Medal Award to Petros Esapov at London Expo, 1909

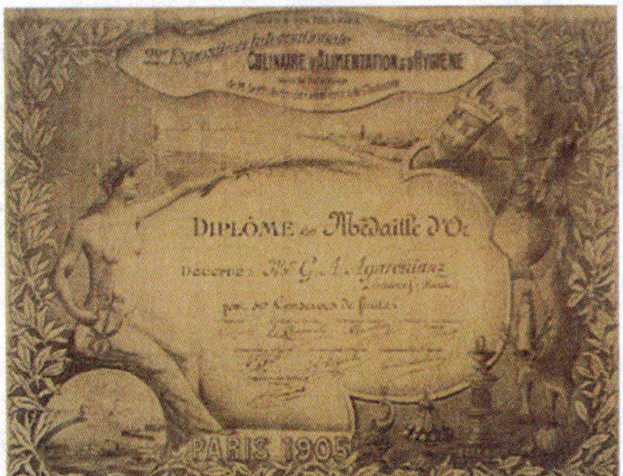

Certificate of Gold Medal Award to G. Aharonian at Paris Expo, 1907

Al. Mantashev

A original bottle of Cognac produced in 1894 at Tairiants brendy factory

Kokhb and Nakhichevan also increased their production. The impoverished peasants and small land-owners moved to Tiflis and Baku joining the newly-formed class of proletariat.

In 1887, the production of Armenian brandy was established in Yerevan. The first brandy factory was opened in Yerevan by Armenian industrialist **Nerses Tairiants.** There were other entrepreneurs involved in brandy production. **"Ararat" brandy manufactured at the factory owned by N. Shustov and cultivated by winegrower P. Musiniants** became the most famous one. It was awarded diplomas at international exhibitions and exported to Russia and Europe.

2. The Ottoman Empire at the Turn of the 19th century. Anti-Armenian Policy of Sultan Abdul-Hamid II

At the end of the 19th century the once powerful Ottoman Empire suffered economic and political decline. In fact, it turned into a semi-colony of the European powers, which artificially supported its territorial integrity in their own interest. **At the end of the Russo-Turkish war of 1877-1878 the Armenian Question became an issue of international politics. The European powers had no intention to solve it, but only used it as leverage to put a pressure on Turkey.**

The Sultans' government radicalized its policy of economic and national oppression of the Armenian population. In a number of cities there were people killed in the clashes between local Armenians and police. **In the summer of 1890, there was a demonstration organized at the initiative of the Hunchakian party in the Goum Gapu** district of Constantinopole with demands to punish those responsible for the murders, as well as to carry out the reforms regarding the Armenian population in keeping with Article 61 of the Treaty of Berlin. The demonstrators moved towards the Sultan's Palace to present their petition to the government. The police opened fire at the demonstrators and the organizers were arrested.

Disillusioned and deprived of any realistic hope to find a diplomatic solution to the Armenian cause wider circles of Armenian society tended to consider revolutionary methods. **In 1894, the Armenian population of the mountainous region of Sasun rebel against the Sultan's policy of oppression**. The uprising was led by the members of the Hunchakian party - Mourad, Gevork Chaush, Hrair and others. First, squads of Turkish mercenaries and then regular army regiments were defeated by the defenders of Sasun. Yet soon, the many times superior regular forces surrounded and seized the city of Sasun. Over seven thousand Armenians were massacred. The surviving leaders were prosecuted and exiled.

However, the Ottoman Empire was not able to break the will of the people of Sasun. Many participants of the uprising continued their struggle joining small Haiduk units.

The uprising in Sasun had a goal of attracting the attention of super powers to the resolution of the Armenian Question. But the reaction of the European powers was limited to the establishment of an ad hoc fact-finding commission. In May, 1895 Great Britian, Russia and France submitted a program of reforms to the Sultans' government on the improvement of the conditions of the Armenian population and also demanded to punish those responsible for the Armenian massacres.

The Sultan promised to carry out the so-called "May, 1895 Program of Reforms". However, nothing was done.

In September, 1895, seeing that the government had no intention of implementing the reforms, **the Hunchakian party organized a mass demonstration in the capital.** Foreign diplomats had been given an advance notice that the objective of the peaceful demonstration was to attract the attention of the super powers to the resolution of the Armenian Question. The demonstrators moved in the direction of the government offices in Bab Ali to present a petition. They were dispersed by the police. With the connivance of the government, massacres started in Constantinople during which about 6000 Armenians were killed. Although the Sultan had to eventually accept the "May, 1895 Program of Reforms", he took even a harder line in oppressing the Armenian population.

At the initiative of the Hunchakian party in October, **1895 there was an Armenian uprising in Zeytun,** which rebel against discrimination and oppression.

The elected leader of the uprising was Nazaret Chaush. The Zeytunians arrested the local administration officials, seized the barracks of the Turkish soldiers and took 700 prisoners. The government sent a 30 000-strong army to suppress the uprising. Taking up arms, 6 000 Zeytunians withstood their attacks for about four months. More than half of the defenders were killed. The Turks lost about 20 000 soldiers.

As a result of the mediation by the European powers the defenders of Zeytun and the Ottoman government reached a compromise. The Ottoman government granted amnesty to the leaders of the uprising, recognized partial autonomy of Zeytun and appointed a Christian ruler in exchange for tax collection from the population of Zeytun.

To remove the Armenian Question from the international agenda and suppress the national liberation aspirations of the Armenian people, the government of Abdul-Hamid II would repeatedly instigate Armenian massacres. By the end of 1895 such massacres happened in Erzurum, Trebizond, Bitlis, Sebastia, Edessa and other cities. In the period of 1894-96 more than 300,000 Armenians were slaughtered and about 200,000 Armenians were forcibly converted to Islam or took refuge immigrating to different countries.

Wary of the new massacres, the Armenian political parties began to prepare the Armenian population for self-defense. When in 1896 the Turkish government tried to instigate new massacres, in several regions they faced a well-organized Armenian resistance. The self-defense of

Van, Malatya, and Edessa are but few examples of that resistance.

3. The Armenian Liberation Movement at the Beginning of the 20th Century

In 1901 a group of Haiduks under the command of Andranik caved in the Monastery of Arakelots, trying to attract the attention of the European powers to the trampled rights of the Armenian population in the Ottoman Empire. There were 37 fighters joined by about 20 local peasants in Andranik's unit. During the period of November 3-27, the unit withstood the attacks of the superior Turkish regular army force. During the negotiations the Haiduks demanded to release the political prisoners, disarm the Kurdish squads and return the villages captured from Armenian peasants. Running out of ammunition, the surrounded Haiduks broke through the Turkish lines by night and escaped to the mountains. They proved that the Armenian people had not abandoned their fight for independence.

In 1904, a heroic defense of Sasun took place. To once and for all suppress the resistance of the Sasunians the Ottoman government brought together a large force for a complete capture of the region. On April 1, 1904, a 10 000-strong regular army supported by the Hamidie squads of 5000 people launched an attack on Sasun. The Armenian population of 12 000 people was defended by 200 Hajduks and 1000 local peasants.

Having learned about the plans of the Ottoman government to seize Sasun, the Dashnak and Hunchakian parties sent units of volunteers and ammunition to the region. Haiduk units under the command of Andranik, Mourad, Arakel, Gevork Chaush and others moved their forces to the vicinity of Sasun. A Defense Council was established that elected Andranik as the Commander-in-Chief.

Despite the heroic resistance, Sasun was seized by the regular army forces and Kurdish squads that brutalized the local population.

4. The Policy of Russia and the Armenian Question at the beginning of the 20th century

The Tsar's government feared that the national liberation movement in Western Armenia would trigger a chain reaction in Eastern Armenia. It created all kinds of obstacles for the activity of national political parties, persecuted the leaders of the liberation movement and outlawed Haiduk units on its territory.

As revolutionary ideas spread all over the Russian Empire, the Tsar's government radicalized its policy of national discrimination to divert the attention of its people from revolutionary struggle. The government was convinced that the liberation movement was guided by the Armenian Church. In 1903, by the order of G. Golitsyn, the Governor of the Caucasus, all property of the Armenian Apostolic Church was requisitioned and Armenian schools were shut down.

The Catholicos of All Armenians Mkrtich Khrimian denounced the anti-Armenian policy of Tsarist Russia. Armenian political parties-Dashnaks and Hunchakians together with Russian social democrats got involved in the struggle against the Tsarist regime. There were Armenian public rallies and demonstrations in Yelizavetpol, Baku, Tiflis, Echmiadzin, Alexandrapole, Shushi and Yerevan that led to clashes with local police, as a result of which people were killed and wounded. In several villages, the local population showed resistance against police and Kazaks.

Persecution of public leaders and progressive intellectuals was underway. Many were exiled or thrown to prison. Despite all efforts by the Tsarist government, there was a revolutionary situation in the country.

In **January, 1905, the First Democratic Revolution took place in Russia.** Just like in the rest of the country, there were strikes in the South-Caucasus. During the summer of 1905 there were strikes in Kars, Alexandrapole, Alaverdi and other cities of Eastern Armenia. The Tsar's government, concerned about the developing revolution and Armenian resistance, canceled its previous decree and returned the property requisitioned from the Armenian Church.

The new Governor of the Caucasus, in the conditions of the developing revolution, opted to conduct a more flexible policy. To divert the attention of peoples from the revolutionary struggle, the Tsarist regime started to monger ethnic conflicts. Ethnic clashes between the Armenians and Azerbaijanis were instigated in Baku, Yelizavetpol, Shushi, Nakhichevan and Yerevan.

On October 17, 1905 the Manifesto by Tsar Nikolai II, in which he promised to convene the State Duma, was made public. Russia was transforming into Constitutional Monarchy. In 1906-1907 the revolution recede. The second State Duma was disbanded on July 3, 1907 and absolute monarchy restored. The revolution came to an end.

A period of reaction started in Russia. The reactionary policy was god-fathered by **Prime Minister Stolypin.** At the same time Stolypin was trying to institute reforms for the further development of capitalism in the country. His agrarian reform was aimed at serving that purpose.

Having suppressed the revolution, the Tsarist regime started the persecution of national political parties. Taking advantage of disagreements inside the party, the Tsar's government accused the Dashnaks of anti-governmental and anti-Russian activity. There were mass arrests of the Dashnak party members and a public trial organized by the government.

In January, 1912, the Court Chamber of the Senate in St. Petersburg, began hearings on the case of the Dashnak party. As many as 159 people were charged. But against all expectations, the verdict was very soft. About 100 people were acquitted, while the rest got away with short prison terms and soft sentences.

Such a soft verdict was accounted for by several factors. By that time the new revolutionary movement in Russia was on the rise and Stolypin had already been assassinated. The international situation became quite tense, while the preparation for the war with Germany and its ally Turkey was underway. In such conditions, the Tsarist regime opted not to continue persecution, and it also took a softer line with Armenians to be able to use them in the upcoming war against Turkey.

5. The Coup d'etat of the Young Turks

In 1908, after a coup d'état, the Young Turk party came to power in Turkey. The peoples of the Ottoman Empire supported that party with a hope of democratic changes in the governance of the country.

The fall of the bloody regime of Sultan Abdul-Hamid II was welcomed by all peoples of the Ottoman Empire. There were hopes that the Young Turk government would abolish legal inequality of the Christian and Muslim populations and grant democratic freedoms to the peoples of the Empire. However, the Young Turk government embarked upon the policy of assimilation of other peoples. **Pan-Turkism** and **Pan-Islamism** became the official policy. Coming across the resistance against its plans the Young Turk government tried to implement them by use of force.

In April-May, 1909, by the order of the government massacres of the Armenian population in Adana province and organized robbery of their property were provoked. In several cities and towns the Armenians saved themselves due to heroic self-defense. Yet, over 30 000 Armenians were slaughtered during that time. In 1912, the triumvirate formed of the leaders of the Young Turk party came to power in Turkey. The entire decision-making was monopolized in their hands. Since then all the state issues in the Ottoman Empire had been at the mercy of Talaat –the Prime Minister and Foreign Minister, Enver-the War Minister and Jemal –the Minister of Interior.

6. The Armenian Question in 1912-1914 and the Great Powers. The Position of Russia

In 1911, a **Turkish-Italian war broke out,** as a result of which Turkey lost a large number of territories. In 1912-1913 the **first and second Balkan wars were waged.** The Balkans peoples joined forces to crush their hated enemy, and liberated their national territories, that had been seized by the Turks. Thousands of Turkish refugees from the lost European territories flooded into the Asian parts of Turkey. The Young Turk government began to populate the deserted Armenian villages and urban quarters by Muslim re-settlers from the European regions of the Empire.

After the Balkan wars the Armenian Question was once again included into the agenda of international diplomacy. The Catholicos of All Armenians, Gevork V authorized Poghos-Nubar, the famous Armenian benefactor and public leader, to hold negotiations with the world powers on the resolution of the Armenian Cause. Along with that, through the Governor of the Caucasus the Catholicos sent a petition to the Russian Tsar, in which he asked for the implementation of the resolutions of the Berlin Congress.

In 1913, the Great Powers came to an agreement and demanded that the Young Turk government should carry the corresponding reforms in Western Armenia. Russia took the mission of overseeing the implementation of reforms.

On January 26, 1914 the Russo-Turkish agreement on the implementation of reforms in Western Armenia was signed.

According to the Russo-Turkish agreement, two administrative territorial units with European governors in charge were to be formed from the regions populated by Armenians. The national and religious discrimination was to be replaced by equal rights for all citizens. All nationalities were to be equally represented in administrative authorities, police and courts. By the summer of 1914, governors from Europe had already been appointed. **But they did not have time to take office. Taking advantage of the break- out of WWI, the Young Turk government refused to implement the reforms.**

CHAPTER 17

WORLD WAR I. THE ARMENIAN GENOCIDE

1. The Beginning of WWI. Military Activities in the Caucasian Front

August 1, 1914 marked the beginning of WWI. The war for the new spheres of influence in the world was waged between two coalitions: the Entente that included England, France and Russia and the Triple Alliance of Germany, Austria-Hungary and Turkey. Dozens of states volunteered or were forced to take part in that war. During the war the Ottoman Empire sought to carry out the program of Pan-Turkism, trying to bring under control and unify all the territories populated by the Turkic nations, including those residing in the Trans-Caucasus, southern regions of Russia, Central Asia and Altay. Russia aspired to annex the territory of Western Armenia, seize the straits of Bosporus and Dardanelles and gain access to the Mediterranean Sea. The two coalitions were involved in military activities on different fronts of Europe, Africa and Asia.

On the Caucasian front the Turks concentrated an army of 300 000 under the command of Enver, the War Minister. In October, 1914 the Turkish forces launched a wide-range offensive and were able to capture several border regions. They also invaded into the western regions of Iran. During the winter months in the course of the battles near Sarikamish the Russian army was able to defeat the superior Turkish forces and squeeze them out of Iran. During 1915 neither side was able to gain an advantage. In the beginning of 1916, the Russian army launched a wide-range offensive and crushing the Turks captured Bayazet, Mush, Alashkert, Erzurum and the important Black Sea port of Trebizond. There were no dramatic military activities on the Caucasian front in 1917. The demoralized Turkish army did not try to launch a new offensive, while the February and October revolutions in

Russia which resulted in the change of power did not allow the Russians to advance farther. In 1917 a cease-fire agreement was signed between the Russian and Turkish commands.

2. The Armenian Voluntary Movement. Armenian Battalions.

The Armenian people actively participated in WWI joining the Entente countries. About 200 000 Armenians were drafted into the Russian army. Some 50 000 Armenians served in the armies of the allies. Since Russia's expansionist plans coincided with the aspirations of the Armenian people to liberate Western Armenia, the Armenian political parties launched an active campaign to organize the Voluntary Movement. They were able to put together as many as 7 Armenian voluntary units with the total of about 10 000 men drafted in them.

General Andranik

Drastamat Kanayan (Dro)

The first unit was under the command of Andranik Ozanian, the national hero and prominent leader of the liberation movement who was subsequently granted the rank of General in the Russian army. Other units were commanded by Dro, Hamazasp, Qeri, Vardan, Arshak Janpoladian and Hovsep Argutian. Unit VI was later brought under the command of Hayk Bzhishkian (Guy), who a few years later was to become a legendary Commander in the Red Army. Armenian volunteers from various regions of Russia and other countries got drafted into those units. The Armenian units showed a lot of courage and participated in all battles for the liberation of Western Armenia.

The Tsar's government had been fully behind the Armenian Volunteers Movement until the defeat of the Turkish army became obvious. In the summer of 1916, fearing that the units of Armenian volunteers might provide a basis for the establishment of national army, the Command of the Caucasian Front reorganized them into five light infantry battalions of the Russian army.

3. The Armenian Genocide in the Ottoman Empire

In 1915-1918 the Young Turk government of Turkey planned and implemented the Genocide of the Armenian population in the Ottoman Empire. During the deportation of the Armenians from their historical homeland and mass killings as many as 1.5 million people lost their lives.

Yet in 1911, during a secret meeting in the city of Thessaloniki, the Young Turk party took a decision to turkify all the citizens of the empire. Christians were to be done away with. Taking advantage of the international situation and break–out of WWI, the Young Turk government decided to implement those decisions.

The Genocide was preplanned. First, all Armenian men of conscription age were drafted to the Turkish army to preclude any potential resistance from the Armenian population. They were used only as a work force or foremen and gradually exterminated. Second, Armenian intellectuals, who could have potentially organized and headed the Armenian resistance, were killed. In March-April, 1915, over 800 intellectuals were arrested. Among them were members of the Parliament Onik Vramian and Grigor Zohrab, writers Varuzhan, Siamanto and Rouben Sevak, composer and musicologist Komitas.

Grigor Zohrap

They were subjected to insults and humiliation while being exiled and deported, some died on the road, while those who survived were later brutally killed. On April 24, 1915 the Young Turk government executed 20 Armenian political prisoners. Komitas, the famous composer, who witnessed those horrors, was never able to recover and spent the rest of his life in mental institutions.

After that the Young Turk government began to deport and kill helpless children, women and elderly people. During the forced marches they were subjected to new brutalities-those too weak to walk were killed; women were raped or kidnapped for harems, children died from starvation and thirst. Only 10 % of the Armenians who were exiled to the desert of Deir ez-Zor in Mesopotamia survived the death march.

From the total of 2.5 million –strong Armenian population in the Ottoman Empire, 1.5 million people were killed and the rest were scattered around the world.

Armenian orphans. Photo from the Archives of the U.S. Library of Congress

A portion of the Armenian population was saved with the help of the Russian army. Leaving behind their entire livelihood people had to run away to find shelter in the Russian Empire. Another part of the Armenian refugees found shelter in the Arab countries, Iran and other places. After the defeat of the Turkish army many of them returned to the homeland, but were again brutally attacked or killed. Around 200 000 Armenians were turkified. Thousands of Armenian orphans were saved by American relief and missionary organizations in the Middle East.

In 1920, with the defeat of the Ottomans in WWI and after the key Ittihadist leaders had fled the country, the new government of Ottoman Turkey held investigation and convened tribunals on the crimes committed by the previous regime. The Military Tribunal of Constantinople found Talaat, Enver, Jemal and Behaeddin Shakir (Secretary of the Central Committee of the Young Turk party) guilty of capital crimes and in absentia sentenced them to death for planning and implementing the Armenian Genocide.

The sentence was carried out by Armenian avengers. The Young Turk leaders fled Turkey and found shelter in Germany and other countries. But justice found them there.

Soghomon Tehlerian

Talaat was tracked down in Berlin and assassinated by Soghomon Teylerian on March 15, 1921. The German Court that conducted hearings on that case acquitted Teylerian. Jemal was assassinated by Petros Ter-Petrossian and Artashes Gevorkian on July 25, 1922 in Tiflis.

Behaeddin Shakir was shot dead by Arshavir Shirakian and Aram Yerkanian on April, 1922 in Berlin. Enver was assassinated in August, 1922 in the Central Asia.

4. Self-defence of the Armenian People

In the course of the Genocide the Armenian population in several regions of the empire was saved due to heroic self-defense or died with dignity in the battlefield.

For more than a month the residents of the city of Van and the nearby villages heroically withstood the attacks of the regular Turkish army. The self-defense was under the command of Armenak Yerkanian, Aram Manoukian, Panos Terlemezian and other leaders. There was a complete accord and good coordination in the activities of the Armenian political parties. Facing imminent death, the defenders were eventually saved by the Russian army advancing towards Van in May, 1915. Afterwards 200 000 Armenians from the Villayet of Van had to join the retreating Russian army and abandon their homeland to escape another massacre.

The residents of the mountainous region of Sasun resisted against the regular Turkish forces for almost a year. But the siege was gradually tightening its grip and the majority of the population was massacred. The Russian army that in February, 1916 captured the city of Mush saved the residents of Sasun from complete extermination. Only about 10% of the once 50 000-strong population of Sasun survived the siege. They had to leave their homeland and resettle within the boundaries of the Russian Empire.

Having received the deportation order, Armenian population of the little town of Shapin took up arms and caved in the ruins of the nearby fortress. For 27 days they withstood the attacks of the regular Turkish forces. Having run out of ammunition and food, they decided to make an attempt to break through the enemy lines. About 1000 people were able to escape, the rest were massacred.

Another great example of Armenian resistance was set by the heroic defenders of Musaler (Musa Dagh). Having received the deportation order, the 5000 residents from 7 Armenian villages of the region of Suetia (the coastal Mediterranean region near Antiochia) decided to resist, fell back and trenched upon Musa Mountain. The self-defense was under the command of Tigran Andreassian. For a month and a half the defenders thwarted the repeated attacks of the superior Turkish regular force supported by artillery. The French warship "Gishen", spotting the SOS signal, came to the rescue of the defenders on September 10, 1915, and as many as 4058 Armenian survivors were transported by French and English warships to Egypt. The heroic defense of Musa Dagh inspired Austrian writer **Franz Werfel to write his novel "The Forty Days of Musa Dagh"**.

Franz Werfel

The last center of the heroic resistance was the self-defense of the Armenian quarter in Edessa, which lasted from September 29 to November 15 of 1915. The entire male population died in the battlefield, while 15 000 surviving women and children were deported to the deserts of Mesopotamia.

Henry Morgenthau, U.S. Ambassador to Turkey

The foreigners who witnessed the Genocide of 1915-1918 condemned that outrage and left a description of the attrocities committed by the Young Turk government against the Armenian population. They also refuted all false allegations of the Turkish authorities that the Armenians had plotted an uprising. Among those who voiced their public protest against the first Genocide of the 20th century were Johannes Lepsius,

Anatole France, Henry Morgenthau, Maxim Gorky, Valery Brusov and many others. In the present day, parliaments of many countries have already recognized the Armenian Genocide perpetrated by the Young Turks.

5. The Consequences of the Genocide

During the Genocide the Armenian population residing in its historical homeland was brutally exterminated. The Ittihadist leaders were fully responsible for the Armenian Genocide. The then Prime Minister of Turkey, Talaat would cynically state that the Armenian Question was no more as there were no more Armenians, and boasted that he was able to achieve more in just 3 months, than Sultan Abdul-Hamid II had managed to do in 30 years of his reign.

Kurdish tribes also actively participated in the planned extermination of the Armenians with the aim to capture Armenian territories and loot their property. The German government and Command were also responsible for the Armenian Genocide. Many German officers were in command of the Turkish regiments that took part in the Genocide. The Entente countries had their share of guilt and responsibility. They did nothing to stop the extermination of the Armenian population by the Young Turk authorities.

In the course of the Genocide over 2000 Armenian villages, as well as thousands of churches, monasteries, schools and Armenian quarters in more than 60 cities were exterminated. The Young Turk government appropriated all property and deposits that had been robbed from the Armenians.

After the Genocide there were virtually no Armenians left in Western Armenia.

6. Armenian Culture at the Turn of the 19th and the Beginning of the 20th Century

Before the Genocide Armenian culture had been on the rise. It was accounted for by the rise of the liberation movement and the awakening of national awareness, as well as the development of capitalism in

Armenia and the countries with large and well-organized compact Armenian communities. The division of Armenia into two parts- Western and Eastern had its impact on the development of two independent trends in Armenian culture, eastern Armenian and western Armenian. The important centers of culture were in Moscow, St. Petersburg, Tiflis, Baku, Constantinopole, Izmir, Venice, Paris and other cities, where the class of Armenian intellectuals was concentrated.

Armenian educational institutions made a significant contribution to the development of culture. Over 300 hundred Armenian elementary and high schools for girls and boys operated in Eastern Armenia, in the key cities of the South-Caucasus and North Caucasus, as well as in several Russian cities such as Rostov-on-Don and Astrakhan. In some rural regions there were primary schools, where pupils were taught to read, write, count, and also Russian language.

There were about 400 hundred elementary, middle and high schools in the towns of Western Armenia and the big cities of the Ottoman Empire. There was no government support for Armenian schools in Russia, moreover in the Ottoman Empire. Those schools functioned due to the financial support of the Armenian Apostolic Church, various public organizations and benefactors. The most famous among Armenian educational institutions were the Nersissian School in Tiflis, Mourad Rafaelian College in Venice and Lazarev Institute of Oriental Languages in Moscow.

The development of education paved the way for a higher demand on Armenian periodicals. In the beginning of the 20th century over 300 Armenian newspapers and magazines of various political orientations were being published. The Armenian national parties published periodicals such as "Droshak", "Hunchak", "Proletariat", etc. Besides, there were also newspapers and magazines covering cultural and social life.

At the turn of the 19th and the beginning of the 20th century Constantinople and Tiflis became the main centers of the publication of Armenian periodicals. The most popular ones were newspaper "Mushak" published in Tiflis (edited by Gr. Artsruni), "Murch"

Vahan Terian

Hakob Paronian

Avetik Isahakian

magazine published in Constantinople (edited by Av. Araskhaniants), as well as newspapers "Meghu" (edited by Haroutyun Svachian and "Masis" (edited by Karapet Utunjian). In Moscow Stepanos Nazarian published "Hyusisapayl" (Northern Lights) magazine.

At the end of the 19th and the beginning of the 20th century Armenian literature was on the rise. A large group of young poets and novelists came to the fore both in Eastern and Western Armenia. Their creative work was inspired by patriotism and a desire to see their homeland free and unified. It is no accident, that in their literary work many Armenian writers would address the heroic pages of Armenian history which proved inspirational in the struggle for the independence and unification of the country. Due to their writing two independent literary Armenian languages- Eastern and Western, were formed. Among those who wrote in Eastern Armenian were poets **Rafael Patkanian, Hovhaness Hovhannisyan, Vahan Teryan, poets and prose writers Avetik Isahakian, Ghazaros Aghayan, Perch Proshian, playwright Gabriel Soundukian, novelists Nar-Dos, Muratsan** and others. Among those who composed their work in Western Armenian were poets **Petros Durian, Misak Metsarents, Siamanto (Atom Yardjanian), Daniel Varuzhan,** as well as poet, prose writer and playwright **Levon Shant,** novelist **Grikor Zohrab,** a great satirist **Hakop Paronian** and others.

The roles of poet and prose writer **Hovhaness Tumanian** and novelist **Raffi** in the Armenian literature of that time cannot be overestimated.

In his work Tumanian adapted a great number of Folk legends and myths and paid tribute to national traditions, way of life and customs. The most famous of his works are poems "Anush" and "Maro", legends "Akhtamar" and "The Fall of Tumpkaberd", etc.

Raffi

Raffi is famous for his historical novels "Samvel", "Jalal-ed-din", "Khent", etc. His novel "Kaytser" (Sparks) had a special popularity among his contemporaries, as it called for national liberation struggle without counting on a helping hand from the world powers. Professor of the Lazarev Institute **Mkrtich Emin** published his translation of ancient Armenian manuscripts into Russian. The same original sources were translated into French and published in Paris with the sponsorship of Armenian benefactor **Nubar-pasha,** who was the Prime Minister of Egypt. **Ghevond Alishan,** a member of the Mechitarist congregation published comprehensive work on the history of Armenia, giving a detailed list and description of historical monuments, many of which were destroyed in the upcoming years. **Grikor Khalatian** was the first to publish the complete history of Armenia in Russian. During his travels in Eastern and Western Armenia, **Garegin Srvanztian** collected invaluable samples of Armenian folklore. He was the one who discovered, made the transcription and organized the first publication of the medieval Armenian epos "Sasuntsi David". Scholar **Manuk Abeghian** studied Armenian folklore and ancient Armenian history. Famous philologist

Hovhannes Tumanian

Hrachia Acharian

and linguist **Hrachia Acharian** conducted a research of Armenian lexicon and did comparative analysis of Armenian and other Indo-European languages. Famous historian **Nikolai Adontz** authored and published a book "Armenia in the Epoch of Justinian" in Russian, which was an overview of the Armenian-Byzantine relations and Armenian history of the middle ages. This comprehensive work published as far back as in 1909 is still academically valid today. Well-known historian and philologist **Leo (Arakel Babakhanian)** authored a number of works on Armenian history and literature, and also compiled and published a collection of documents regarding the Armenian Cause.

Nikoghayos Adonts

Komitas

Hovhannes Aivazovsky

Armenian music was also on the rise. The art of gousans (people's poet, composer and singer) was perfected by **Gousan Jivani, Gousan Sheram** and others. Armenian composers who had received classical music education came to the fore. **Tigran Chukhajian** (1837-1898) wrote the first Armenian opera "Arshak II", a great number of operettas, as well as symphony and chamber music. Composer Armen Tirgranian (1879-1950) wrote opera "Anush" based on the famous poem by Hovhaness Tumanian. Famous composer and musicologist **Komitas** (1869-1935) laid the foundation stone for the study of musical folklore as he transcribed the music and words of about 3000 folk songs. Komitas performed and lectured extensively in European countries familiarizing European audiences with idiosyncrasy of Armenian folk music.

Armenian art was also on the rise by the end of the 19th and the beginning of the 20th century. Among most famous Armenian artists the name of the seascape painter **Hovhaness Aivazovsky** (1817 -1900) must be mentioned first. He lived and worked in Feodossia (the Crimea) and most of his paintings are seascapes and coastal scenes. His most famous paintings are "The Ninth Wave", "Noah Descends the Ararat Mountain", "The Armenian Massacre in Trebizond", etc.

Other prominent artists were **Gevork Bashinjaghian, Panos Terlemezian and Vardges Surenyants.**

Vardges Surenyants would also paint frescos in many Armenian churches in Russia. His most famous paintings are "Shamiram and Ara the Beautiful" and "Salome". A copy of his painting "Armenian Madonna" is kept in the new Cathedral of Yerevan.

***Armenian Madonna** by*
Vardges Sureniants

The Genocide of 1915-1918 was a serious blow to Armenian culture as not only great works of art and culture were destroyed, but also many people of culture and arts were physically exterminated.

CHAPTER 18

THE FALL OF THE RUSSIAN EMPIRE AND ARMENIA

1. The February Revolution and Armenia

On February 27, 1917 the Second Democratic Revolution took place in Russia, which brought about the collapse of the autocracy. Before the convocation of the Constituent Assembly the Provisional government was formed.

By the decree of the Provisional government the post of the Governor of the South-Caucasus was abolished in March, 1917, while the 5 deputies from the South-Caucasus to the State Duma formed local provisional government- the **Special Trans-Caucasus Committee (STC).** Regional, province, city and rural commissariats were established as local government institutions.

By another decree of the Provisional government the territories of Western Armenia occupied by the Russian army were granted special status. The Provisional government appointed General P. Averyanov as Commissar of Western Armenia. Conditions were created for the return of Armenian refugees to their homeland. The first Congress of the Western Armenians elected the National Committee of Western Armenians.

The Armenian political parties in Eastern Armenia concerted their efforts. In Yerevan, Tiflis and Baku Armenian National Councils were established. The leading role was given to the National Council in Tiflis headed by a well-known writer **Avetis Aharonian.**

The Provisional government continued to participate in WWI, which was very unpopular in Russia. Against the expectations of Russian peasants the land ownership issue was not resolved. The Bolshevik party capitalized on that, and during the armed revolt overthrew the Provisional government in October, 1917. Soviet power was established in Russia.

2. The October Revolution and Armenia

Stepan Shahumian

In the national provinces of the empire Soviet power was not recognized. With the support of local national councils the Trans-Caucasus Commissariat, consisting of the former deputies of the State Duma, was established as a local government institution. In turn, the Soviet government did not recognize the Commissariat and appointed a well-known Bolshevik **Stepan Shahoumian** as provisional Extraordinary Commissar for the Caucasus Affairs.

The Soviet government declared that it was exiting from WWI. It also stated that all land was granted to peasants, recognized the right to self-determination of the peoples of the Russian Empire and even their right to establish independent states. The Caucasian front began to collapse. Russia soldiers made haste to return home to get their share of the distributed land. Toward the end of 1917 the ceasefire with Germany and its ally Turkey was signed and negotiations on peace agreement got underway.

On December 19, 1917, by a special decree, the Soviet government granted the right to self-determination to Western Armenia, which had been occupied by the Russian army during WWI. Provisional government of Western Armenia was to be formed together with local administration and police. However, in the conditions of anarchy and the imminent threat of Turkish offensive it was impossible to bring that decree to life.

By the order of the Russian Command Special Armenian Corps was formed under the command of General **Tovmas Nazarbekian** to defend the Front after the withdrawal of the Russian forces. By the decision of the National Council a division of Armenian volunteers was created under the command of the national hero, General Andranik. Haiduk units commanded by Mourad, Sepouh and Torgom, as well as

Aram Manoukian

local volunteers also helped to defend the borders.

The Armenian National Council of Yerevan headed by **Aram Manoukian** was in charge of stabilizing the situation in Eastern and Western Armenia. The formation of national armed forces was underway. Armenian officers who had served in the Russian Army, such as General M.Silikian, Colonel D. Bek-Pirumian, P. Zalinian, N. Gorganian and others, began to gather in Yerevan.

3. The Armenian Question at the Negotiations in Brest-Litovsk and Trebizond

On March 3, 1918 the Peace Treaty of Brest-Litovsk was signed between Soviet Russia and Germany and its allies, which had grave consequences for the Armenian people. By Article 4 of the peace treaty Russia was taking an obligation to withdraw from the occupied territories in Western Armenia. The provinces of Kars, Ardahan and Batum were also ceded to Turkey. As soon as the treaty had been signed, the Turkish forces lost no time to move into the aforementioned territories, while the Armenian Corps began to retreat showing resistance along the way. The Turks seized Yerzinka, Trebizond, Van, Erzurum and Baberd, and moved in the direction of Kars. **The Armenian people were subjected to another massacre. Thousands of new refugees flooded Eastern Armenia and the South-Caucasus. Once again the Armenian people suffered a huge moral and physical blow.**

It was on February10, 1918 that the Transcaucasian Seym was convened in Tiflis with the participation of the deputies of the Constituent Assembly, elected from the South-Caucasus. The Seym was declared the highest authority in the South-Caucasus, and on March 1, 1918 it initiated separate peace negotiations with Turkey in Trebizond. The delegation of the Seym was headed by A. Chkhenkeli. The Armenian National Council was represented by Alexander Khatisian and Hovhaness Kajaznuni. The Turkish side stated that the territories of Eastern Anatolia (i.e. Western Armenia) were inalienable part of Turkey and demanded that the Seym should declare independence of the South-Caucasus from Russia.

On April 9, 1918, under the pressure by the Georgian and Muslim delegates and against the will of the Armenian representatives, the Seym declared independence of the South-Caucasus from Russia. The Transcaucasian Federative Democratic Republic was established.

4. The Turkish Invasion into Armenia and the Trans-Caucasus

The demand of the Turkish side to separate the South-Caucasus from Russia was a diplomatic trap to prevent possible Russian interference in the upcoming developments. Turkey's ultimate goal was the capture of the entire territory of the South-Caucasus, and the seizure of the oil-rich Baku in particular.

The declaration of independence by the Transcaucasian Federal Republic did not stop the Turkish offensive. The Turkish Command demanded the surrender of the Kars fortress, which had a potential to withstand a durable siege. Despite the protests of General T. Nazarbekian, the Head of the Transcaucasian Federation A. Chkhenkeli gave an order to surrender the city of Kars only to preserve Georgia's territorial integrity.

Although the negotiations with Turkey had been underway since May. 1918, the Turkish army continued the offensive and unexpectedly captured the city of Alexandrople. The government of the Transcaucasian Federation ordered to surrender the city to the Turks. The population was subjected to massacre, robbery and violence. The Turkish army continued to advance moving in the direction of Yerevan and on May 20, 1918 seized Sardarapat gaining control over the railway.

There was an imminent threat of the complete physical extermination of the surviving portion of the Armenian people.

5. The Self-Defense of the Armenian people in Sardarapat, Karaklis and Bash-Aparan in May, 1918

On the brink of national disaster, the entire Armenian people rose to defend themselves. There was a concerted effort by all layers of the population and political parties. The National Council of Yerevan headed by Aram Manoukian was in complete control and spared no effort to organize the defense. The Armenian military regiments were reorganized and reinforced with volunteers. The Yerevan corps was under the command of General Movses Silikian. The other corps under the command of Dro (Drastamat Kanayan) was sent to drive out the enemy from Bash-Aparan. The Armenian regiment that had retreated from Alexandrople was on a mission to defend the road to Karaklis (modern Vanadzor).

On May 22, 1918, the Armenian forces in Sardarapat under the command of Colonel **Daniel Bek-Pirumian** and with the support from the population of the nearby villages crushed the Turks and drove them out of Sardarapat. The panicking Turkish forces retreated all the way back to the Arax River. That victory raised the fighting spirit of the Armenian forces and people at large. In the battle of May 26 the Turkish forces suffered an ultimate defeat.

Memorial for heroes of Sardarapat Battle

164. *Armenia on the Eve of the Fi*

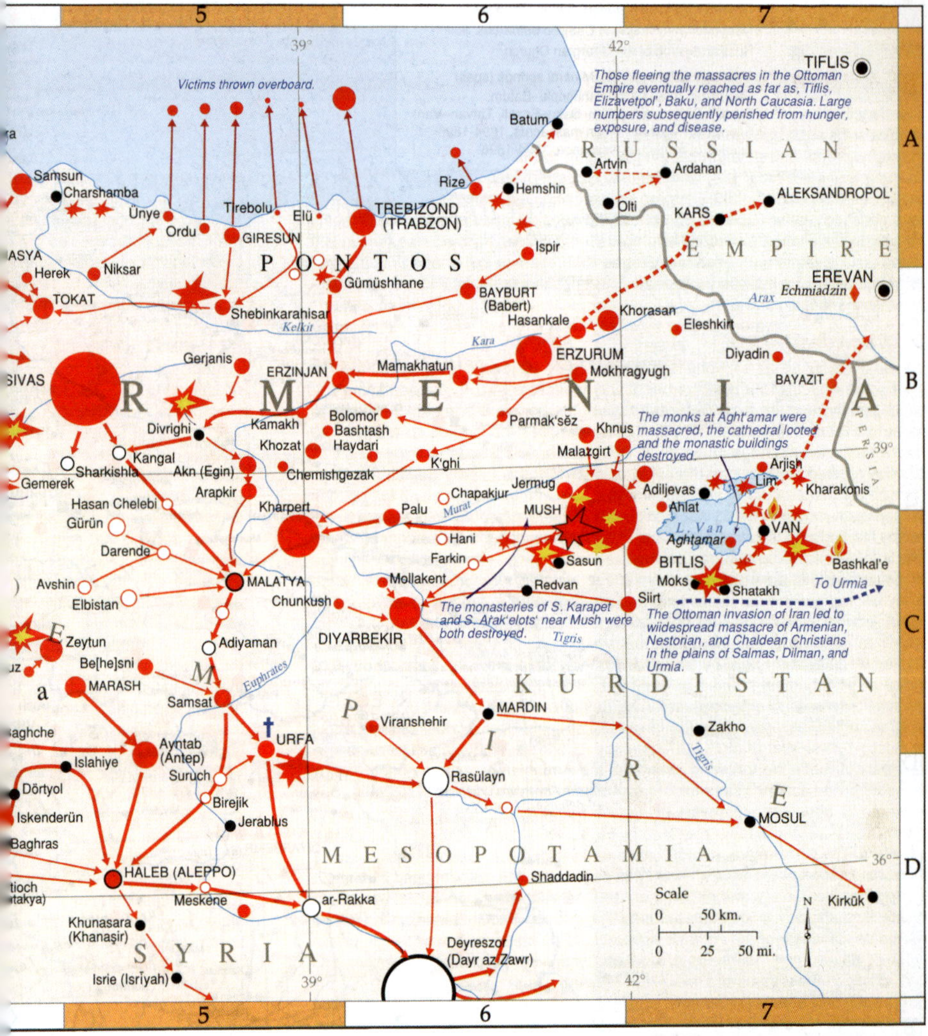
5
6
7
A
B
C
D
39°
42°
36°
Victims thrown overboard.
Those fleeing the massacres in the Ottoman Empire eventually reached as far as, Tiflis, Elizavetpol', Baku, and North Caucasia. Large numbers subsequently perished from hunger, exposure, and disease.
TIFLIS
Batum
RUSSIAN
Artvin
Ardahan
Hemshin
Olti
KARS
ALEKSANDROPOL'
EMPIRE
EREVAN
Echmiadzin
Arax
Rize
TREBIZOND
(TRABZON)
Samsun
Charshamba
Ünye
Ordu
Tirebolu
Elü
GIRESUN
PONTOS
Ispir
Niksar
Herek
TOKAT
Gümüshhane
BAYBURT
(Babert)
Shebinkarahisar
Kelkit
Hasankale
Khorasan
Eleshkirt
Kara
ERZURUM
Diyadin
Mokhragyugh
BAYAZIT
Gerjanis
ERZINJAN
Mamakhatun
SIVAS
ARMENIA
PERSIA
Divrighi
Kamakh
Bolomor
Bashtash
Haydari
Khozat
Parmak'sēz
Khnus
Malazgirt
The monks at Aght'amar were massacred, the cathedral looted and the monastic buildings destroyed.
Kangal
Sharkishla
Gemerek
Akn (Egin)
Chemishgezak
K'ghi
Arjish
Lim
Kharakonis
Adiljevas
Ahlat
Jermug
Arapkir
Chapakjur
Murat
MUSH
Hasan Chelebi
Gürün
Kharpert
Palu
L. Van
Aghtamar
VAN
Hani
Darende
Farkin
Sasun
BITLIS
Bashkal'e
Moks
Shatakh
To Urmia
Avshin
Elbistan
MALATYA
Mollakent
Redvan
Siirt
Chunkush
The monasteries of S. Karapet and S. Arak'elots' near Mush were both destroyed.
The Ottoman invasion of Iran led to wiidespread massacre of Armenian, Nestorian, and Chaldean Christians in the plains of Salmas, Dilman, and Urmia.
Zeytun
Adiyaman
DIYARBEKIR
Tigris
Be[he]sni
Euphrates
KURDISTAN
MARASH
Samsat
MARDIN
Viranshehir
Zakho
Ayntab
(Antep)
URFA
Islahiye
Suruch
Rasülayn
Dörtyol
Birejik
Iskenderün
Jerablus
MOSUL
Baghras
MESOPOTAMIA
HALEB (ALEPPO)
Shaddadin
Meskene
ar-Rakka
Scale
0
50 km.
25
50 mi.
N
Kirkük
Khunasara
(Khanaşir)
Deyreszor
(Dayr az Zawr)
SYRIA
Isrie (Isriyah)

In the heavy battles of May 24-29, the Armenian corps under the command of **Dro** crushed the Turkish forces near **Bash-Aparan** and drove them back to Alexandrople.

The Turkish command concentrated significant force to invade Karaklis, from where the road to Tiflis was open. On May 24-28, 1918 heavy battles were waged near **Karaklis**. The regiments of Colonel A. Bey-Mamikonian and Colonel N. Gorganian as well as the squadron commanded by Lieutenant Njdeh showed a lot of courage. The enemy suffered huge losses. The Armenian forces had to retreat after they had run out of ammunition, and on May 30 the Turks seized Karaklis. Yet their losses were so significant that they were not able to start an offensive on Tiflis.

By its victories in May, 1918 the Armenian people proved its will to survive, defended its independence and helped to abort the expansionist plans of the Young Turk government.

6. The Republic of Armenia Declares Independence. The Treaty of Batum

Under the military and political pressure of Germany and its ally Turkey the Transcaucasian Federative Republic was disbanded. On May 26 Georgia and on May 28 Azerbaijan declared independence. Under the circumstances, on **May 28, 1918 the Armenian National Council declare independence of the Republic of Armenia.** Until the elections the functions of the Parliament were temporarily performed by the Armenian National Council of Tiflis headed by Avetis Aharonian. **Hovhaness Kajaznuni** was appointed as Prime Minister and Alexander Khatisian became the Minister of Foreign Affairs. Before the newly-formed government would have moved from Tiflis to Yerevan, the de facto leader of the Republic was Aram Manoukian the Chairman of the National Council of Yerevan.

The May victories of the Armenian people were of historic importance. Due to them the Turkish position at the negotiations became more flexible. On **June 4, 1918 the Peace Treaty of Batum** was signed between Turkey and the newly-independent Republic of Armenia.

Armenia retained its independence but had to cede a lot of territories. The territory of Armenia was reduced to 12 000 sq. kilometers around Lake Sevan. It was allowed to have small national guard. Its foreign policy and railway communications were brought under Turkey's control. Turkey was given the right to use that territory and communications to transport its military force to Baku, where it planned to overthrow the Baku Commune.

Yet in the late April of 1918 Soviet power was established in Baku. The Soviet of People's Commissars was formed, which was headed by Stepan Shahumian. Soviet power did not extend to the rest of Azerbaijan, but was limited to Baku. This is how the name the Baku Commune originated.

The defense of the Baku Commune was coordinated by General Hakop Bagratuni and other commanders of Armenian descent. There were about 18 000 Armenian soldiers and volunteers among the defenders. Withstanding the attacks of the Turkish forces they realized that they were simultaneously defending the independence of the Republic of Armenia. Upon the capture of Baku, the Young Turk government planned to once and for all do away with the Republic of Armenia, which they had only recognized for tactical purposes.

The Baku Commune held on for about three months. Receiving no assistance from Soviet Russia, the population surrendered the city to the English forces that executed the 26 Commissars of Baku. But the English could not hold the city for long. On September 15, 1918, the Turks invaded Baku and subjected the Armenian population to massacres and robbery. However, the Turks failed to bring their plans to completion. Soon, defeated by the Entente powers in World War I, Turkey had to surrender.

CHAPTER 19

THE FIRST REPUBLIC OF ARMENIA

1. The Establishment of Government Institutions

The first Republic of Armenia was born in difficult internal and external conditions. Stopping the Turkish offensive cost many lives and losses. The conditions of the Peace Treaty of Batum were also very hard. The country was flooded with refugees and homeless children. There was lack of food. The economy was ruined, there were no financial resources, while railway and road communications were either destroyed or controlled by the enemy.

Independence of Armenia was declared in Tiflis on May 28, 1918. A pre-Parliament and government were formed on the basis of the Armenian National Council. Before the government would have moved from Tiflis to Yerevan on July 17, 1918, Aram Manoukian, the Chairman of the National Council of Yerevan was de facto in charge of all government operations.

Hovhannes Kajaznuni

In Yerevan a number of local political activists were included into the pre-Parliament. On August 1, 1918, the first session of the Armenian pre-Parliament, where all national minorities residing in the Republic were represented, was opened in a solemn atmosphere. The pre-Parliament had 47 members, of whom 6 were Muslims, 1 Russian and 1 Ezid. All Armenian political parties had their representatives - Cadets, Mensheviks, Socialist-Revolutionaries, Hunchakians and there was even 1 Bolshevik. The majority in the pre-Parliament was held by the Dashnak party, which formed the government headed by Hovhaness Kajaznuni.

In fact, the pre-Parliament played the role of Constituent Assembly.

An ad hoc group was formed to work on the draft of the Armenian Constitution. Before it had been drafted and adopted by the Armenian Parliament, the old laws of the Russian Empire continued to be in force. Courts also functioned in keeping with the Russian laws. Until the year of 1920 the old Russian court system had been in place, after which it was replaced by a Jury system. A declaration on the commitment to democratic values- freedoms of speech, conscience and religion was made. All citizens over the age of 20 irrespective of their sex, worship or nationality were given the right to vote. The symbols of national statehood-colors, coat of arms and anthem were adopted.

In the Armenian tricolor the color of red symbolized the blood spilled for freedom; blue was the color of the Armenian skies, while the golden color of apricot stood for labor. The coat of arms was adopted by the second half of 1920. It was designed by Alexander Tamanian and Hakob Kojoyan. In its center was a shield divided into 4 sections with coats of arms of 4 Armenian dynasties in each of them. The shield was held by an eagle and a lion. The same coat of arms has been adopted by modern Armenia.

Alexander Khatissian

In June, 1919 the first and only elections to the Armenian parliament were held. 80 members, most of whom were representatives of the Dashnak party, were elected. The new government was formed, which was headed by Alexander Khatisian, the former Mayor of Tiflis.

2. The Establishment of the Armenian National Army

The most important attribute of independent statehood was the Armenian army. It was built around the Armenian Corps and Division of Volunteers that had yet been established in the second half of 1917. According to the Treaty of Batum Armenia was allowed to have only one division. At the demand of Turkey, the Armenian corps was disbanded and Haiduks units were outlawed. General Movses Silikian was appointed the Commander of the Armenian Division.

After the defeat and capitulation of Ottoman Turkey in World War I, the Treaty of Batum was declared void and Armenia got an opportunity build its own army. A conscription law was passed and 25 000 men were drafted into the Armenian Army under the command of General Tovmas Nazarbekian.

The decision to disband Haiduk units remained in force, because those units were insubordinate to the central command and often acted on their own causing internal disagreements.

National hero General Andranik, the Commander of the Volunteers Division was unhappy both with that decision and the government's policy at large. In 1919, he disbanded his division and surrendering all ammunition to the Catholicos in Echmiadzin, left the country. He died in 1927 in the city of Fresno (the US) and was buried in Paris. In 2000, his ashes were reburied in Armenia.

3. The Internal Situation in Armenia

Since the very moment of its foundation and during two and a half years of existence the Republic of Armenia had to survive in most difficult economic conditions. The past war and economic collapse brought about famine and epidemics of typhus and cholera that started at the end of 1918 and lasted for almost a year. Over 180 000 people died as a result of that.

The government of the Republic took emergency measures to improve the situation. A state monopoly on bread and other basic

U.S. 28th President Woodrow Wilson

products was declared. To obtain a credit and purchase wheat an Armenian delegation headed by Prime Minister H. Kajaznuni paid a visit to the United States. With the support of the **Woodrow Wilson** administration Armenia was given a credit of 10 million dollars and with the help of the American Committee for Armenian and Syrian Relief by the second half of 1919 wheat, medical supplies and basic goods were shipped to Armenia. By the end of 1919 famine and epidemics were overcome.

Poster by the American Committee for Near East Relief

Measures were taken to re-settle more than 200 000 refugees from Western Armenia and Azerbaijan. They settled in the abandoned and semi-destroyed villages. The American Committee for Relief in the Near East took care of 50 000 homeless children.

In Alexandrapole, Kars, Yerevan, Tiflis, Trebizond, Bitlis, Beirut and other cities American shelters and orphanages were opened mainly for homeless Armenian orphans and also for adult refugees. In turn, the government of Armenia also built several orphanages to accommodate those in need. The government was taking steps for agricultural development of the country. In 1919 sowing wheat was purchased and distributed among peasants. In 1920 the law on land nationalization, its expropriation from large landowners and distribution among the rural population was passed. Another law on redistribution and division of arable land between neighboring villages was adopted. The concept of agricultural development was based upon establishment of farms.

A preliminary program for the economic development of the country was drafted, according to which the government encouraged the establishment of small enterprises producing brandy, wine, cheese, canned fruit and vegetables. Serious attention was paid to agricultural cooperation. In 1919, HayCop (Armenian Cooperation Agency) was organized.

Humanitarian assistance from various American committees for Armenian relief, Armenian entrepreneurs and private citizens was shipped to the country. It was planned to build power stations, irrigation canals, roads and a network of internal railway communications.

A lot was accomplished in the field of education. Elementary, middle and high schools were opened in the country. In 1919, preparations for the opening of national university began. **In January, 1920 the university was opened in festive atmosphere in Alexandrapole.** It was later moved to Yerevan. National library was also established and began operating. By the decision of the Parliament Armenian was given the status of the official language in the country. The process of its purification form the excess of foreign borrowings was initiated. Government spending was reduced to the minimum. All political parties and movements operated freely and often cooperated for the sake of the national interest. Socio-political life developed democratically.

However, in such a short period of time the government could not achieve tangible economic results because of the continuing wars and domestic turmoil. The destabilizing factor was the unrest and repeated armed clashes instigated by Turkey and Azerbaijan in the regions with mixed Muslim and Armenian populations of the Republic of Armenia such as Vedi, Masis, etc.

Another destabilizing factor was the activity of Armenian Bolsheviks, who sought to establish Soviet power in Armenia, just like it happened in Russia.

4. Armenia's Relations with Neighbor States

Armenia's relations with the neighboring countries were quite complicated. While good-neighborly relations were maintained with Iran, the relations with Turkey had been hostile from day one. There were serious territorial disputes with Georgia and Azerbaijan, which led to military collisions.

At the time of the administrative division of the South-Caucasus the Tsarist government ignored the national and ethnic factors. After the collapse of the Tsarist regime and establishment of independent states territorial disputes related to demarcation of borders occurred among Armenia, Georgia and Azerbaijan.

The regions of Akhalkalak and Lori with predominant Armenian population had once been under the administrative jurisdiction of the province of Tiflis. Based on that, the Georgian government had claims to those territories. Yet at the end of 1918, when after the capitulation the Turkish army had withdrawn from the South-Caucasus, the Georgian forces moved in and seized the regions of Lori and Akhalkalak. In December 1918, the Armenian forces liberated Lori. Due to the interference by the English Command, the region of Lori was declared a neutral zone governed by an English Commissar. The territorial dispute was resolved only after the establishment of Soviet power in the region. Lori was ceded to Armenia, while Akhalkalak was recognized as part of Georgia.

The relations with Azerbaijan were even more complicated, as it had territorial claims to the regions of Nakhichevan, Karabagh and Zangezur with predominant Armenian population. At the end of 1918 during their march on Baku, the Turkish forces also massacred the Armenian population of Nakhichevan, thus changing the ethnic composition of that region. The Turks also tried to invade Karabagh and make it part of Azerbaijan. But they failed to do that coming across the heroic self-defense of the local Armenian population.

Andranik's Volunteers Division had defended Zangezur from the Turkish invasion since August, 1918. After the signing of the Treaty of Batum, Andranik retreated to Iran. There were 20 000 refugees gathered under the protection of his division, whom Andranik helped to move to Nakhichevan and Zangezur, where he continued to protect them until the establishment of the Armenian state authority there.

After the withdrawal of the Turkish forces from the Trans-Caucasus, the English army moved in and seized Baku. England was trying to establish its control of the oil resources in Baku. The English were quite comfortable with the anti-Bolshevik and anti-Russian policy of the Azerbaijani government. Just like Turkey had done in the past, pursuing its own interest the English Command tried to resolve the regional territorial disputes in favor of Azerbaijan, bringing Karabagh, Zangezur and Nakhichevan under Baku's jurisdiction.

After the retreat of the Turkish army, the Armenian population of Karabagh, that constituted 90% of the entire population of the region, convened a congress of its representatives who decided to call on the government of Armenia to recognize the region as inalienable part of Armenia. At the request of the local population Andranik's division moved to Karabagh to prevent the enforced unification of the region with Azerbaijan. The Commander of the English forces in Baku demanded that Andranik should withdraw from Karabagh, and in case he refused to comply threatened that it would be viewed as a hostile act against England. Andranik returned to Zangezur and controlled the region until April, 1919. After the Armenian government had declared the establishment of Independent and Unified Armenia, he transferred the regional power to the official representative of Armenia Colonel Arsen Shahmazian and soon left the country.

In 1919, the English declared Karabagh and Zangezur part of Azerbaijan and appointed Azerbaijani General Sultanov as governor of those regions. Only after a long siege, the Armenian population of

Karabagh had to recognize the jurisdiction of Azerbaijan. With the support of the English, at the end of 1919 Azerbaijan also tried to invade Zangezur and Nakhichevan.

The Armenian government sent official protest regarding the hostile actions of the English and Azerbaijan to the Paris Peace Conference. Having received the official support of the allies, Armenia took decisive steps. The government appointed Dro as official representative to Northern Zangezur and Karabagh, while Captain Njdeh became the official representative in Southern Zangezur and the eastern part of Nakhichevan. Organizing the self-defense of the local population, they were able to crush the advancing Azerbaijani forces and counterattack. Njdeh established full control on the territory of Zangezur, while Dro's regiment moved into Karabagh in March, 1919 and began to liberate it. The retreating Azerbaijani forces massacred the Armenian population of Shushi and burnt to ashes the Armenian quarter of the city. **By 1920, Karabagh, Zangezur and Nakhichevan came under the jurisdiction of the Republic of Armenia.**

5. International situation of the Republic of Armenia. The Armenian Question at the Paris Peace Conference

The Republic of Armenia established diplomatic relations and had its representations in Turkey, the US, France, Switzerland, Bulgaria, Japan and other countries. The priority vector of its foreign policy was the Entente countries and their western allies.

After the capitulation of Germany and the Ottoman Turkey in World War I the treaties of Brest-Litovsk and Batum were declared void. In March, 1919, with the support of the English forces the Armenian army liberated the Kars region and Surmalu that had been under illegal Turkish occupation. De jure the territories of Western Armenia came under the jurisdiction of the Entente powers, but de facto they continued to remain under the Turkish rule.

Yet in February, 1919 the Second Congress of the representatives of the population of Western Armenia (the Genocide survivors) adopted a resolution on the need to unify Western and Eastern Armenia in one state. Based on that, **on May 28, 1919, the Armenian Parliament declared the establishment of Independent and Unified Armenia, exercising the legal rights of the Armenian people residing in their historical homeland. The aspiration to unify the territories of Eastern and Western Armenia in one state became the main priority of Armenia's foreign policy.**

Poghos Nubar Pasha

In January, 1919, the Peace Conference of the Entente countries was convened in Paris to set peace terms and sign peace treaties with the defeated nations. The Republic of Armenia also sent a delegation to the Paris Conference, headed by Avetis Aharonian. Also present in Paris was the National Delegation of Armenians, headed by Poghos-Nubar Pasha. Established yet in 1912, it represented the interests of the Armenian population of Western Armenia and Cilicia. Despite some disagreements and different interpretation regarding the priority list of the demands of the Armenian people, the Armenian delegations were able to jointly draft and submit a Memorandum on the territorial demands and expectations of the Armenian people, which was discussed at the Conference.

Avetis Aharonian

At the Paris Conference the fate of international issues was mainly decided by the leaders of the US, France, England and Italy. For the division of power and spheres of influence in the world they established a system of states-under-mandate, according to which the leading powers became transitional trustees responsible for the welfare and governance of small, newly-independent countries.

The Armenian delegations made numerous contacts with the leaders of the world powers to find a fair solution for the Armenian Question. The President of the US Woodrow Wilson expressed the

Maj. Gen. (U.S. Army) James G. Harbord, Head of Mission to Armenia, 1919

readiness of his country to take the mandate for Armenia. The US opened a state credit for the government of Armenia. During 1919-1920, Armenia received large amount of humanitarian assistance from the US. American Colonel Haskell was appointed as representative of allied countries to Armenia. In August, 1919, special American relief mission headed by General James Harbord was sent to Armenia. Harbord mission of 50 people traveled from Constantinopole via Cilicia to Western Armenia. From there it headed to Kars, Alexandrapole and Yerevan. The mission had meetings with the Armenian government, and upon completing a comprehensive fact-finding study of the situation, presented its report to the US President on the issue of taking Armenia mandate.

The Armenian Question was discussed in April, 1920 at the Conference of the Allied Supreme Council in San Remo, Italy. The participants of the Conference made an official appeal to President Wilson to take Armenia mandate and define the future borders of a unified Armenia. Woodrow Wilson gave his consent and defined the borders of Armenia that included ports at the Black Sea. The US Congress officially recognized the independence of Armenia within the borders defined by President Wilson, but on June 1, 1920 voted against taking Armenia mandate.

6. The May 1920 Revolt of the Bolsheviks

After on April 28 Soviet power had been established in Azerbaijan, in May 1920 the Armenian Bolsheviks launched an armed revolt to establish Soviet power in Armenia. In Alexandrople (modern Gyumri) a Revolutionary Military Council was formed, which on May 10, declared about the seizure of power. The army showed no resistance to the revolt. The Bolsheviks also seized power in Kars, Karaklis, Igdir, Gavar and other cities. Sarkis Musaelian, the commander of the armored train "Vardan Zoravar", assumed the military command of the revolt.

In conditions of political crisis the Dashnak party formed a new government headed by **Hamazasp Ohanjanian.** State of emergency was declared. The parliament was temporarily disbanded and its members were sent to the regions to work with the population there. A special force under the command of khumbapet (unit leader) Sepouh was formed to suppress the revolt. In a few days, receiving no assistance from the Red Army the revolt leadership in Alexandrapole surrendered their arms without any serious resistance. The other hotbeds of the revolt were easily suppressed. By the verdict of the Military Tribunal many of the revolt leaders and participants were put against the firing squad. The Bolshevik party was banned.

Hamazasp Ohanjanian, 3rd Prime Minister of Armenia

The May 1920 revolt failed because of poor organization and no assistance from Soviet Russia. The defeat of the revolt further aggravated the internal and external situation of Armenia.

7. Armenia after the Treaty of Sevres. The Position of Soviet Russia

On August 10, 1920, in Sevres (suburb of Paris) the Allied powers signed the Peace Treaty with Ottoman Turkey. The Treaty of Sevres was also signed by the head of the Armenian delegation Avetis Aharonian.

By the Treaty of Sevres the Allied powers and Ottoman Turkey recognized Armenia within the borders defined by President Woodrow Wilson. The territory of Armenia was equal to 150 000 sq. kilometers and included the regions of Van, Bitlis, Trebizond, Erzurum and access to the Black Sea. However, the Treaty did not envisage a mechanism of ceding those territories to Armenia. The Allied powers did not take any obligations for the implementation of the Treaty, while the US Congress had already refused to take Armenia mandate.

Meanwhile the process of national consolidation was well underway in Turkey and a new power came to the fore. The National Assembly headed by Mustafa Kemal in Ankara declared that the Sultan's power had been overthrown and embarked upon confrontation with the Entente countries. It refused to recognize the Treaty of Sevres that had been signed by the Sultanate government.

Soviet Russia established close relations with the Kemalist government, giving diplomatic and political support for its struggle against the Entente powers. To establish a land border with Turkey, Soviet Russia sought to include the Southcaucasian republics into the sphere of its influence.

Mustapha Kemal Ataturk

The Armenian government failed to show proper diplomatic flexibility and make adequate decisions in complex international relations. It continued to count on assistance and support of the Entente powers in bringing a fair solution to the territorial problems of Armenia. This is why Kemalist Turkey viewed Armenia as a hostile country.

Until the time when the US refused to take Armenia mandate, Turkey had been afraid to engage into open military confrontation. Kemalist Turkey was also restrained by the position of Soviet Russia, which sought to establish Soviet power in the South-Caucasus and include the region into the sphere of its influence.

It can be assumed that had the May 1920 revolt been successful and had Soviet power been established in Armenia, the Armenian-Turkish war would not have been waged. Soviet Armenia could have counted on the support of Soviet Russia in the resolution of its territorial problems.

CHAPTER 20

THE FALL OF THE FIRST REPUBLIC. THE ESTABLISHMENT OF SOVIET RULE IN ARMENIA

1. The Turko-Armenian War of 1920

Taking advantage of the favorable international situation, on September 28, 1920, Kemalist Turkey waged a war against Armenia. Turkey mobilized its 15th Army Corps under the command of Kyazim Karabekir against Armenia. The Armenian army under the command of Tovmas Nazarbekian retreated, showing resistance against the superior force of the enemy. By the end of September the Turkish forces seized Kagzvan and Sarykamysh.

The morale within the Armenian forces was gradually down as none of the Entente countries showed assistance, while the position of Soviet Russia was obviously pro-Turkish. On October 31, the Turkish army seized Kars taking many prisoners. On November 7, they invaded Alexandrapole and on November 18, Armenia had to accept the Turkish ultimatum and sign a ceasefire agreement. According to official data, as many as 60 000 Armenians were killed during the war.

Simon Vratsian

Georgia, taking advantage of Armenia's predicament and making a secret deal with Turkey, seized the Lori region.

After government crisis in Armenia **Simon Vratsian's** team came to power. On November 25, peace negotiations were started with the Turkish command in Alexandrople. The Armenian delegation was headed by Alexander Khatisian.

2. The Armenian –Russian Talks. The Agreement on the Transfer of Power to the Revolutionary Committee.

Abandoned by the allies and left without any other alternative, Armenia requested Soviet Russia to mediate peace negotiations with Turkey.

The relations between the Republic of Armenia and Soviet Russia were hostile. By remaining allied with Entente, Armenia was, in fact, supporting the White Army of General Denikin and later the government of Baron Wrangel. Independent Armenia, being an ally of the Entente, was an obstacle for the establishment of closer ties between Soviet Russia and Kemalist Turkey.

Levon Shant

After the establishment of Soviet power in Azerbaijan in late April, 1920, Soviet Russia began to support its territorial claims to Armenia. The Bolshevik 11th Red Army invaded Karabagh and Zangezur. In May, 1920, an Armenian delegation headed by **Levon Shant,** Vice-Chairman of the Parliament, was sent to Moscow to negotiate an agreement with Soviet Russia. But Soviet Russia was in no hurry to recognize the Republic of Armenia and sign agreement with it, considering the suppression of the May 1920 revolt and execution of Armenian Bolsheviks as another hostile act by Armenia. Taking advantage of such a position by Soviet Russia, Kemalist Turkey waged a war against Armenia.

When after the defeat in the war, Armenia asked for Russian mediation, Russia capitalized on it to carry out its own agenda. During the negotiations, Soviet Russia's plenipotentiary Boris Legran demanded that the government of Armenia should transfer power to the Bolsheviks.

The Armenian Bolsheviks formed the **Revolutionary Committee**

of Armenia (Revcom), which on November 29, 1920 with the support of the 11th Red Army that had moved into Armenia from Azerbaijan **declared the establishment of Soviet Rule in Armenia.** Soviet Azerbaijan, showing its support to the Armenian Revcom made a declaration recognizing Nakhichevan, Zangezur and Karabagh as part of Soviet Armenia.

Trying to preserve the territorial integrity and very existence of the Republic of Armenia, on December 2, 1920, Simon Vratsian's government signed an agreement with plenipotentiary B. Legran on the transfer of power to the Revcom and resigned from office. Until the arrival of the Revcom in Yerevan, General Dro, the Commander-in- Chief of the Armenian army was put in charge of the government.

On the night of December 2, in Alexandrapole the delegation headed by Alexander Khatisian on behalf of the already resigned government of Armenia signed a peace treaty with Kemalist Turkey, which could no more have any legal force.

According to the Treaty of Alexandrapole, Armenia was renouncing the Treaty of Sevres and the regions of Kars, Nakhichevan and Surmalu with Mount Ararat were ceded to Turkey. The new border was established along the Arax and Akhurian rivers.

3. First Steps of Soviet Power

Having come to power, the Revcom of Armenia lost no time to engage into revolutionary activity. A wide-spread propaganda campaign to discredit the previous government was launched. In cities, towns and villages new local government institutions were formed-regional and district Soviets of workers. The laws of the Republic of Armenia were replaced by the laws of Soviet Russia. EC (Extraordinary Commission) for combating counter-revolutionary forces was established. It was headed by Gevork Atarbekian. Repressions began against the members of the previous government, officers of the Armenian army and national activists. Over 1400 officers of various military ranks were arrested and exiled, including Commander-in-Chief Dro.

The population was extremely unhappy about the policy of "military communism", when the entire stock of grain and sowing wheat was taken by force from peasants. Any disagreement with the policy of the new government was labeled as counter-revolutionary activity. The "Revolutionary Tribunal" would throw people to prison or even shoot them dead without a trial.

4. The February 1921 Revolt

Poorly planned and extremist actions of the Revcom, trampling on national values and mass repressions led to an all-around disillusionment with Soviet power and triggered a **spontaneous popular revolt in February, 1921.**

The revolt started in the districts of Garni, Aparan and Daralagyaz and soon became nation-wide. Seizing power in the regions, on February 16-17, the participants of the revolt started an advance to Yerevan. The people in Yerevan also took up arms and on February 18, seized power in the city. The Dashnak party assumed the leadership of the revolt. In Yerevan a **Homeland Salvation Committee headed by Simon Vratsian** was established. The Committee sent a cable to Moscow informing the Soviet government about the change of power in Armenia and revoked the credentials of the Armenian delegation that was there for peace negotiations with Turkey.

The Revcom and Red army forces retreated from downtown Yerevan to the railway station where armored trains provided cover for them. They boarded the trains, which took them to the district of Vedi (modern Ararat) and Ghamarlu (modern Artashat), all the way to the border with Iran. It was there that they took defense positions and thwarted poorly-organized attacks of the rebels until the arrival of the Red army's main force.

It was yet in December, 1920 that the main force of the 11th Red Army was sent to the region of Lori –Gugark to support the uprising of the local population against the Menshevik government of Georgia that had claims to those territories. Upon the establishment of Soviet power in Georgia in February, 1921, the Red army forces were sent to suppress the revolt in Armenia.

The Homeland Salvation Committee did not receive the expected support from the Entente powers. Because of the numerical superiority of the Red army advancing to Yerevan, the rebels retreated to Daralagyaz and from there to Zangezur and joined forces with the regiments of Garegin Njdeh, who was defending the region against the assaults of Azerbaijan and the Red army. In early April, 1921 the revolt was suppressed. Soviet power was restored in Armenia.

5. The Russo-Turkish Talks. The Moscow and Kars Treaties

Toward the end of 1920, Soviet Russia and Kemalist Turkey joined efforts to do away with the independent Republic of Armenia, which both viewed as an obstacle for their plans. To strengthen mutual ties between Turkey and Russia, bilateral talks were held in Moscow on March 16, 1921. Armenia's participation in those negotiations had also been envisaged, that's why a delegation from Soviet Armenia (Alexander Bekzadian and Sahak Ter-Gabrielian) arrived in Moscow. However, upon the demand of the Turkish side the talks were limited to a bilateral format only. The Armenian delegation was not allowed to participate, because, formally, during the February revolt new power had been established in Armenia, which hurried to send a cable to Moscow informing the government of Soviet Russia, that it had revoked the credentials of the delegation from Soviet Armenia.

As a result of the talks a friendship and cooperation treaty was signed between Soviet Russia and Turkey. Without any legal right to do it, Soviet Russia recognized the Kars region and district of Surmalu as inalienable part of Turkey. Turkey ceded the Nakhichevan region to Soviet Azerbaijan precluding its further transfer to a third party (i.e. Armenia). The new Turkish-Armenian border was established along the Arax and Akhurian rivers. From 60 000 sq. kilometers of the territory of the Republic of Armenia, Soviet Armenia was allowed to retain only 29.600 sq. kilometers. Upon Russia's demand, the Turks were to return the city of Alexandrapole-an important railway communication point, back to Soviet Armenia. The Turkish forces had remained in Alexandrople until April 22, 1921 and withdrew only after repeated demands by Soviet Russia.

Since formally Soviet republics of the South-Caucasus were sovereign states, the territorial concessions to Turkey made at their cost by Soviet Russia, needed to be ratified by their governments.

Under the auspices of Soviet Russia, from September 26 to October 13, 1921, a conference between Soviet republics of the South-Caucasus and Turkey took place in the city of Kars, which was under Turkish occupation. The Armenian delegation was headed by Askanaz Mravian. The Turkish side refused to make any territorial concessions. In fact, the Treaty of Kars, signed during the conference, augmented the Treaty of Moscow without changing any of its basic provisions.

The Treaty of Kars demonstrated that the Soviet republics of the South-Caucasus were, in fact, under the absolute domination of Soviet Russia. Russia hoped that by making those concessions it could gain the support of Kemalist Turkey and use it in the struggle against international imperialism. It also cherished illusions that Turkey might become a center for the future revolution of the nations of the Orient.

In fact, in 1921 as a result of the Russo-Turkish bargain, a new partition of Armenian territory took place between its more powerful neighbors. One part of that territory was seized by Kemalist Turkey, while in the other the establishment of Soviet republic was proclaimed under Soviet Russia's control.

6. The Defense of Zangezur in 1920-1921. Garegin Njdeh

After the establishment of Soviet power in all Southcaucasian countries, the last remaining province that retained independence was the Armenian region of Zangezur. The defense of Zangezur was coordinated by the plenipotentiary of already non-existent Republic of Armenia, **Garegin Njdeh.** Having organized the self-defense of the region, he thwarted the attempts of the Azerbaijani forces supported by the Red army to conquer Zangezur.

In late 1920, the Red army Command demanded that Garegin Njdeh put down his arms. However, Njdeh was in no hurry to surrender and demanded guarantees for Zangezur and Karabagh to become part of Soviet Armenia. On December 25, 1920 in the Monastery of Tatev the First Congress of the representatives of the population of Zangezur took place, which decided to continue the resistance. **Njdeh was proclaimed the Sparapet (Commander-in- Chief) of Syunik.** After the February revolt had been suppressed, part of the rebels retreated to Zangezur. On April 27, 1921 the Second Congress of Zangezur's representatives declared independence, establishing the **Republic of Mountainous Armenia with Njdeh as a ruler** and decided to continue the resistance. The events that followed proved Garegin Njdeh to be right.

Garegin Nzhdeh

Very soon Soviet Azerbaijan backpedalled from its declaration that had promised to recognize Nakhichevan, Zangezur and Karabagh as part of Soviet Armenia. According to the Treaty of Moscow, Nakhichevan was ceded to Azerbaijan, while Karabagh was occupied by the Red army and also brought under the jurisdiction of Azerbaijan.

After the February revolt had been suppressed in 1921, the government of Soviet Armenia demanded that Njdeh stopped the resistance and transferred power in the region to Armenia proper. In June, 1921, the numerically superior forces of the Red army launched an offensive against Zangezur, both from the territory of Armenia and Azerbaijan. Taking into account the gravity of the situation and the promises that Zangezur would become part of Soviet Armenia, Garegin Njdeh stopped the resistance and retreated to Iran.

7. The Nagorno Karabagh Problem in 1920-1921

After the establishment of Soviet power in Armenia and Azerbaijan's declaration of November 30, 1920, the population of Nagorno Karabagh stopped the armed resistance. The 11th Red army moved into Karabagh. Local Armenians that constituted 90% of the total population of the region hoped that Soviet power would find a fair solution to the Karabagh problem.

On June 3, 1921 the Plenum of the Caucasian Bureau of the Communist party adopted a resolution recognizing Karabagh as part of Armenia. On June 12, in keeping with that resolution, the government of Soviet Armenia appointed A. Mravian as Plenipotentiary Commissar in Nagorno Karabagh. However, the government of Soviet Azerbaijan backpedalling from its previous statement demanded that Karabagh should be unified with Azerbaijan. Upon its demand, a special commission headed by S. Kirov was formed to resolve territorial disputes between the republics. Taking into account the ethnic factor (90% Armenian population), the commission expressed its support for the unification of Karabagh with Armenia.

The issue was once again included into the agenda of the Plenum of the Caucasian Bureau of the Communist party. At its July 4, 1921 sitting a decision was taken to make Karabagh part of Armenia. Nariman Narimanov, the Head of the Azerbaijani government spoke against it. Upon his demand, the final decision on that issued was to be taken in Moscow, by the Central Committee of the Communist party. However, next day, under Stalin's influence, the Plenum of the Caucasian Bureau opted to revise its previous decision.

On July 5, 1921, the Caucasian Bureau of the Communist party passed a resolution affixing Nagorno Karabagh's to Azerbaijan. Based on the ethnic factor, Nagorno Karabagh was granted a status of "autonomous region".

8. The Adoption of the First Constitution of Armenia. Alexander Myasnikyan

Alexander Myasnikian

After the suppression of the revolt, the Soviet leadership in Armenia drew certain conclusions and began to conduct a more flexible policy. **Alexander Myasnikyan,** a well-known Bolshevik with solid political experience, was sent to Armenia. He was elected the **Chairman of the Council of People's Commissars of Soviet Armenia.** In December, 1921 elections to the local Soviets were held. Soviet Armenia was divided into 9 administrative districts.

In January-February, 1922 the First Congress of Soviets of Armenia was convened, which adopted the **First Constitution** of the country. Armenia was declared a Soviet Socialist Republic, where highest power belonged to the Soviets of workers. Land, natural resources, factories and plants, banks and railways were nationalized. Land was given to peasants without compensation. The Church was separated from the state, while schools were no longer under the jurisdiction of the Church.

Coat of Arms of the Armenian SSR

All workers who reached the age of 18 had voting rights. Private entrepreneurs, traders and farm hands were deprived of voting rights. Elections were open. The new flag, coat of arms and national anthem were adopted. The author of the round coat of arms with Mount Ararat and vine in the middle was famous painter Martiros Saryan. For a country that had been deprived of statehood for 500 years the adoption of the Constitution was a historic event.

9. The Establishment of the Transcaucasian Federation

After the establishment of Soviet power in the Trans-Caucasus, the Communist party and the government of Soviet Russia became ideological leaders in the political life of the republics. At Vladimir Lenin's initiative the Soviet republics of the Trans-Caucasus were to establish close relations in order to overcome ethnic animosity, stand together against external enemies and join forces in rebuilding the ruined economy.

Putting those ideas into practice, on **March 12, 1922** the Soviet republics of Armenia, Georgia and Azerbaijan signed an agreement on the establishment of the **Transcaucasian Federation.** Federal government institutions on the basis of equal representation of each republic were formed. On paper, each of the republics preserved independent statehood. The Transcaucasian Federation served as a role model for the unification of the rest of Soviet republics into a common state.

The Transcaucasian Federation existed from 1922 to 1937. After the adoption of the Second Constitution of the USSR in 1936, it was decided that each of the Transcaucasian republics would join the USSR as a sovereign state. In 1937 the Transcaucasian Federation ceased to exist, because Armenia, Georgia and Azerbaijan became members of the USSR.

On December 30, 1922 the First Congress of Soviets of the USSR was convened in Moscow, during which the RSFSR, Ukraine, Belorussia and the Transcaucasian Federation signed a declaration on the establishment of the USSR -the Union of the Soviet Socialist Republics. The federal government institutions were formed and the Union Treaty was signed.

According to the draft of the Constitution, submitted by Stalin all Soviet republics were to become part of Soviet Russia. But with Lenin's support, a decision was taken to establish a federation of Soviet republics, where each republic would retain some independence in internal and foreign policy and have a right to secede from the USSR. The first Soviet Constitution was adopted in 1924 during the Second Congress of Soviets of the USSR.

CHAPTER 21

THE SECOND (SOVIET) REPUBLIC OF ARMENIA PARTICIPATION OF THE ARMENIANS IN WWII

1. The Rebuilding of the Country's Economy. The New Economic Policy (NEP)

After the establishment of Soviet power the Second republic began to rebuild its ruined economy. The country was suffering from lack of food products, continuous famine and epidemics. The Turks ruined and looted Armenia's only railway depot in Alexandrapole. The state budget was void and the money devaluated.

Alexander Myasnikyan's government established an ad hoc Emergency commission responsible for purchase and distribution of sowing wheat. Since June, 1921, the HayCop (Armenian Cooperatives' Union), which provided barter exchange between rural and urban areas, has been back in operation. Toward the end of 1921, wine and brandy factories, tanneries and canneries began to produce goods. In 1921, under the supervision of national poet Hovhaness Tumanian an **Armenian Relief Committee** was established, which mobilized charity and fundraising efforts to overcome famine and assist the population. The American Committee for Near East Relief continued to ship humanitarian assistance to the country.

Large assistance was received from Soviet Russia and other Soviet republics. In 1921, Russia granted Armenia 3.5 ml. rubles in gold. Apparel, shoes, medical supplies, inventory and sowing wheat were sent to Armenia. Oil, crude oil and fuel were shipped from Azerbaijan.

Engineers with special equipment were sent to Armenia to assist in rebuilding industrial enterprises. New equipment was brought and assembled at the factory of mechanical engineering in Alexandrapole.

With the technical assistance of textile workers from the city of

Ivanovo a textile factory was established. Construction of hydro power plants and irrigation canals was underway. In 1924, the copper factory in Kapan that had been out of business since 1916 began to operate again. In 1925, the Yerevan tobacco factory began to operate. The first MTS (Machinery and Tractor Station) was established in the country.

Since the summer of 1922 Armenia began to implement the New Economic Policy (NEP), which had already been in place in Soviet Russia and other Soviet republics. Establishment of cooperatives was encouraged both in rural and urban areas.

The NEP allowed the development of private entrepreneurship. Upon paying a pre-calculated tax on future harvest, peasants were allowed to sell the surplus at local markets. Private entrepreneurs in urban districts had the same privilege. In general terms, in 1928, Armenia's economy reached the levels of 1913, although several industrial branches were still dragging behind and reached those levels at a later stage.

2. Industrialization and Collectivization of Armenia

According to Lenin's plan, to accomplish building socialist society it was necessary to industrialize the economy, collectivize agriculture and perform a cultural revolution.

When the main part of the Soviet Union's economy had been rebuilt, the Communist party began to implement Lenin's plan to build socialism. In 1925, the 14th Congress of the Communist party decided to begin industrializing the country. The objective was to make the USSR a country of developed heavy industry.

Long-term construction of heavy industry enterprises made it necessary to have a planned economy. The first five-year plan for the development of the Soviet economy was elaborated and adopted at that time. Planned economy meant a retreat from the NEP, transition from market economy to a centrally planned economy and command and control system.

Although the process of economic rehabilitation had not as yet been completed in Armenia, it was decided to simultaneously begin industrializing the republic. During the first five-year plan (1928-1932) of planned economy as many as 18 new enterprises began operating, such as the Yerevan soap and dairy factory (1926), sewing factory (1926) and carbide factory, etc. In 1928, the Artik tufa and Ani limestone plants, and the Leninakan textile factory launched their production. The hydro power plants in Yerevan (1926) and Leninakan (1928), and the Dzorages Hydro plant (1932), etc. were built. The construction of the Sevan-Hrazdan Power Cascade was underway.

During the second five-year plan (1933-1937) 26 new enterprises began operating in Armenia, such as a mining factory in Kapan, chemical plants in Alaverdi and Kirovakan (Vanadzor) and cement factory in Davalu (Ararat). The construction of synthetic rubber plant began in Yerevan.

Industrialization needed huge financial investments. To be able to finance it an internal loan was provided by the government, the export of wheat to foreign countries was increased and expropriation of the Church property and land was launched. In Armenia alone, as many as 800 churches were shut down, while the clergy were thrown to prison, exiled or even executed.

In 1927, the XV Congress of the Communist party decided to begin collectivization of agriculture that had to be run parallel to industrialization. The objective to liquidate the class of land-owners was set, while peasants were to be united in so-called soviet and collective farms.

Collectivization in Armenia began in 1928 when the first 55 collective farms were organized. In 1929, upon Moscow's instruction a nation-wide collectivization began which was scheduled to be completed by 1933-the end of second five-year plan.

The country-wide collectivization significantly harmed Armenia's agriculture and brought about economic and human losses. Armenia's specific landscape, which made the use of agricultural machinery in some parts of the country virtually impossible, was not taken into account. Collectivization was carried out by violent means, as it was often accompanied by score settling between neighbors, liquidation of private farms and dispossession of local wealthy land-owners. All property was confiscated by collective farms, while the families of land-owners were banished from their villages. Those who ventured to resist were exiled to Siberia. As result of nation-wide collectivization, the size of arable land was reduced and cattle numbers also decreased.

Although, by 1932 there were already as many as 540 tractors used in Armenia's agriculture, the harvest dropped twice. The agricultural production decreased significantly and in 1931-1932 famine began. A ration-card system for foodstuffs was introduced which lasted until 1936. Even after that the consequences of the crisis were not fully overcome.

Forced collectivization was resisted by peasants all over the territory of the USSR. There were spontaneous revolts, sabotage and terrorist acts. The Communist party and government had to slow down the forced collectivization campaign replacing it with the methods of economic coercion. Toward the end of the second five-year plan, about 80% of Armenian agriculture was collectivized. There were 1074 collective farms, 16 soviet farms and 24 Machine and Tractor Stations. The country-wide collectivization of Armenia was completed by 1940.

During the collectivization campaign the land-owners' class was liquidated, part of the peasantry joined the rank of the working class and agriculture was centralized and controlled by the government.

3. Liquidation of Illiteracy. Development of Education

One of the first steps made by Soviet power in Armenia was nationalization of all cultural and educational institutions. By doing this Soviet power was establishing a monopoly in the fields of education and culture. Private publishing houses, newspapers and magazines were shut down. Only party and state-controlled media was published. For propaganda and indoctrination of the communist ideology it was important to liquidate illiteracy.

By the Revcom's Decree of December 9, 1920 Armenian was declared the official language of the republic. By the special decree of the Armenian government adopted in September, 1921, all illiterate and semi-literate persons between the ages of 16 to 50 were obligated to learn how to read and write in their native language. In cities and villages centers for liquidation of illiteracy were organized. According to the census of 1926, there were 200 000 illiterates in Armenia.

During the first two five-year plans great work was done towards that end and by 1940 80% of the population of Armenia was literate. The percentage of illiteracy remained high among the Azerbaijanis and Kurds residing in Armenia.

The government paid serious attention to the development of school education. Elementary and middle schools were established. For national minorities Azerbaijani, Russian and Assyrian schools were opened in Armenia. In rural area construction of school buildings was underway, text- books were translated and published. To prepare teachers pedagogical colleges were established in Yerevan and other cities, while at the State University since 1922 a pedagogical department has begun operating. In 1928, steps to introduce compulsory education were made. By 1932 compulsory elementary education was already been introduced, while steps were taken to make a transition towards compulsory 7-year education.

In the course of rebuilding the economy and industrialization there was an increasing need for skilled workers and well-educated engineers. To achieve that, in 1923 so- called workers' faculties were established in Armenia ,where workers could receive a 7-year education and technical specialization. After 1930, on the basis of those faculties professional technical schools were established.

In the 20s and 30s the network of higher education institutions was enhanced. Since 1921 the Armenian University has become a state institution. After History and Law departments, the Department of

Natural Sciences, Medical school, Agriculture and Pedagogical departments were opened. State Conservatory was established in 1923. In 1928, Zoo-Veterinarian Institute was opened. In 1940, there were already 9 higher education institutions with 11 000 students in Armenia.

4. Participation of the Armenian People in the Great Patriotic War (WWII)

Hovhannes Baghramian

On June 22, 1941, Fascist Germany began the invasion of the USSR. Hitler planned to crush and conquer the Soviet Union before the winter of 1941. The 1930s repressions against the high command and officers had a negative impact on the defensive capacity of the Red Army. During the first months of the war the enemy was able to invade the entire European part of the country. The Soviet army suffered heavy losses and was retreating after fierce battles. All peoples of the Soviet Union rose to fight the enemy. Soviet Armenia mobilized its entire material and human resources for the needs of the war. Industrial enterprises were converted and re-adjusted to meet the demands of the war. For the needs of the army Armenia produced synthetic rubber, various kinds of ammunition and weaponry, and foodstuffs. The Armenian people raised funds to build aircraft squadrons, tanks and armored trains.

Sergey Khudiakov

Hamazasp Babajanian

Yet in the very beginning of the war, 6 Armenian divisions were formed, which made a

Ivan Isakov

significant contribution to the victory. Most famous were the 89th and 409th divisions. The 409th division began its victorious march in the Northern Caucasus and finished the war after taking part in the battles for the liberation of Austria and Czechoslovakia. The 89th Tamanskaya division became famous after battling its way from the Northern Caucasus to Berlin. Many Armenians fought in the resistance units in the occupied territories.

The Armenians also earned fame fighting in other divisions and were among legendary defenders of the Brest Fortress. As many as107 Armenians (36 post mortem) were decorated with the high rank of a Hero of the Soviet Union. 27 were awarded the Order of Glory of three degrees. 10 representatives of national minorities of Armenia were also granted the rank of a Hero of the Soviet Union. Nelson Stepanian, a military pilot, who participated in the defense of Leningrad, was made a Hero of the USSR twice.

Nelson Stepanian

During the war, there were over 60 high-ranking commanders of Armenian descent, who became generals such as Nver Safarian, Sarkis Martirossian, Michael Parsegov, Askanaz Karapetian, Hayk Martirossian, Ivan Vekilov and others. Four Armenians had the rank of marshal: Marshal of the Soviet Union, twice a Hero of the USSR, **Hovhannes Bagramian** (1897-1982); a Hero of the USSR, Navy Admiral **Ivan Isakov** (1894-1967); Chief Marshal of the heavy armored forces **Hamazasp Babajanian** (1906-1977); Marshal of Aviation **Sergey Khudyakov** (real name-**Armenak Khanferiants**, 1902-1950).

5. Socio-economic Development of Armenia in 1945-1985

After the end of the war it was necessary to convert the economy back, readjusting it to peace time and to develop agriculture to provide the population and demobilized war veterans with food supplies. Armenia was actively involved in helping to rebuild the ruined economies of the Soviet republics of Russia, Ukraine and Belorussia.

During the three post-war five-year plans (1946-1960) Armenia's economy was on a significant rise. The construction of new plants and factories was well underway. In 1949, the construction of copper and molybdenum plant began in Kajaran and 1950 the Yerevan aluminum plant launched its production. Armenia began to export machinery, generators, transformers and condensers, etc. To develop heavy industry the energy base was expanded. In 1949, the construction of the Sevan underground hydro power plant was finished and in 1953 the Gyumush hydro plant began to operate within the Sevan-Hrazdan Energy Cascade. In 1958, it was decided to make Armenia a country of developed chemical industry. A large plant of superphosphates was built in Alaverdi and a "Polyvinyl acetate" factory was opened in Yerevan, etc. In 1960-1985, large industrial enterprises were established in Charentsavan, Abovian, Sevan and Hrazdan. Thermo plants were built in Yerevan, Vanadzor and Hrazdan. Highways were built and railway communications network expanded. The development of industry required a further expansion of the energy base. In 1960, the construction of the **nuclear power plant began in Armavir and in 1980 it was ready for exploitation.** The NPP was producing electricity not only for Armenia but also for the neighboring republics. To save Lake Sevan, the level of which dropped twice after the construction of the Sevan-Hrazdan Energy Cascade, a unique 50 kilometer-long underground **Arpa-Sevan canal was built in 1962-1968.**

Armenian NPP

Armenia's agricultural development was very much behind the industrial progress. During the post-war five-year plans the country took the course of electrification and mechanization of agriculture. It began the construction of small local power plants, water reservoirs and irrigation canals in Kotayk, Talin, Ashtarak, Artik and Akhurian.

The development of agriculture took a much faster pace after the death of Stalin. It was then that the government raised retail prices on agricultural products, and peasants were allowed to have small livestock of their own. By 1958 all MTS-s were disbanded and all their machinery and equipment was given to collective and soviet farms. In the late 60s, the electrification and mechanization of the rural areas were completed. The work conditions of the rural population were very much improved.

The development of industry and agriculture in the post-war years created conditions for raising the living standards of the population. At the end of 1947, the ration-card system was abolished, and the monetary reform was made. By the end of the 50s, the income of the population increased. The quality of life began to improve significantly with items such as radio and TV sets, refrigerators, sewing machines, pianos, etc. becoming accessible and affordable.

Vigorous industrial development changed the demographic composition of the population in Armenia. By 1960, the urban population increased to 1/3 and by 1985 already constituted 2/3 of the total population of the republic. There was a growing need to provide the urban population with living quarters. By the mid 60s, the first phase of that problem was resolved. New districts with apartment blocks were built in Yerevan: Komitas, Zeytun, Arabkir, Achapnyak, etc. But by the early 80s the population of Yerevan reached 1 million, and to provide the people with living quarters more new districts were built: Erebuni, Davitashen, Nork, Ararat, etc. By 1985, the construction of the first, five-station line of the Yerevan subway was completed.

Despite the country-wide construction, and significant increase of the living standards the quality of life of the people was much lower than in the developed countries.

6. Socio-political Life in the Years of the Second Republic

With Soviet power already in place, by the mid 20s the dictatorship of the Communist party was established in the USSR. The severe struggle in the leadership of the party resulted in the establishment of Stalin's autocracy. Fabricating various charges of national treason, betrayal of party principles, sabotage, etc., Stalin gradually got rid of other leaders of the party and by the early 30s established his own dictatorship. Stalin fostered a cult of personality around himself, when achievements of the party and people were attributed to the power of his intellect and wisdom. To strengthen his power, Stalin launched a wide-spread repression campaign. There were mass arrests, show trials and executions. The wave of repressions reached its peak in 1936-1938. Many well-respected state and party leaders, intellectuals, writers and scholars were convicted and sentenced on the basis of fabricated evidence.

Among the victims of repressions in Armenia were Catholicos Khoren Mouradbekian, First Secretary of the Communist party of Armenia Aghasi Khanjian, state and party leaders Sahak Ter-Gabrielian and Nerses Stepanian, writers Yeghishe Charents, Axel Bakunts, Mkrtich Armen, Gourgen Mahari and many others. In 1936, about 25 000 Armenians, who disagreed with the policy of collectivization, were exiled to the Central Asia and the Altay region of Siberia. The total number of those subjected to repressions in Armenia during the years of Stalin's dictatorship was 42 000 people. In the following years the repressions were somewhat softened, but never entirely stopped.

Aghasi Khanjian

After the victory in the Great Patriotic War, Stalin's dictatorship became even stronger. Securing the support of the party leadership and KGB (NKVD) apparatchiks headed by L. Beria, Stalin took even a harder line in domestic political life. Mass arrests, repressions and show trials started again. Upon Stalin's instruction, in June, 1949 the Central Committee of the Communist party of Armenia decided to exile so-called unreliable elements to the Altay region. During 24 hours over 13 000 people were arrested and exiled. Most of them were those who had already been repressed in the past, their relatives, former POWs of WWII, as well as Armenian expatriates, who had returned to the Homeland in 1946-1948. Fabricated charges were incriminated against them, such as membership in clandestine anti-government organizations, espionage on behalf of capitalist countries, etc.

Yeghishe Charents

Repressions were stopped only after J. Stalin's death and the arrest of L. Beria. The new leaders of the country headed by First Secretary of the Central Committee of the Communist party Nikita Khrushchev denounced the personality cult of Stalin during the XX Congress held in June, 1956 and took measures to overcome the consequences of his policy. Special ad hoc commissions were created to review the cases of the unjustly convicted and almost all of those who had survived the Gulag were rehabilitated. They returned home where they were provided with jobs, living quarters and pensions.

Axel Bakunts

Just like in the rest of the country, socio-political life in Armenia during Khrushchev's time in office was very much democratized. The command and control system became somewhat softer, while some criticism and difference of opinions were allowed.

However, the reforms of the late 50s and early 60s could not be entirely democratic, as the one-party system did not provide necessary conditions for that. In 1964, during the coup-d'état by party apparatchiks N. Khrushchev was removed from power. The conservatives who came to power under the leadership of L. Brezhnev gradually abolished all would-be freedoms and restored the control and command system in the country. Soon the signs of socio-political crisis and societal stagnation became obvious. Persecutions against dissidence, commitment to national values and historical memory of peoples began.

Armenian Genocide Memorial in Tsitsernakaberd

On **April 24, 1965, on the 50th anniversary of the Genocide** there was a nation-wide demonstration in Armenia, in which all layers of Armenian society participated. It was for the first time in Soviet history that such a mass, spontaneous public rally took place. The rally was dispersed by the militia and KGB, while its organizers and participants were subject to persecution and punishment. However, those events triggered the awakening of national awareness. At the initiative of Yakov Zarobian, First Secretary of the Communist party of Armenia, a decision was taken to erect a special monument in memory of the Genocide victims. The building of the monument was completed in 1967 and became a Shrine for national pilgrimage.

Yakov Zarobian

In1968, the victory of the Armenian people in the Sardarapat battle was celebrated in the festive atmosphere. In Sardarapat a memorial for the Armenian participants of the battle was built and ethnographic museum was opened.

In the following years with the deepening of the socio-economic and moral- psychological crisis the social activity in the country became barely noticeable.

7. Development of Cultural Life during the Years of the Second Republic

Hovsep Orbeli

Periods of durable peace had a positive impact on the development of cultural life in Armenia. By the end of 1921, ancient manuscripts and valuable artifacts that had been taken from the Museum of Echmiadzin to Moscow during WWI were returned to Armenia. The libraries and artifact collections of the Lazarev Institute as well as the Armenian schools of Astrakhan and New Nakhichevan were also sent to Armenia. The latter served as a basis for the establishment of the State Science and Arts Research Institute in 1925. In 1935, the Institute was converted into the Armenian Branch of the Soviet Academy of Sciences, which in **1943** was reorganized into **Armenian Academy of Sciences.** From 1938 the Branch was headed by a prominent scholar, the then director of the Hermitage Museum in St. Petersburg, Academician **Joseph Orbeli** (1887-1961).

Armenian literature was also on the impetuous rise. Writers A. Isahakian, A. Shirvanzade, Nar-dos, D. Demirchian, S. Zoryan and others were in their prime. The star of **Yeghishe Charents's** poetic talent (1897-1937) had already been shining, when he became a victim of the Stalinist repressions. Composers **Alexander Spendiarian, Romanos Melikian and Armen Tigranian** made an invaluable contribution to the development of musical arts in Armenia. In 1932, the Armenian Philharmonic was founded and in 1938 the Ballet and Opera House and National Ensemble of Folk Dance and Song were established.

Hamo Bek-Nazarian

In 1922, the Armenian State Drama Theater and in 1937, the Russian Drama Theater were opened. In the early 20s, the **Armenfilm (Ar-**

menian Motion Picture Company) was established. In 1925, the first Armenian silent movie "Namus" was directed. In 1935, film director **Hamo Bek-Nazarian** made the first Armenian sync-sound motion picture "Pepo".

Sergey Mergelian

In 1924, a famous architect **Alexander Tamanian** designed a building development plan for the city of Yerevan. The construction of government buildings, Opera House, apartment and public buildings was underway. There were other talented architects on Tamanian's team such as T. Toromanian, K. Halabian and S.Safarian.

Al. Tamanian Memorial

The political thaw of the 50-60s provided an impetus for the new rise of science and culture. Natural sciences made a great progress. A great number of young talented scholars came to the fore. In 1958, there were already 64 various science and research institutes operating in Armenia, and in 1985, that number grew to 90 with 22.000 researchers and staff employed there. By the efforts of **Victor Hambartsumian the Byurakan Astrophysical Observatory was established.** Under the supervision of **Sergey Mergelyan Automated Control Systems Scientific Research Institute** was founded, while due to the efforts of **Artem Alikhanian a Synchrotron Particle Accelerator** was built in Yerevan, in 1967.

Artem Alikhanian

Victor Hambartsumian

Main Telescope, Byurakan Observatory

A great progress was registered in the development of humanities. Archaeological excavations of the monuments of Urartian and Hellenistic periods were begun. In **1958, the Matenadaran – Research Institute of Ancient Manuscripts** moved to a new, specially-built facility. Today over 20 000 manuscripts are reposed and studied there. In the 70s, academic editions of "History of the Armenian People" (in 8 volumes), "History of Armenian literature" (in 5 volumes) and Armenian Encyclopedia (in 12 volumes) were published.

Matenadaran, Institute of Ancient Manuscripts

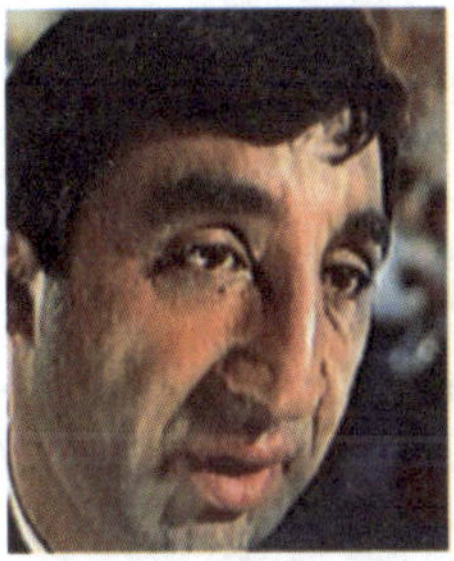
Mher Mkrtchian

The number of schools and technical high schools increased significantly. In 1965, the transition to compulsory secondary education was completed. In the 80s, there were as many as 13 higher education institutions with 60 000 students in Armenia. But the stagnation times had a negative impact on the system of education. Schools could no more meet the demands of modern life, while a university diploma would not always adequately reflect the level of knowledge and preparation of those who graduated.

Aram Khachaturian

Public library network was expanded. New museums, theaters and movie theaters were opened. On **November 29, 1957 the Armenian State Television aired its first program.** In 1965, a new drama theater was opened, and in 1982 the Yerevan State Chamber Theater was established.

Sergey Paradjanov

Prominent actors **Vahram Papazian, Hrachya Nersissian, Avet Avetian and Gourgen Janibekian** continued their stellar performances. New talents began to emerge, such as Metaksia Simonian, Khoren Abrahamian, Sos Sargsian, Mher Mkrtchyan and Hrachya Ghaplanian. In cinematography a talented film director **Sergey Parajanov** became world famous. Films by Frunze Dovlatian and Henrich Malian made Armenian cinematography very popular in the country. Armenian literature also achieved a lot

Martiros Sarian

Tigran Petrosian,
9th World Chess Champion

of success. After the years of Stalin's personality cult had been over, books by the previously banned authors such as Raffi, Charents, Bakunts, Mahari and Paronian began to be published. A. Isahakian, D. Demirchian, S. Zoryan continued their fruitful literary activity. Prose writers Hrachya Kochar, Sero Khanzadian, Khachik Dashtents and poet Gevork Emin became famous. The verse and poems by **Hovhaness Shiraz and Paruyr Sevak** were especially popular. In the 70-80s works by new talented writers such as Perch Zeytuntsian, Razmik Davoyan, Hrant Matevossian, Mushegh Galshoyan, Vardkes Petrossian began to be published.

Musical arts were on the impetuous rise. The talent of **Aram Khachaturian** was in its prime. He had the privilege to compose the first national ballet "Gayane", while his "Spartacus" became one of the most prominent works in ballet art at large. Talented works were created by composers **Arno Babajanian, Mikayel Tariverdiyev,** Eduard Mirzoyan, Tigran Mansourian, **Konstantin Orbelian** and many others.

Arno Babajanian

Famous opera singers were Pavel Lisitsian, **Gohar Gasparian,** Tatevik Sazandarian, Zara Dolukhanova, Lusine Zakarian, Mihran Yerkat and others. The patriarch of Armenian art, **Martiros Saryan** continued his work. Rich traditions were developed by talented painters **Minas Avetisian, Grikor Khanjian,** Hovhaness Zardarian and others. In the art of sculpture the names of Ghukas Chubarian and Ara Haroutyunian became famous. The talent of **Yervand Kochar** was fully expressed in his famous sculpture of the epic hero Sasuntsi Davit.

Radio telescope at the Byurakan Observatory

In architecture national traditions continued to develop. Construction of new buildings in Yerevan in keeping with Tamanian's general design was underway. In the 70-80s unique architectural projects such as the building of stadium "Hrazdan", Chamber Music House , "Zvartnots" airport, Sports and Concert Center and subway stations, etc. were carried out in Yerevan.

This is only a short list of achievements of Armenian culture.

Hrazdan Stadium

CHAPTER 22

THE THIRD REPUBLIC OF ARMENIA

1. The Policy of Perestroika. The Beginning of the Artsakh Movement

By the mid 80s the USSR entered into a deep socio-economic crisis. As a result of economic stagnation the population incomes dropped drastically. Even for the party leadership it became obvious that reforms were necessary. In April, 1985, the General Secretary of the Central Committee of the CPSU Mikhail Gorbachev declared the policy of **perestroika and glasnost**. It was aimed to boost economic development and democratize socio-political life. However, the attempt to overcome the crisis by control and command half-measures was unsuccessful. Socio-economic crisis transgressed into political turmoil, and the process of the collapse of the USSR began. Ethnic enmity and conflicts, deteriorated relations between the republics and the Kremlin administration- those were the problems of that time.

Inspired by the declared policy of reforms, the Armenian population of Nagorno Karabagh started to believe in the possibility of finding a fair solution to the Karabagh problem. On February 20, 1988, the Session of the Regional Soviet of Nagorno Karabagh adopted a resolution on the secession of the region from Azerbaijan and its unification with Armenia. From February 20 to February 27, there were huge public rallies summoned under the leadership of Igor Mouradian, Sylva Kaputikian and N.Saroukhanian at the Opera Square in Yerevan in support of the just demand of the Karabagh population.

The Soviet leadership proved to be unprepared to deal with inter-ethnic problems. M. Gorbachev made an appeal to the Armenian and Azerbaijani peoples to remain calm and keep law and order. Giving the central authorities time to respond and come up with a solution of the problem, public rallies in Armenia were stopped. Meanwhile, the

Azerbaijani leadership tried to solve the Karabagh problem by use of force, organizing the Genocide of the Armenians residing in Azerbaijan.

On February 27-29, in the city of Sumgait (near Baku) pogroms of the Armenian population were organized. 32 people were brutally killed, over 100 were wounded, raped, beaten up, while their property and homes were looted. The central authorities interfered only on the third day of the pogroms, bringing in the army force that helped to evacuate three thousand Armenian refugees who had gone through horrendous atrocities and lost their property. The Moscow administration concealed or falsified information about those attrocities. Under the public pressure an investigation was held, as a result of which some 2-3 organizers of the pogroms were charged and put on trial. No political reaction was given to those events and afterwards similar events took place in other regions of Azerbaijan and Nagorno Karabagh.

After the Sumgait tragedy, there was a new wave of demonstrations and public rallies in Armenia. The "Karabagh Committee" was formed, which coordinated demonstrations, strikes, hunger-strikes and the support of the Karabagh movement at large. In late May, the first secretaries of the Communist parties of Armenia and Azerbaijan, K. Demirchian and M. Bagirov were relieved of duty and replaced by Suren Haroutyunian and A. Vezirov respectively. By doing that the central authority tried to bring the popular movement under its control.

Rally in Yerevan

On June 15, 1988, under the popular pressure the Supreme Council of Armenia adopted a resolution on unification of Nagorno Karabagh with Armenia and sent a request to the Supreme Council of the USSR to ratify that decision. However, on July 18, the Presidium of the Supreme Council declined the request and took a decision to leave Nagorno Karabagh under Azerbaijan's jurisdiction.

After that, new, even more powerful mass demonstrations, public rallies and strikes were held in Armenia and **Artsakh** (the Armenian name for Karabagh). The "Karabagh Committee" was headed by Levon Ter-Petrossian, Vazgen Manoukian, Babken Ararktsian, Ashot Manoucharian and other leaders. The committee had its branches in almost every enterprise and institution of the republic.

In Azerbaijan, since May, 1988 new Armenian pogroms and deportations were organized. In response, persecution of the Azerbaijani population began in Armenia. Toward the end of 1988, 300 000 people were deported from Azerbaijan to Armenia and around 200 000 Azerbaijanis left Armenia for Azerbaijan.

On November 24, 1988, state of emergency was declared in Yerevan by USSR Government. Special policy force was brought into the city. Curfew was imposed and all public rallies and demonstrations were banned.

2. The Spitak Earthquake

On December 7, 1988, an earthquake with a magnitude of 6.9 by the Richter scale took place near the town of Spitak. According to the official data, 25 000 people were killed, about 30 000 were disabled and over 500 000 lost their homes during the earthquake. 40 % of the territory of Armenia was in ruins.

In those difficult days, many republics of the Soviet Union, foreign countries and international organizations showed invaluable support to Armenia. Humanitarian assistance-tents, food supplies, medical equipment, basic products were shipped to Armenia from all over the world. The victims of the earthquake were sent for treatment and rehabilitation to the leading medical centers and sanatoriums of the Soviet Union.

Doctors from many countries of the world volunteered to show first aid and assist in the long-term treatment. Huge financial and material assistance was sent by the Armenian Diaspora from around the world. Over 2000 Armenians from the Diaspora volunteered to come to Armenia to assist their compatriots. Many of them would stay there for many years or establish permanent residence.

Baroness Caroline Cox

After the earthquake Charles Aznavour made numerous visits to Armenia. The wife and son of President George Bush –senior, Great Britain's Prime Minister Margaret Thatcher, Baroness Caroline Cox, Joseph Rigler and many other leaders came to Armenia bringing medical and food supplies, equipment, personal donations, as well as government or private financial assistance. Today many schools, hospitals, entire quarters built in the cities and towns struck by the earthquake bear the names of the countries, nations and individuals who helped to rebuild them.

Nikolay Ryzhkov

On December 8, 1988 a special ad hoc state commission headed by the Chairman of the Government **Nikolai Ryzhkov** arrived in the disaster zone. Under his leadership immediate assistance and measures to liquidate the consequences of the earthquake were organized. Over 40 000 skilled workers arrived in Armenia to assist in the rebuilding and rehabilitation process. On December 10, 1988, M. Gorbachev visited the disaster zone. He promised to spare neither effort nor expense to rebuild the ruins in two years time.

Even in those dire conditions, the Armenian people did not abandon the hopes to find a fair solution to the Artsakh problem. This burning issue was raised at the meeting with Gorbachev, who was taken aback and became infuriated as he failed to understand the vital importance of the Artsakh issue for the Armenian people.

3. Armenia on the Road to Independence

Upon Gorbachev's instruction, by the end of 1988 all members of the "Karabagh Committee" were arrested and thrown to prison in Moscow. Yet neither natural, nor man-made disasters could stop the Artsakh movement which had already transformed into the national liberation struggle. Russian intellectuals, such as Nobel Prize winner Academician **Andrey Sakharov** and his wife **Yelena Bonner,** journalist **Genrikh Borovik,** ethnographer **Galina Starovoytova,** poet **Mikhail Dudin** voiced their support in solidarity with the just demands of the Armenian people.

Andrey Sakharov

On January 12, 1989, the Presidium of the Supreme Council of the USSR passed a resolution to create Special Governance Committee of Nagorno Karabagh under the supervision of Arcady Volskiy. The activity of the party and government institutions of the autonomous region was suspended. The Committee existed for less than a year failing to prevent further deterioration of the ethnic standoff.

Genrikh Borovik

Under the public pressure, in spring 1989, the authorities had to release the members of the "Karabagh Committee". Back at home, they were welcomed as heroes. Since that moment a consolidation of all political forces and groups

to be unified in one organization began. In November, 1989, t founding Congress of the **Armenian Pan-National Moveme (APNM)** was convened.

The AAM brought together different people with various visions the country's future. There were many currents in the APNM, ea trying to take its own path. This is why the movement could not avo making mistakes, running to the extremes, taking short-sighted and, times, irresponsible steps. It was at the APNM demand that the Nai synthetics rubber factory, mining metallurgical plant in Alaverdi a Armenian nuclear power plant were shut down. Great harm was do to the country's economy, as thousands of people lost their jobs. crown it all, since 1989 Azerbaijan had imposed transport a communication blockade on Armenia. The shipment of buildi materials for the reconstruction of the disaster zone was interrupte There was a severe shortage of fuel. Armenia was in critical situation

The situation in Nagorno Karabagh was also difficult. The regi was in complete blockade by Azerbaijan and could only connect wi the outer world by air travel. In August, 1989, in Stepanakert, Congress of representatives of Nagorno Karabagh was convene which elected the **National Council of Artsakh.** In response, speci Administrative Council of the Azerbaijan Republic headed by t second secretary of the Central Committee of Communist party Polyanichko was established in Azerbaijan to coordinate the policy ethnic cleansing of the Armenians in Artsakh. In those conditions, **December 1, 1989 the Supreme Council of Armenia and t National Council of Artsakh adopted a resolution on the unificati of Artsakh with Armenia.**

On January 10, 1990, the Presidium of the Supreme Council of t USSR declared that decision void. Inspired by such turn of events, t government of Azerbaijan together with the representatives of t Azerbaijani Popular Front organized mass pogroms and deportation the Armenian population of Baku that began on January 13, 1990 a lasted for more than a week. After that, there were no more Armenia left in Azerbaijan. The central authorities interfered only after t

armed units of the Popular Front had made an attempt to overthrow Soviet power in Azerbaijan and when the pogroms against the Russian, Jewish and other minorities had also started. Special army force was brought to Baku and the armed units were liquidated. A. Mutalibov was appointed first secretary of the Central Committee of the Communist party of Azerbaijan. However, it was already too late to establish any control over the armed units of the Popular Front.

In February, the armed units of the Azerbaijani Popular Front launched attacks on the border villages and towns of Armenia and Artsakh. Taking prisoners and exchange of hostages became a repeated action. Spontaneously, self-defense units were formed in Armenia that took the responsibility to defend the population in the border districts against the attacks of Azerbaijani gangs.

Since the summer of 1990, the blockade of Armenia had become permanent. In fact, **Azerbaijan waged an undeclared war against Armenia.** All reconstruction work in the disaster zone was stopped. There was no fuel. The gas pipe-line to Armenia was blown up repeatedly.

4. Declaration of Independence. The Collapse of the USSR

The idea of secession from the USSR and restoration of independence became more and more popular in Armenia. On May 20, 1990, elections to the Supreme Council of the republic took place in Armenia. Those were the first democratic elections. During the elections, the APNM that united all opposition forces got 36% of the votes. On August 4, 1990 with additional support of the majority of the deputies from the Communist party, the APNM's candidate and one of the leaders of the "Karabagh Committee" **Levon Ter-Petrossian** was elected Chairman of the Supreme Council of Armenia.

On August 23, 1990, at its first session, the Supreme Council of Armenia adopted the "Declaration of Independence of the Republic of Armenia".

The Declaration proclaimed the beginning of the process of establishing independent statehood with the purpose to restore full sovereignty. The tricolor, coat of arms and national anthem of the first

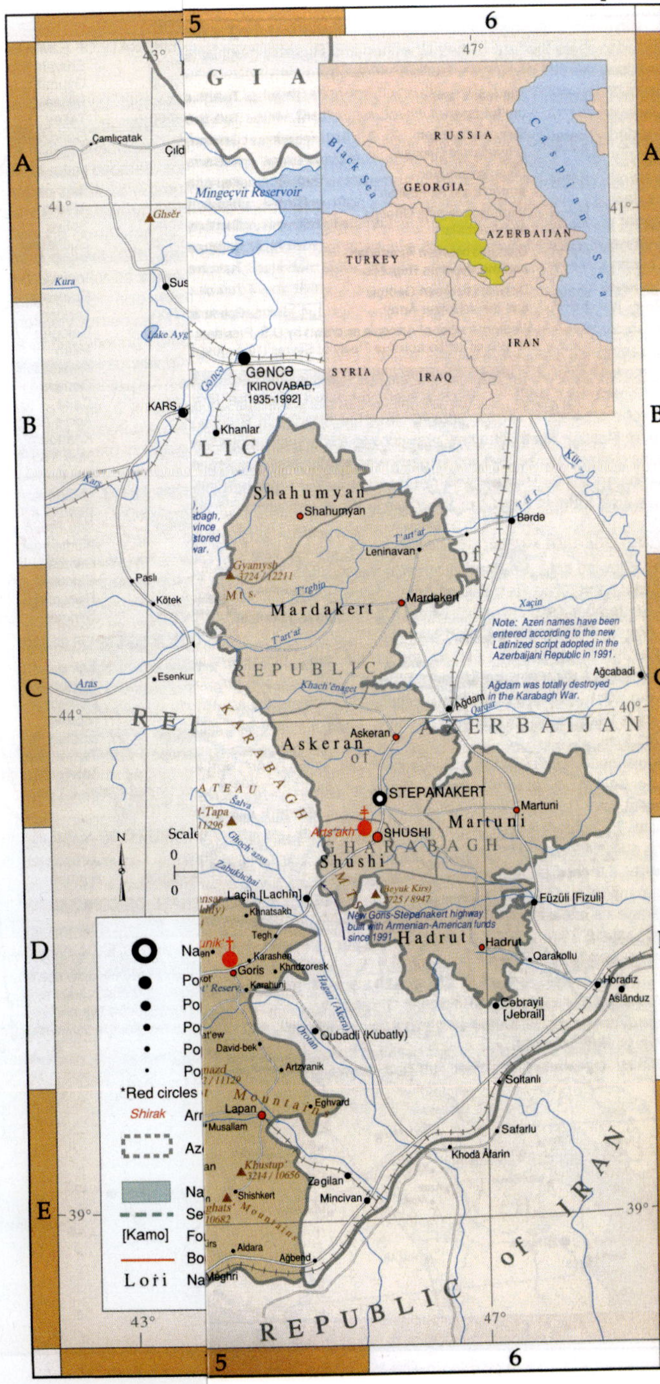

republic were restored. Land, natural resources and all economic capabilities were declared the property of the Republic of Armenia. As the subject of international law, the Republic of Armenia decided to conduct an independent foreign policy and participate in international organizations. Independent Armenia decided to achieve international recognition of the Genocide of 1915.

In March 1991, Armenia refused to participate in the referendum on signing the new union treaty of the USSR and decided to hold its own referendum on independence.

On August 19, the reactionary forces of the USSR made a coup-d'état attempt. The Soviet President M. Gorbachev was put under house arrest at his summer residence in Faros (Crimea). Special army forces were brought to Moscow. The SCSE -State Committee of the State of Emergency was formed. But the democratic forces of Russia were able to suppress the putsch and defend the democracy in the country. The failure of the putsch accelerated the process of disintegration of the USSR.

On September 21, 1991, a national referendum was held in Armenia, during which 94 % of the population cast their votes to secede from the Soviet Union and establish independent statehood. Fulfilling the will of the people, the Supreme Council of the Republic of Armenia declared independence of the Republic of Armenia.

Levon Ter-Petrossian,
First President of Armenia

On October 16, 1991 presidential on elections were held in Armenia. **Levon Ter-Petrossian** was elected the first President of the third Republic of Armenia. Gagik Harutyunyan became the Vice-President.

On December 8, 1991, the presidents of Russia, Ukraine and Belarus signed a memorandum on the dissolution of the Soviet Union. Instead the Commonwealth of Independent States was established (CIS). On December 21, Armenia together with 10 former Soviet republics signed an agreement on joining the CIS. Georgia and the Baltic republics did not sign the agreement.

Many countries of the world recognized Armenia's independence-the US, Greece, France, Canada, Turkey, Russia, Great Britain, China, etc. On May 2, 1992 Armenia became a member of the United Nations (UN).

5. Declaration of Independence of the Nagorno Karabagh Republic

During the year of 1991Azerbaijan was formally part of the Soviet Union, and that is why the Soviet leadership gave its full support to the acts of Azerbaijani aggression against Armenia.

In April-May, 1991, military units of Azerbaijan supported by the Soviet army launched an attack on the village of Getashen known as operation "Ring". As a result of it, the Armenian population was forced out of the Getashen district. In the summer of 1992, the Armenian population was driven out from the Shahoumian and Mardakert districts. Despite territorial losses, the people of Artsakh continued their courageous struggle. In fact, an undeclared war was waged in the region. In those conditions, on **September 2, 1991 the Congress of representatives of the Nagorno Karabagh population declared the Karabagh region an independent republic.**

The international community was concerned about the developments in and around Karabagh. The CSCE/OSCE (Conference/Organization on Security and Cooperation in Europe) discussed the Karabagh problem at the meeting of its representatives in Minsk, in March, 1992 and assumed the mission of mediating the conflict. In turn, the UN adopted a resolution calling on the conflicting parties to resolve the Karabagh problem by peaceful means.

After the collapse of the Soviet Union, during national elections the Popular Front came to power in Azerbaijan. Its leader, Abulfaz Elchibey was elected the President of the country. The leadership of independent Azerbaijan rejected all recommendations and proposals of international organizations opting to resolve the issue by use of force. The attempt of the presidents of Russia and Kazakhstan to mediate a peaceful settlement of the problem was rejected by Azerbaijan. A wide-range war against Artsakh and Armenia was waged. Artsakh was completely surrounded by the Azerbaijani army that subjected its capital Stepanakert and other towns and villages to artillery bombardments and missile strikes. During the bombardments there were casualties among the civilian population.

Arkady Ter-Tadevossian

The self-defense forces of Artsakh under the command of **Arcady Ter-Tadevosian** (Commandos) took resolute actions against the Azerbaijani army. **On May 9, 1992, they liberated the city of Shushi-** the ancient capital of Artsakh. On May 18, the Azerbaijani forces were driven out from the Lachin district. The Lachin corridor was secured to break the blockade and link Karabagh with Armenia.

A poor coordination between the self-defense units allowed Azerbaijan to occupy the Shahoumian and Mardakert districts. In the summer of **1992, the National Defense Committee of Artsakh was established under the supervision of Robert Kocharian** to coordinate the activities of the self-defense units.

In 1993-1994 the self-defense units of Artsakh drove the Azerbaijani forces out of the Mardakert, Kelbajar, Fizuli, Kubatli and Zangelan districts. The defeat lead to a political crisis in Azerbaijan. Suret Husseinov, one of the Azerbaijani commanders launched an anti-governmental revolt. The government was overthrown, and President Elchibey fled the capital. An experienced Communist leader Heidar Aliyev came to power. Convinced that the Karabagh problem could not be resolved by use of force, Aliyev's government signed a ceasefire agreement in July, 1994. With Russia's mediation Armenia, Karabagh and Azerbaijan signed an agreement on the cessation of military activities. Under the auspices of the OSCE, peace negotiations have begun between Armenia, Karabagh and Azerbaijan, which are still underway today.

In 1996, national elections were held in Artsakh. Robert Kocharian was elected President of Artsakh. In 1999, Arcady Ghukassian became the second President, and in 2007 Bako Sahakian was elected the third President of Artsakh.

CHAPTER 23

ARMENIA AT THE THRESHOLD OF THE THIRD MILLENNIUM

1. The First Steps of Independent Armenia

The top priority of the newly-independent Armenia was to end the Karabagh war and liquidate of the blockade of the country imposed by Azerbaijan and its ally, Turkey. To overcome the economic crisis it was absolutely necessary to make a transition to market economy. In October, 1990, the law on "State Property of the Republic of Armenia" was passed.

Armenian Dram

Privatization in Armenia started from the agricultural field. Its purpose was to provide the population with foodstuffs and make the peasantry see their own interest. During 1991-1992 almost 80 % of the agricultural land was privatized and given to peasants. As a result, about 320 000 individual and corporate farms were created. However, the process of privatization was marred by certain violations, as there was no clear-cut plan or adequate technical support. This is why the agricultural field remained in crisis for quite a long time.

The disintegration of the Soviet Union brought about the rupture of economic ties, while the blockade by Azerbaijan led to the economic crisis in Armenia. Transportation of fuel or raw materials to Armenia was interrupted. Because of the economic collapse the financial system of the country was in crisis and inflation started. In November, 1993, the government had no choice but to introduce its national currency- **Armenian dram.** In conditions of continuous economic crisis, dram rapidly devaluated.

The main factors that had caused the socio-economic crisis were the collapse of the USSR and interruption of economic ties, earthquake of 1988, blockade imposed by Turkey and Azerbaijan and inexperienced management. To overcome the energy crises, the government had to re-open the Armenian Nuclear Power Plant.

The most important guarantee of independent statehood and security of Armenia was the establishment of effective national army. Under the supervision of **Vazgen Sargssian (1959-1999)** and due to the efforts of regular (former Soviet) army officers and field commanders, in a short period of time a strong national army equipped with modern hardware was created.

The socio-political life of the country developed in democratic atmosphere. Not only the traditional Armenian parties –the Dashnaks, Hunchaks and Ramkavar- Azatakan (former Armenakan) but also the new ones that had been formed in the era of independence such as "Azgayin Inknoroshum (National Self-Determination), Republican party, etc were active. Their activity had a positive impact on the democratization of domestic political life. The ban on the activity of Dashnak party in December, 1994 and shutting down of several opposition papers, as well as challenged results of the parliamentary elections of 1995 and the national referendum on the Constitution had a negative impact on the democracy-building process.

On July 5, 1995 as a result of the national referendum the Constitution of independent Armenia was adopted, according to which Armenia was becoming a republic with mixed presidential and parliamentary system of governance. The President's power was enhanced at the cost of the reduction of the power of the Parliament.

The Head of State- the President of the Republic is elected by the citizens of the Republic of Armenia for a five year term of office. A president can be elected any person having attained the age of thirty five, having been a citizen of the Republic of Armenia for the preceding ten years, having permanently resided in the Republic for the preceding ten years. The President is the guarantor of the Constitution, territorial integrity and security of the Republic.

The legislative power is vested in the National Assembly (NA, one-chamber Parliament). It has 190 members who are elected for a four year term. 150 are elected by majoritarian system (one deputy from each district) and 40 members are elected by proportional system (from the list of candidates representing the parties that have overcome the 5% barrier). Every citizen who has attained the age of 18 having permanently resided in Armenia for a year before the Election Day has a right to vote.

Any citizen of Armenia having attained the age of twenty five, having permanently resided in the Republic for no less than preceding 3 years may be elected as a Deputy.

The executive power is vested in the Government of Armenia. The Prime Minister is appointed by the President. The cabinet members are appointed by the President upon the recommendation of the Prime Minister. The decrees of the government are signed by the Prime Minister and ratified by the President.

On December 1, 1995 the law on the new administrative and territorial division of Armenia was passed. In keeping with this law, the territory of the Republic is divided into 10 regions, the city of Yerevan, which has the status of the region and communities. Regions have rural and urban communities, while Yerevan is divided into quarters.

In the regions state governance is carried out by marzpets (governors), who are appointed by the government. The Mayor of Yerevan is appointed by the President upon the recommendation of the Prime Minister. The communities elect their representatives to local self –governance bodies for a three year term (council of elders, head of the community, village elder or city mayor). Their responsibilities include managing community property and other community problems, such as adoption of the budget and oversight of its administration, as well as local tax legislation and collection. Each head of a community forms his/her own administration. In Yerevan, local self-governance is carried out in quarter communities.

2. The Consequences of the Socio-Economic and Political Crisis

The first years of Armenia's independence turned out to be the most difficult. The country suffered through a socio-economic crisis. From 1992 to 1997, the size of the arable land decreased by 25%, unemployment was wide-spread, the living standards of the population dropped drastically. Academic and artistic elite would live the country. During the period of 1990-1995, the number of academic research workers dropped by 4 times, from 22 000 to 5.500. Trying to make both ends meet people were immigrating to Russia, the US and European countries.

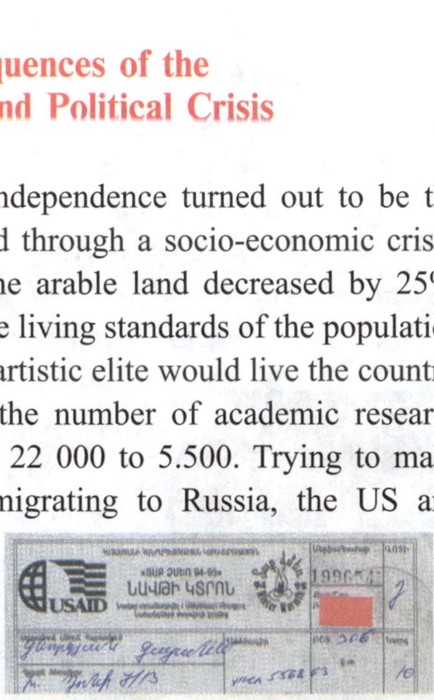

Rationed oil stamps

During the energy crisis the population would only receive 1-2 hours electricity per day. The ration-card system for bread and other foodstuffs was introduced. To crown it all, there were thousands of refugees from Azerbaijan that needed to be accommodated. In the disaster zone, people were living in tents for years. The minimum salary and pension could not even cover the basic needs, and most of the population lived beyond the poverty level.

In 1993-1995, Armenia had to apply for foreign credits. The World Bank provided a loan of 12 ml. dollars, the US allocated 1 ml. dollars for the purchase of sowing wheat and Russia gave a 5 ml. dollar credit to purchase Russian oil and agricultural products. However, most of this money was poorly managed by the inexperienced government or pocketed by corrupt officials. In socio-political life, polarization of the society led to all-around disillusionment with the activities of the APNM, as well as to a split inside the movement and establishment of new political parties disassociated from the APNM.

In September, 1996, the second presidential elections were held in Armenia, the results of which were rigged. The main struggle was between the incumbent president and the leader of the National Democratic Union (NDU), Vazgen Manoukian. President Ter-Petrossian was elected for the second term.

The people hoped that the change of power would improve the situation in the country. However, the APNM leadership was reluctant to leave office. There were serious violations and pressure by power ministries during the elections. Disillusioned, the opposition supporters stormed the building of the National Assembly and forced their way in protesting against the falsified elections. There were incidents of violence. The political climate in the republic became unhealthy.

Robert Kocharian,
2nd President of Armenia

Armenia entered a period of crisis. There was a split in the government with regard to the issues of foreign and domestic policy. In early 1998, President L. Ter-Petrossian and some of the team of the APNM leaders had to resign.

Pre-term presidential elections were held in Armenia. The main rivalry was between Prime Minister Robert Kocharian, who had been in office since May, 1997 and former Communist leader Karen Demirchian. **In April, 1998, Robert Kocharian became the second President of Armenia.**

Armenia was gradually overcoming the crisis. Political life was normalized. Democracy in domestic politics was restored, as the criminal proceedings against the Dashnak party were halted and political prisoners were released. New political parties were formed such as Democratic, People's, Iravunk yev Miabanutyun (Right and Unity), Orinats Yerkir (Country of Law), Azgayin Miabanutyun (National Unity), etc. New laws were adopted to accelerate the development of the country, including the Law on Education.

Since 1998 the system of education has been reformed. A 15 ml. dollar loan was provided by the World Bank towards that end. The programs of school education have been reconsidered and scores of new textbooks have been published. According to statistical data, in the academic year of 2003-2004, 18 state higher education institutions with 55 000 students and 73 private universities with 22 000 students operated in Armenia. In 1991, with the support of the University of South California the American University of Armenia was established. In 1999, the Russian-Armenian (Slavonic) University was opened in Yerevan. In 2000, the French University of Armenia was established. European two-phase system of higher education has been put into practice in Armenia.

Karen Demirchian

Vazgen Sargssian

In the summer of 1999, regular parliamentary elections took place in Armenia. The political block of "Unity" (alliance of Republican and People's party), headed by Vazgen Sargssian and Karen Demirchian won the elections. It formed the Majority in the new National Assembly. K. Demirchian was elected

Speaker of the NA and Vazgen Sargssian was appointed Prime Minister.

The new leadership began taking steps to improve the living standards of the population. Many factories and plants that had been out of business for a long time resumed operation. The domestic and external situations were improving. But the natural course of events was interrupted by the new crisis.

On October 27, 1999, an armed gang of extremists broke into the NA building and in cold blood assassinated the leadership of the NA and government. Karen Demirchian, Vazgen Sargssian and 6 other state officials were killed. The members of the NA were taken hostage. After 24-hour long negotiations all of them were released and the terrorists surrendered.

Armenia suffered through a very difficult night. President Kocharian personally supervised the negotiations with the terrorists to free the hostages. In those difficult days several former leaders returned to the stage. There were attempts to organize a revolt within the army. It took months before crisis was overcome and life returned back to normal. The trial of the terrorists lasted for over two years, all of them receiving life sentences in 2003, as capital punishment had already been abolished in Armenia.

3. Armenia at the Threshold of the Third Millennium

The dawn of the new millennium has been the time of new hope in Armenia. In May, 2000, Andranik Markarian, the Chairman of the Republican party became Prime Minister. Internal disagreements had not been overcome yet, and the new Prime Minister did a lot to stabilize the situation after the assassination of the leaders of the "Unity". The country's economy was gradually put on track due to foreign investment. Armenia became a member of the WTO.

Financial assistance to Armenia continued to be provided by the UN, US, Japan, Russia and other countries. Due to foreign investment and assistance from the IMF, it has become possible to resume the operation of several industrial enterprises, maintain mining and processing of building materials, resume the operation of the copper plant in Alaverdi and begin excavation of copper mines in Kapan, Kajaran, Agarak and Akhtala. Excavations and mining of other local natural resources such as molybdenum, aluminum and gold has been underway. Food industry has been on the rise and production of wine and brandy has also increased.

Computer technology and software production has been put on track. Hundreds of new small and medium size enterprises, especially in services, have been opened.

In August-September, 2001, festivities dedicated to the 1700th anniversary of the adoption of Christianity as state religion in Armenia were organized in the country. On this occasion, Pope John Paul II paid an official visit to Armenia. Numerous government delegations from foreign countries and a lot of compatriots from the Diaspora arrived in Armenia to participate in the festivities.

Two nation-wide Diaspora-Armenia conferences to elaborate development strategy and joint plans for Armenia were convened. **Pan-Armenian Games,** in which sportsmen from Armenia and the Diaspora participate were inaugurated and are now held biannually. The previous Games were held in 2001, 2003, 2005, 2007 and 2009.

Pope John Paul II in Armenia

In 2003, new presidential and parliamentary elections were held in Armenia. The incumbent President, Robert Kocharian was elected for the second term in February-March 2003. In May, the block of the Republican party, Dashnaks and Orinats Yerkir won the Majority during the parliamentary elections. Artur Baghdasarian, the Chairman of the Orinats Yerkir was elected Speaker of the NA.

The Chairman of the Republican party, Andranik Markarian was re-appointed Prime Minister. As a result of the national referendum of **November 27, 2005 important amendments to the Constitution were adopted, which changed the text significantly.**

The power of the NA was enhanced at the cost of the presidential power. Also enhanced was the power of courts, human rights and rights of public organizations. The number of deputies was reduced from 190 to 131, of whom two thirds are now elected by proportional system from the lists of candidates submitted by political parties and organizations that have overcome the 5% barrier.

In May, 2006 there was a crisis in the ruling coalition- Artur Baghdasarian resigned from the post of the Speaker of the NA for political motives. Tigran Torossian, a representative of the Republican party became a new Speaker.

Stabilization of the political climate had a positive impact on the country's economy. Transport communications are developing rapidly. Highways and local roads are being repaired and reconstructed. Trade with neighbors is also on the rise. Armenian currency- dram has been stabilized.

In early March, 2007, in a festive atmosphere the grand opening of the Iran-Armenia gas pipe-line took place, which would provide about 40 % of the total gas demand in Armenia. Near the city of Meghri, a bridge was built over the Arax river connecting Armenia with Iran. The trade turnover with Russia through the ferry communication via the Georgian port of Batumi is being enhanced. Since May 25, 2007, a new terminal was put into operation at the Zvartnots airport, which allows servicing about 2 ml. passengers a year.

Armenia strengthened its position at the international arena. It became a full member of the Council of Europe. Armenian peace-keepers take part in international missions in Kosovo and Iraq.

On the eve of the new parliamentary election, on March 27, 2007 Prime Minister Andranik Markarian passed away.

Markarian was the tenth Prime Minister of the Republic and headed the government for 7 years. He did a lot to stabilize the economy of the country. During his time in office many problems were solved such as construction of irrigation systems, state budget growth and increase of teachers' salaries, etc.

The Congress of the Republican party elected Serge Sargsyan, the then Minister of Defense, as its Chairman. On May, 2007, regular parliamentary elections were held. Only 5 parties –Republican, Bargavach Hayastan (Prosperous Armenia), Dashnak, Orinats Yerkir and Zharangutyun (Heritage) were able to overcome the 5% barrier. Tigran Torossian, a representative of the Republican party was re-elected Speaker of the NA. Serge Sargssian, the Chairman of the Republican party became Prime Minister.

From 131 seats, the Republican party won 67 mandates. Although it had a right to form the government by itself, the party opted to establish a coalition with Bargavach Hayastan and the Dashnak party. It was probably done to secure full quorum during debates on vital issues.

On February 19, 2008, regular presidential elections were held in Armenia. This time, there were six candidates for the post. **Serge Sargsyan was elected the third President of Armenia.** Presidential candidate Levon Ter-Petrossian (the ex-President of Armenia) and his supporters refused to recognize the results of the elections. After the elections, opposition held non-stop public rallies for ten days at the Opera Square. Levon Ter-Petrossian claimed victory. The demonstrators stayed in tents assembled at the Opera Square around the clock.

Serge Sargsyan, 3rd President of Armenia

In the early morning of March 1, 2008 the police force dispersed the demonstrators forcing them out from the Opera Square. There were clashes with the police and several people were arrested. There was public unrest in Yerevan, which by the evening hours grew into a mass protest rally.

Since the downtown was surrounded by the police, the demonstrators moved and began to assemble at the Myasnikian Square across the street from the Mayor's office and near the Embassy of France. By night, the demonstrators and the police engaged into an open confrontation. The people were arming themselves with anything they could get hold of, barricading themselves behind overturned buses and trams. The special police force surrounded the area. Stones, metal objects were thrown at the police, cars were burnt down. Shots were fired in response. Pressured by the people, the police had to retreat to the Mesrop Mashtots Ave. Some stores were looted.

The March1-2 events were a serious blow to Armenia's international image and undermined the country's internal stability. State of Emergency was declared in Yerevan and arrests of the opposition leaders made, who were charged with instigating the unrest. According to the official data, there were ten people killed. The number of the wounded was impossible to assess. The situation in Armenia was discussed by the Council of Europe and other international institutions. After the State of Emergency was lifted, the opposition rallies resumed, but the revolutionary activity of the people was down.

Tigran Sargsyan

In April, a transfer of power to the newly-elected President was made. In May, 2008, the formation of the new government began, which was headed by the former Chairman of the Central Bank, **Tigran Sargsyan.** In conditions of mass social protest, the new government launched an active campaign to fulfill the promises made during the presidential elections, such as improvement of tax and customs administration, increase of social security payments and strive against corruption. The future development of the country and restoration of its international image very much depends on how civilized, balanced and consistent the activity of the new government can become to resolve the aforementioned problems.

CHAPTER 24

THE ARMENIAN DIASPORA: THE PAST AND PRESENT

1. The Formation of the Armenian Diaspora

After the Genocide in the Ottoman Empire, over 1 000000 Armenians who were dispossessed of their homeland and survived the massacres by miracle were scattered all around the world. Those exiled joined the already existing Armenian colonies in different countries and formed the Armenian Diaspora.[1]

Armenian orphans, survivors of the genocide, are sent to America. Photo form the Archives of the U.S. Library of Congress

By he early 20s, of 2.5 million Armenians who had once lived in Turkey only one tenth was left, that was mainly concentrated in Constantinople. The largest Armenian colonies were formed in the Balkan countries (Greece, Bulgaria, and Romania), the Middle East (Syria, Lebanon and Egypt), Georgia, Iran, Russia (the Northern Caucasus, Black Sea region), the US, France and South America (Uruguay, Argentina).

[1] Greek term "Diaspora" means "spread out," and is used to identify large expatriate communities.

In those countries where Armenian colonies had already been in existence, the new settlers received support from their compatriots, were more easily integrated and were quick to find jobs. In less developed countries such as Iran, Egypt, Syria and Lebanon Armenian refugees were more easily integrated and very soon started playing an important role in the development of crafts and trade. In more developed countries, such as the US and France, Armenian refugees with no knowledge of the language of the new country of residence and impossibility to receive social security support from the state, settled in with difficulty.

2. The Armenian Question and International Relations in 1922-1923

The Armenian Question was still included in the agenda of international conferences of the super powers in 1921-1923. It was only the Diasporan organizations that pursued the promotion of the Armenian Question. For the government of Soviet Armenia that was part of the Soviet Union and was under ideological guidance of the Communist party, it was impossible to conduct independent policy. Therefore, it could not take part in those conferences. Soviet Russia and, later, the USSR continued to support the claims of Kemalist Turkey believing that it stood against international imperialism.

In February-March, 1921, a conference of the Great Powers took place in London. Armenian delegation headed by Avetis Aharonian that represented the already non-existent first Republic of Armenia, and the National delegation headed by Poghos-Nubar took part in the conference. During the conference they raised the issue of putting into practice the Treaty of Sevres and establishment of an independent Armenian state in Western Armenia. However, the conference only complied with an indistinct formulation of the right to have "Armenian national homeland" within the bounds of Turkey's eastern provinces, which was not recognized by the Turkish delegation.

From November 1922 to July 1923 an International Conference was convened in Lausanne (Switzerland). It ended up by signing the

Lausanne Peace Treaty which determined today's boundaries of Turkey and as a matter of fact substituted Peace Treaty of Sevres. The Turkish delegation decidedly rejected the idea of creating the Armenian national homeland reasoning that both Turkey's eastern provinces and Cilicia were populated mainly by Turks. In the already concluded Lausanne Treaty there wasn't any mentioning of Armenia or Armenians. The Armenian Question was turned into an issue of Armenian refugees and was delivered to the League of Nations, which turned out to be unable to do anything.

For more than a decade the League of Nations was "trying to solve" the problem of Armenian refugees. Many resolutions were adopted, but no concrete steps taken. At the League's request, Fridtjof Nansen, a famous Norwegian scholar took a long-term commitment to deal with the problem of Armenian refugees. Due to his personal efforts, under the auspices of the League of Nations special stateless status and UN passports (also known as Nansen passports) were given to Armenian refugees. Due to that, many refugees were able to find jobs and later receive citizenship in their new countries of residence. Eventually, Nansen came to a conclusion that it was impossible to solve the problem within the framework of the League of Nations and suggested that the question should be removed from the agenda as it had no prospect of resolution. In his book "The Deceived People" he exposed the cynicism and treacherous policy of the Great Powers with regard to the Armenian Question.

Fritjof Nansen

3. The Armenian Diaspora between the World Wars

In difficult socio-economic conditions, Armenian communities aspired to preserve their national idiosyncrasy. In each more or less large colony the Armenians built churches, opened schools and published newspapers. Public charity organizations were established in the Diaspora to help the refugees. The most influential among them was the Armenian General Benevolent Union (AGBU), which sponsored schools, hospitals, orphanages and helped to establish craft shops and factories to provide the refugees with jobs.

Armenian intellectuals realized the importance of establishing ties between the Diaspora and Armenia to preserve national identity. In 1921, the Armenian Relief Committee (ARC) headed by national poet Hovhaness Tumanian was established in Soviet Armenia. Famous activists were sent to the Diaspora to organize the repatriation of refugees to the Homeland. Through its branches the ARC sent books and textbooks to the Diaspora. In turn, intellectuals from the Diaspora also realized the necessity of maintaining ties with the Homeland.

In 1921, the first caravan of refugees from Iraq arrived in Armenia. In 1925-1926, over 20 000 Armenians from Constantinople, Greece, France and Iran repatriated to Armenia.

In 1931-1936, the total number of the repatriated reached 42 000. Farmers were settled in rural districts, while craftsmen and intellectuals were accommodated in urban area. The government helped them to settle in. Around Yerevan and other cities new settlements of expatriates were established, which were given the names of the cities and towns in Western Armenia, such as Arabkir, Butania, Sebastia, Malatsia, Zeytun, etc. Reaching the Homeland, the expatriates were involved in peaceful work and had the opportunity to receive education and specialization.

4.The Armenian Diaspora in the Years of WWII

The Armenian Diaspora made a significant contribution to the struggle against Nazism during WWII (1939-1945). Many representatives of the Armenian Diaspora fought against Nazism serving in the US, British and French armies, as well as participating in the resistance movement and underground organizations.

In 1943 -1944, Armenian communities around the world raised funds to assist the Soviet army. Those funds were spent to build "Sasuntsi Davit" Tank Corps and a squadron of bombers.

The unit of Misak Manushian took active part in the French Resistance. Post mortem he became a national hero of France. The Armenian unit “Freedom” glorified its name participating in the Greek Resistance.

In the war against the USSR Germany tried to use POWs organizing them into national legions. Dro, Njdeh and other Armenian leaders of the past participated in the establishment of the Armenian legion under the German Command. They tried to secure Germany’s patronage for Armenia, should the USSR have been defeated and against Turkey’s possible entry into the war. Many Armenian POWs used that chance to be rescued from suffering and imminent death in the Nazi concentration camps. The majority of Armenian legionnaires used every opportunity to desert and join local resistance to continue fighting against Nazism.

5. Mass Repatriation of Armenians in 1946-1948

At the Potsdam Conference of the victor-powers in 1945, the Soviet leadership raised the issue of the return of the territories of Western Armenia by Turkey. To support those demands, the government of Soviet Armenia launched a mass repatriation campaign among Armenian communities in different countries. The public organizations of the Armenian Diaspora made repeated appeals to the governments of the US, France, Great Britain, USSR, as well as the UN to restore the historical justice and return the territories of Western Armenia to the Armenian people. The raise of the international image of the Soviet Union and the hope to attract international attention to the defense of the rights of the Armenian people made a lot of Diasporan Armenians agree to repatriate to Soviet Armenia.

The first group of expatriates arrived from Lebanon. They took a ship to Batum and reached Armenia in June, 1946. By October, new caravans of expatriates came to Armenia. Mass repatriation continued for some time and only slowed down in 1947-1948. The total number of expatriates that came to Armenia from 12 countries reached 90 000. Repatriation, although not so active, continued in the 50s and 60s. The expatriates were provided with lodging or loans to build homes. They received free specialization and various privileges.

However, Armenia's economy was not strong enough to provide adequate living standards for the expatriates. On the other hand, many expatriates became victims of the Stalinist mass repressions and were exiled to the Altay region in Siberia. All these factors had a negative impact on the future process of repatriation. Moreover, in the following years, some of the expatriates left Soviet Armenia and immigrated to foreign countries.

6. The Armenian Diaspora Today

In the second half of the 20th century there were serious demographic changes in the Armenian Diaspora. With the change of the international political situation in the 50-70s, national liberation struggle, revolutions, ethnic and religious conflicts began to unfold in the Middle East. In conditions of political instability, mass exodus of the Armenians from those countries began. They moved to more developed, politically stable countries, such as the US, France, England, Canada, Germany, Australia, Austria and Sweden.

After the fall of the Stalin's dictatorship and end of the Cold war, permanent multifaceted ties were established between Armenia and the Diaspora. There were text-books on Armenian literature and history published in Armenia for the schools in the Diaspora. Young people from the Diaspora were given an opportunity to study at higher education institutions in Armenia. In 1960-1980, over 1000 Armenian youngsters from all over the world received their degrees in Armenia. In 1992, their number reached 1200, and today there are as many as 3000 students from the Diaspora.

Scientific cooperation and ties were established between Armenian scholars in the Diaspora and research centers in Armenia. An exchange of researchers and guest lecturers took place. Many scholars from the Diaspora were elected to the Armenian Academy of Sciences. Due to Diaspora efforts and fund raising Armenian studies programs and courses exist in several American universities.

In 1964, a Committee for Cultural Ties with the Diaspora was established in Armenia. "Hayreniki Dzayn" (Voice of the Homeland) newspaper began to be published, which covered the news in Armenia and the Diaspora.

Literary ties between writers in Armenia and the Diaspora were strengthened. Works by William Saroyan, Alicia Kirakossian, Charles Aznavour, Karapet Sital, Levon Mesrop and other writers were published in Armenia.

William Saroyan

Theater troupes, music and folklore ensembles from Armenia were on regular tours to the countries that had Armenian communities. Art exhibitions were organized. The Armenian Apostolic Church played a very important role in strengthening the ties between Armenia and the Diaspora.

In 1965, both in Armenia and the Diaspora events were organized to commemorate the 50th anniversary of the Armenian Genocide. In many countries Armenian communities build monuments in memory of the Genocide victims. In Yerevan, the Tsitsernakaberd Memorial and, later, the Genocide museum were built.

Charles Aznavour

The new Armenian generation in the Diaspora was brought up in different conditions and has different mind-set. Continuing the struggle for the fair solution of the Armenian Question they began using different tactics and approach, which secured the support of many countries for the just demands of the Armenian people. The Armenian Genocide in the Ottoman Empire has already been recognized and condemned by the parliaments of Uruguay, Cyprus, Greece, Russia, France, Switzerland and other countries. In 1987, the European Parliament condemned the Genocide and called on the government of modern Turkey to recognize it. The public organizations of the Diaspora continue to publish relevant materials in different languages, seeking the recognition of the Armenian Genocide by other countries as well.

Bearing in mind the importance of the Armenian language and culture for the preservation of national identity, Armenian communities around the world spared no effort to establish and maintain education institutions, folklore groups and ensembles. The most famous among education institutions in the Diaspora are the Haykazian College in Beirut (est. in 1955), the Melkonian College School in Cyprus (est. in 1924) and the Moorad Rafaelian College in Venice (est. in 1836). Students from the Diaspora have a chance to receive Armenian education there. Armenian elementary, middle and high schools operate in Latin America, the US, Canada and Australia.

Carzou

The development of literature was important to preserve national identity. Famous writers of the Diaspora were Levon Shant, Vahan Tekeyan, Arshak Chopanian, Hakop Oshakan, William Saroyan, Mushegh Ishkhan and many others. Diasporan literature is an inalienable part of Armenian culture.

Many Armenian art and music workers became world famous. French Armenian artists-engraver Edgar Shahin, landscapist Armis (Armenak Misirian), abstractionists Carzou (Garnik Zulumian) and Jansem (Hovhaness Semerjian), sculptor Hakop Gyurjian reached international acclaim. American Armenian artists Arshile Gorky (Vostanik Adoyan), Hovsep Pushman, film director Rouben Mamoulian became international celebrities. Lebanese Armenian painter Haroutyun Kalents, Italian Armenian artist

Arshile Gorky

Gerardo Orazian, sculptor Nvard Zarian and film director Jean-Carlo Kuyumjian also reached international acclaim.

In different countries with Armenian communities numerous music ensembles, composers and soloists of Armenian descent continue to perform. American Armenian singers Lili Chukaszian and Lucine Amara, French Armenian chansonnier Charles Aznavour, composer Georges Garvarents and organist Perj Zhamkochian became world famous.

Rouben Mamulian

There are many amateur theater troupes and folklore ensembles that continue operating in Armenian communities around the world. Many of the supervisors of those groups received or advanced their education in Armenia. In the XX century newspapers and magazines in Armenian were published in many countries. It is also the case today. The new phenomenon is the publication of bilingual press and Armenian magazines in foreign languages. This is done because the younger generation of the Diaspora does not have a good command of the Armenian language. Because of the migration of the Diaspora population from one country to another, many Armenian newspapers and magazines stopped being published in Egypt, Lebanon, Bulgaria, Iran, Greece and France.

Henri Verneuil

The oldest Armenian journal is "Bazmavep" that has been published by the Mechitarist Congregation of Venice since 1843. "Hayrenik" (New York), "Armenian Review" (Boston), "Asbarez" (Fresno), "Alik" (Tehran), "Marmara" (Istanbul), "Ashkhar" (Paris) , "Ararat" (Beirut) and many other Diasporan Armenian newspapers continue being published today.

After the disintegration of the Soviet Union in 1991, the former Soviet republics were added to the list of countries with Armenian communities. Socio-economic hardships and political situation in the Homeland brought about a new wave of emigration and made a part of the population of Armenia seek for better living conditions abroad.

Today the number of the Armenians living in the Diaspora significantly exceeds the number of the population in Armenia proper. The Armenian Diaspora population is currently estimated to be 5 ml. with 2 ml. residing in Russia, 0.5 ml. in the CIS, 1 ml. in the US and Canada, 0,5 ml in EU and 1ml. in the rest of the world. According to the census of 2003, the population of Armenia proper is 3.210.300.

The ties between the Diaspora and Armenia year by year are becoming stronger.

"L'Esperance" (Hope) by Hovsep Pushman: Portrait of an Armenian girl presented to the President of the United States Woodrow Wilson. Wilson House, Washington D.C.

CHRONOLOGY

15th c. BC	Hittite sources provide the earliest reference to the country of Hayasa
13th c. BC	Assyrian sources provide the earliest reference to the country of Nairi
860 BC	Emergence of the Van Kingdom (Urartu) – the earliest known unified state on the territory of Armenia
782 BC	Founding of the city-fortress Erebuni (Yerevan) by King Argishti I
714 BC	Campaign of King Sargon II of Assyria to the Van Kingdom
585 BC	Demise of the Van Kingdom
6th c. BC	Emergence of the Yervanduni Kingdom in Armenia
521-520 BC	Armenian rebellion against King Darius I of Achaemenia
401-400 BC	Retreat of 10,000 Greek soldiers through Armenia
330 BC	Emergence of independent kingdoms on the territory of Armenia
240 BC	Emergence of the independent Armenian Kingdom of Tsopk (Sophene)
215 BC	Armenia and Tsopk fall under Seleucid rule
189 BC	Armenia and Tsopk regain independence
189-160 BC	Reign of King Artashes I. Unification of Armenian lands
188 BC	Founding of Artashat – Armenia's new capital
95-55 BC	Reign of King Tigran II the Great

89-71 BC	Conquests of Tigran the Great. Armenia's ascension to the status of major power
77 BC	Founding of Tigranakert – Armenia's new capital
69-68 BC	Campaign of Lucullus to Armenia. Battle of Tigranakert
66 BC	Campaign of Pompeius to Armenia. Treaty of Artashat
55-34 BC	Reign of King Artavazd II
54 BC	Parthian campaign of Crassus. Parthian-Armenian Alliance
34 BC	Campaign of Marcus Antonius to Armenia. Imprisonment of King Artavazd II
20 BC	Armenia becomes a Roman Protectorate
1 AD	Fall of the Artashisian Dynasty in Armenia
52	Parthian-Armenian Alliance. Assumption of Trdat I Arshakuni to the Armenian Throne
64	Roman Army defeated. Treaty of Randea
66	Coronation of Trdat I as King of Armenia by Emperor Nero in Rome
66-428	Reign of the Arshakuni Dynasty in Armenia
226	Rise of the Sassanid Dynasty in Iran
298	Treaty of Mtsbin (Nisibis). Rome and Persia recognize Trdat III as Sovereign of Armenia
301	Proclamation of Christianity as Armenia's State Religion
387	First division of Armenia between Rome and Persia

406	Mesrop Mashtots creates the Armenian alphabet
450-451	Vardan Mamikonian leads Armenia's war of liberation against Persia
481-484	Vahan Mamikonian leads Armenia's war of liberation against Persia
591	Second division of Armenia between Rome and Persia
640	Arab invasion to Armenia. Fall of the capital city Dvin
652	Armenian-Arab Treaty between Theodoros Rshtuni and Omayyad Emir Muawia
End of 7th c.	Armenia comes under Arab rule
703	Armenia rebels against Arab rule. Armenian Nakharars are burned on fire in Nakhijevan
850-852	Province of Sasun rebels against Arab rule
855	Ashot Bagratuni appointed Governor of Armenia
885	Armenia regains independence. Ashot I crowned as King of Armenia
885-1045	Reign of the Bagratuni Dynasty in Armenia
962	City of Ani declared the capital of Armenia
1045	Byzantium takes over Ani. Fall of the Bagratuni Dynasty.
1071	Battle of Manazkert. Armenia comes under Seljuk rule
1081-1375	Armenian Kingdom of Cilicia
1185-1240	Georgian-Armenian Alliance. Rise of the Zakarian ruling family in Eastern Armenia

1198	Levon II crowned as King of Cilician Armenia
1245	Cilician Armenia's alliance with Mongols. King Hetum I travels to Karakorum
13-14th cc.	Armenia Major comes under Mongol rule
1375	Armenian Kingdom of Cilicia conquered by Mameluks of Egypt
1441	The Holy Sea of the Armenian Church moves from Cilicia to Echmiatsin
1453	Fall of Byzantium. Founding of the Ottoman Empire
15th c.	Armenia comes under the rule of Turkic nomadic tribes
16-18th cc.	Turkish-Persian Wars on the territory of Armenia
1512	Hakob Meghapart publishes 'Urbatagirk' - the first book in Armenian print
1555	First Division of Armenia between Turkey and Persia
1639	Second Division of Armenia between Turkey and Persia
1717	Founding of the Armenian Mkhitarist (Catholic) Congregation in Venice
1722-1728	War of liberation in Syunik led by Davit Bek
1771	Founding of the Echmiatsin Typography – the first publishing house in Armenia
1773	Publication of 'Vorogait Parats' - a draft Constitution for independent Armenia
1794	Publication of 'Azdarar' in Madras – the first Armenian newspaper
1804-1813	First Russian-Persian War

1815	Founding of the Lazarian Seminary in Moscow
1826-1828	Second Russian-Persian War. Russia annexes Eastern Armenia
1828-1829	First Russian-Turkish War
1828-1840	'Armenian Oblast' within the Russian Empire
1862	Popular Rebellion in Zeitun
1863	Western Armenians adopt the 'National Constitution'
1874	Founding of the Gevorgian Seminary in Echmiatsin
1877-1878	Second Russian-Turkish War. Russia acquires the Kars Province
1885	'Armenakan' Party founded in Van
1887	'Hunchakian' Party founded in Geneva
1890	Dashnaktsutiun (Armenian Revolutionary Federation) founded in Tiflis
1895-1896	Armenian Massacres in Ottoman Turkey
1917	Revolution in Russia. The Bolshevik Decree 'On Western Armenia'
1918 March	Treaty of Brest-Litovsk
1918 May	Armenia declares independence. Battles of Sardarapat, Bash-Aparan, and Karakilisa
1920 January	Founding of the Armenian University
1920 Aug 10	Treaty of Sevres. Western territories are recognized as part of the Armenian Republic
1920 Nov 29	Soviet rule established in Armenia
1920 Dec 2	Transfer of authority to Revkom (Revolutionary Committee). Treaty of Alexandropol

1920 Dec	Syunik declare sovereignty under the command of Garegin Nzhdeh
1921 Feb-Mar	Civil War in Armenia. Founding of the Committee on the Salvation of the Homeland
1921 Mar-Oct	Treaty of Moscow between Russia and Turkey. Treaty of Kars
1922	Founding of the Trans-Caucasian Federation, and the U.S.S.R.
1943	Founding of the Academy of Sciences of Armenia
1946-1948	Worldwide repatriation of Armenians to Soviet Armenia
1965	Demonstrations in Yerevan in commemoration of the 50th Anniversary of the Genocide
1967	Construction in Yerevan of the Monument to the Victims of the Genocide
1976-1979	Armenia commissions the 1st and 2nd reactors of the Metsamor Nuclear Power Plant
1981	Completion of the Arpa-Sevan Tunnel construction
1988, Feb	Nagorno Karabakh's legislature adopts a Resolution on Reunification with Armenia. Armenian Pogroms in Sumgait, Azerbaijan
1988	Mass exodus and deportation of Armenians from Azerbaijan
1988 Dec 7	Devastating Earthquake hits Northern Armenia
1989 Nov	Founding Congress of the Armenian Pan-National Movement (APNM)

1989 Dec 1	Armenia's Supreme Council adopts a Resolution on Unification with Nagorno Karabakh
1990 Jan	Armenian pogroms in Baku. Armenia's blockade, and outbreak of war with Azerbaijan
1990 May	Armenian Pan-National Movement wins in Soviet Armenia's Parliamentary elections
1990 Aug 23	Armenia's Parliament adopts the Declaration of Independence
1991 Sep 2	Nagorno Karabakh declares independence, and reforms as Nagorno Karabakh Republic
1991 Sep 21	Armenia holds a Referendum on Independence
1991 Oct 16	Levon Ter-Petrossian elected the First President of Armenia
1992 May 2	Armenia joins the United Nations
1992 May 9	Armenian forces liberate Shushi – ancient capital of Karabakh
1995 Apr 5	Armenia adopts a new Constitution through Referendum
1996	Restart of the Armenian NPP
1998 Apr	Robert Kocharian elected the 2nd President of Armenia
1999 Oct 27	Terrorists attack the Armenian Parliament while in expanded session. Seven high level officials assassinated, including Prime Minister Vazgen Sargssian, and Speaker of the Parliament Karen Demirchian.
2001	Armenia became a member of the WTO
2001	Opening of the Davitashen Bridge in Yerevan

2001 Aug	Celebration of 1700 anniversary of adoption Christianity as state religion
2003	Presidential and Parliamentary elections in Armenia
2005 Nov 27	Referendum on Constitutional amendments
2007 Mar	Opening Iran – Armenia gas transmission pipeline
2007 May	Parliamentary elections in Armenia
2008 Feb	Serge Sargsyan elected the 3rd President of Armenia

NOTES

NOTES

NOTES

ABOUT THE AUTHOR

Dr. Armen Khachikyan is Associate Professor of History at Yerevan State Linguistic University named after V. Brussov. He gains his PhD in 1988 from Institute of Oriental Studies of National Academy of Sciences and in 1991 was awarded with academic status of Docent (Associate Professor) by USSR State Committee on Education.

Earlier in his career Mr. Khachikyan taught at the Armenian State Pedagogical University and at the European Regional Academy in Armenia. He is the author of a monograph titled "Armenia in the sphere of international policy at the threshold and beginning of our Era" (1999) and over 20 scholarly articles and studies on the methodology of instruction of history, published in Armenian, Russian and English. His research focuses on K-12 curriculum and textbook development for the subject of History.

Mr. Khachikyan has co-authored a textbook on "Ancient history" for fifth form which was in use at Armenian schools in 2000-2008, and a Civic Education Course for Distance Learning for secondary schools in Armenia. Together with Georgian and Azerbaijani colleagues, he has also co-authored a book titled "History of the South Caucasus Countries: a multiperspective view on history" (2009).

In 2003, Mr. Khachikyan was a Fulbright Senior Program Scholar at the U.S. Library of Congress. He is an active participant and contributor to numerous international conferences, seminars, symposia and workshops on issues related to education, from preschool to graduate. Mr. Khachikyan serves as a Member of the Working Group on National Curriculum and Textbook Development for World History, and an Advisor on Curriculum Development at the Armenian Fulbright Fellows Association.

Mr. Khachikyan is married, has two daughters.

NOTES